Panasonic

Microwave Oven Cookbook

Contents

PLEASE NOTE:
Cooking times vary by model. 600 Watt units cook slightly faster than 500 Watt units.
600 Watt cooking times are mentioned first in each recipe. 500 Watt cooking times are mentioned second and appear in parenthesis ( ).
Check the cover of your operating instruction manual for your model's wattage output.

Introduction

COOKING WITH MICROWAVES

How Does It Work?
Microwaves are a form of energy similar to radio and TV waves. As they pass through food placed in the Microwave Oven, microwaves cause moisture molecules within the food to vibrate at extremely high speeds. This friction produces the intense heat which cooks the food. The high speed of the vibration accounts for the dramatic savings in cooking time possible with a Microwave Oven. Microwave cooking can reduce regular cooking times by up to 70%.

Another reason for the speed of microwave cooking is the fact that a Microwave Oven cooks by two methods— penetration and conduction. While waves penetrate food surfaces — usually to a depth of 1 to 3 inches — internal cooking is done by conduction. Conventional ovens cook only by conduction. The magnetron tube and stirrer blade of a Microwave Oven circulate microwaves throughout the oven cavity to penetrate food from all sides simultaneously, so cooking is off to a faster start.

Microwaves are odorless and tasteless, so they can't affect the flavor of the foods you cook. In fact, microwave-cooked foods will usually taste better than those cooked by slower methods.

Microwave Cooking
microwave heating
microwave ovens

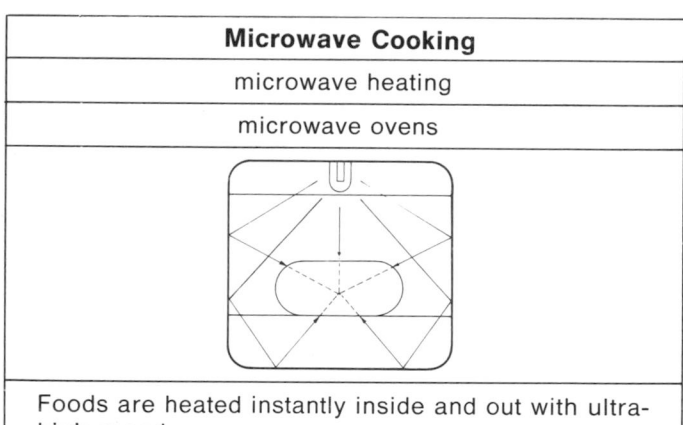

Foods are heated instantly inside and out with ultra-high speed.
Foods start cooking the instant cook button is pressed. The exterior and interior of the Microwave Oven DO NOT BECOME HOT.

BENEFITS YOU'LL APPRECIATE

Dramatic Time Savings
Your Microwave Oven can save up to 70% of the cooking times for most foods. Sometimes even more. A big 5-lb. roast takes only 30 (40) minutes in the Microwave Oven — 2½ hours conventionally!

No Pre-heating
Your Microwave Oven saves time in other ways, too. For instance, no 15-minute wait while the oven warms up. Just place your food in the Microwave Oven, set timer and press "Cook" button. Microwave cooking starts immediately!

No Temperature to Set
Cooking time is all that matters, not temperature.

So there's just one thing to set before cooking — the convenient timer. With the correct time setting, food's perfectly cooked every time.

Oven Automatically Turns Off
A pleasant bell signals the end of the cooking time. And the oven shuts itself off automatically. You can't overcook as long as you've set the correct time.

Rapid Defrosting
Microwave thawing is super-efficient. A frozen turkey can be thawed in minutes instead of hours—or days. You can plan more meals around frozen food, take unexpected company right in stride. (See "Defrosting" page 8)

New World of Cooking Utensils
Microwaves are not absorbed by ceramics, glass, paper or some plastics. So utensils of these materials can be used in your Microwave Oven. The only heat to be absorbed will be that from the food itself. Dishes remain cool. (See "Utensils", page 2.)

Nutritive Value Retained
Microwave cooking is so remarkably fast that foods retain greater vitamin and nutritive potency than with slower conventional methods. Dehydration is kept to a minimum, so delicious natural juices are preserved.

Fresh-Tasting Leftovers
Foods reheated in the Microwave Oven taste as fresh and delicious as they did the first time they were cooked. Reheating is so speedy there's almost no dehydration. You can make more efficient use of your food dollar by creating great-tasting leftovers.

Makes Meals Easier for a Busy Family
The Microwave Oven is so fast that it's easy to prepare servings of the same meal at different times. So when the family can't sit down to dinner together, everyone still gets a hot, nourishing meal. Ideal for instant snacks, special diets, or preparing foods for freezing.

Quick Cleanup, Cool Kitchen
Microwaves don't emit heat, so air inside the oven — and oven surfaces — stay cool. Food spatters can't burn on. A damp cloth is all that's needed for cleaning. A cool oven means the kitchen stays cool and smokeless.

Who Says Cooks Belong in the Kitchen?
You can take your oven anywhere there is an adequately wired grounded household circuit. Your oven fits neatly on a counter top or roll-about cart. So meal preparation can be as relaxed and versatile as your lifestyle.

Long Dependable Service
Your Microwave Ovens are designed with very few moving parts. And every part of the oven is precision-crafted, so you can expect long, dependable service.

SAFETY FEATURES

Microwave cooking offers many advantages over conventional cooking methods. And thanks to modern technology, your Microwave Oven is fast, efficient and safe. It's been designed with your total safety in mind, and we are proud of the results. You can operate your oven with the same confidence you have in using any conventional oven. Our safety features operate independently of each other to assure you complete peace of mind.

Door Catch Safety Switch
When you pull the convenient Door Handle to open the oven door, all microwave activity immediately ceases. There's no way to open the door without releasing the Door Catch Safety Switch, thus shutting off all microwaves.

Independent Door Safety Locks
A Second Safety Switch built into the door operates independently from the Door Catch Safety Switch. This lock will completely turn off all microwave activity the instant the door is opened.

Short Circuit Safety Switch
A third safety switch assures shut down of microwave activity when the door is opened.

Ferrite Door Liner and Choke System
Special ferrite material surrounding the oven door safely absorbs microwaves near the door. Capacitive seal and choke system effectively prevent microwave leakage at door edges. This design renders microwave activity completely harmless at the important contact points where the door meets the sides of the oven.

PRECAUTIONS TO AVOID POSSIBLE EXPOSURE TO EXCESSIVE MICROWAVE ENERGY

(a) Do not attempt to operate this oven with the door open since open-door operation can result in harmful exposure to microwave energy. It is important not to defeat or tamper with the safety interlocks.

(b) Do not place any object between the oven front face and the door or allow soil or cleaner residue to accumulate on sealing surfaces.

(c) Do not operate the oven if it is damaged. It is particularly important that the oven door close properly and that there is no damage to the;
    (1) door (bent)
    (2) hinges and latches (broken or loosened),
    (3) door seals and sealing surfaces.

(d) The oven should not be adjusted or repaired by anyone except properly qualified service personnel.

UTENSILS

In the use of utensils, microwave cooking opens new possibilities for convenience and flexibility in the kitchen.
Different substances react differently to microwaves. Some substances absorb, some reflect, and others are transparent to microwaves. Foods, because of their water content, absorb microwaves.

Glass, ceramics, paper and some plastics are essentially transparent to microwaves, so microwaves pass through them freely as they cook the food. This means dishes made of these materials are excellent for use in the Microwave Oven.

A good way to determine whether utensils are safe for use in the Microwave Oven is to test for heat caused by microwave absorption. Place the empty utensils in the oven for 15 to 30 (20 to 40) seconds. If the utensil becomes very hot it should not be used in the Microwave Oven.

Since microwave cooking is a relatively new technology, developments in microwave cookware are occurring almost daily. More and more manufacturers are adding cookware products designed specifically for use in Microwave Ovens. So watch for new labels and read them carefully.

Information in this section about brand-names and materials was supplied by some of the manufacturers interested in Microwave Oven cookware.

Glass, Ceramic and China Utensils
Most glass, glass ceramic and china utensils are excellent for use in the Microwave Ovens. Many manufacturers are now identifying their Microwave-Oven-safe dishes, either by a mark right on the utensil or a note in the product literature.

Heat-resistant glassware, unless it has metallic trim, can almost always be used in your Microwave Oven. However, be careful about using delicate glassware since it may crack from the heat of the food.

Pyrex® and Corning® products with the (*) symbol "Good for Microwave" or "Good for Range and Microwave" marks are suitable for use in Microwave Ovens.

Centura® cookware by Corning®, without metallic trim, but with the (*) symbol is Microwave-Oven-Safe. Centura® tableware, however, is generally not Microwave-Oven-Safe. A few accessory items may be used and these are marked with the (*) symbol.

Corelle® Livingware by Corning®, with the exception of the closed-handled cups, is Microwave-Oven-Safe.

Fire King® cookware by Anchor Hocking without metallic trim is Microwave-Oven-Safe, as stated on its product labels.

Glassbake® cookware by Jeanette Glass without metallic trim is Microwave-Oven-Safe.

Heat Proof® cookware by Federal Glass Company without metallic trim is labeled Microwave-Oven-Safe.

Temperware® by Lenox is a new line of cook-and-serve-ware acceptable for use in Microwave Ovens.

With all your new cooking possibilities, for best results just remember to avoid:

Introduction

- Utensils with metallic trim or metal parts such as screws, bands, handles, etc.
- Dishes glazed with high-metallic-content glazes.
- Utensils or dishware with cracked or crazed glazes or chipped parts.
- Ceramic mugs or cups with glued-on handles.
- Delicate glassware.

Paper Goods

For low-heat cooking, reheating, short cooking times and for foods with a low fat or water content, paper is a good utensil for Microwave Oven use. Napkins, towels, plates, cups, cartons, paper freezer wrap and cardboard are great convenience utensils for the oven. Paper is also used in microwave cooking as a moisture absorber.

Avoid wax-coated plates and cups, however, since foods that reach high temperatures may melt the wax.

Note: In using foil, foil containers or metal skewers make sure metal does not touch the sides of the oven, or arcing may occur.

Browning Skillet

When operating the Microwave Oven in combination with the browning skillet, please read the instructions supplied with the dish. The browning skillet is designed with a glaze-coating on the bottom of the dish. When used in the Microwave Oven it becomes very hot, similar to a fry pan.

Never use plastic wrap, wax paper or any paper products to cover or hold foods that are cooking on the browning skillet.

Using the Browning Skillet

Before you use the browning skillet, you must first preheat the dish in your Microwave Oven for 1 to 4 minutes. The grill keeps getting hotter as long as you preheat it. Follow the preheating times suggested in the instruction provided with the dish.

To determine the degree of doneness first check visually, just as you would with a conventional grill, broiler or fry pan. It is important to keep the browning skillet clean, wash thoroughly after each use.

Do not use steel wool or harsh abrasives on the cooking surface. They will damage the surface. Clean the cooking surface with a plastic scouring pad. The bottom of the dish should only be wiped with a damp cloth; do not scour the bottom of the dish, you may damage the special glaze.

Plastic Utensils

Plastic dishes, cups, freezer containers and plastic-coated paper products may be used in the Microwave Oven. Use plastic products with care as some may become soft, disfigured or pitted from the heat of the food.

"Dishwasher safe" is usually a good indicator as to whether a plastic utensil is safe for low-heat Micro-wave Oven cooking. Plastic dishes should not be used for cooking foods with high fat or sugar content.

Cooking pouches designed to withstand boiling and freezing or conventional heat work well in the oven. If the food will become so hot that steam will build up inside the pouch, the bag should be slit to allow steam to escape. Be sure not to use metal twists for closing. *Do not attempt to cook in plastic storage bags.*

Some plastic wrap may be used as a covering, but should not be allowed to touch food as heat from the food may cause it to melt. Stretch plastic wraps are not suitable for use in the Microwave Oven because they form too tight a seal.

Polychina® plastic cookware made from UDEL® Polysulfone by Union Carbide Corporation is suitable for use in the Microwave Oven.

Melamine® is not suitable for use in Microwave Oven since it has a tendency to absorb microwave energy and get hot.

Straw, Wicker and Wood

Straw, wicker, and wood baskets may be used in the oven for short periods of time, for example to warm buns, rolls or bread. Large wooden utensils used in the Microwave Oven for prolonged periods of time have a tendency to dry out.

Metal Utensils

Metal utensils and utensils with metallic trim should not be used in the Microwave Oven. There are several reasons for this. Microwaves are reflected by metals, and so foods in metal containers have a tendency not to cook.

There is also a possibility of "arcing" (a static discharge or spark between gaps in the metal or between the metal utensil and the side of the oven.) If you see arcing inside the oven, there is nothing to be afraid of. Just turn the oven off and transfer food to a non-metallic container.

Although metal is not generally used in microwave cooking, it can be used under the following conditions.

1. *Sheet–type metal foils*
Metal foils may be used if the amount of food is much greater than the amount of foil. Because metal reflects microwaves, it can be used to an advantage in some cooking the Microwave Oven. Foil should be used to prevent or to direct the cooking process. By this we mean you can use small smooth pieces of foil to cover areas such as poultry wings or legs or small ends of meat, or to shield spots that cook too quickly. Foil is used in these cases to slow or stop the cooking process for smaller sections of a food item to prevent overcooking in these parts.

2. *Frozen dinners in foil containers*
When cooking in such containers, all the cooking takes place from the top surface only. Results are more satisfactory if the container is no more than ¾ inch deep. Just remove the foil cover and replace it with wax paper or cook food in its cardboard box. Foods packaged in foil containers deeper than ¾ inch

should be transfered to another container before cooking.

3. *Metal skewers*
Metal skewers can be used if there is a large amount of food in proportion to the amount of metal.
If a small amount of food is put on a metal skewer, it may cause arcing.   .

TIPS AND HINTS FOR EASIER MICROWAVE OVEN USE

Time Variations
Foods vary throughout the country and factors such as size and shape may cause cooking times to differ from those given in the cookbook. For this reason, cooking times given here can only be approximate.

Factors that may affect cooking time include temperature of the food at the beginning of cooking, volume of food, size, and utensils. As you become more familiar with your oven, you will be able to adjust for these factors. Remember in any case that it is always better to undercook than to overcook.

Shells, Skins, and Other Outer Coverings
If foods such as nuts, apples and chicken, the outer covering and the food inside heat at different rates. Because of this, it is advisable to pierce the outside membrane to allow for the heating differences and also to allow any steam to escape. In recipes that require such attention, this added step has been included.

Jars and Bottles
Baby food jars and wide-mouthed bottles can be used for heating small amounts of foods in the Microwave Oven. Covers and metallic bands, however, must be removed.

Bottles with narrow necks should not be used in the Microwave Oven, since heating may cause the food to expand rapidly and break the bottle.

Lids and Covers
Casserole covers, plates, plastic wrap, wax paper, or almost any type of non-metallic covering may be used when "covering" is called for in the recipes. Stretch plastic wraps, however, are not suitable for use in the Microwave Oven. Since they form such a tight seal, they create a vacuum around the foods.

LID    WRAP

When covering foods in a casserole or baking dish, always allow room for foods to expand as they cook.

When using plastic wrap as a cover, be sure the dish is deep enough so that plastic will not touch the food. As the food heats, it may cause the wrap to melt wherever it touches the food.

When removing a tight-fitting cover, always tilt the cover away from you so steam escapes harmlessly.

Stirring
Stirring is sometimes necessary in microwave cooking. Throughout the cookbook we have noted when stirring is helpful, using the words "frequently" and "occasionally" to describe the amount of stirring necessary. In stirring, it is often best to bring the cooked outside edges toward the center and the less-cooked center portions toward the outside.

For More Even Heating

1. Leave space between each food item, such as canapes or hors d'oeuvres. Space them in the oven at least one inch apart.

2. Rotate the dish a quarter or halfway once or twice during cooking time.

3. Turn over the food items like a roast, pork or chicken once or twice during cooking time.

Recipes Containing Milk
Milk, when heated, has a great tendency to bubble up and boil over. Casseroles and baking dishes should be chosen to allow extra room when there is a large quantity of milk in the recipe.

Browning
Foods cooked in the Microwave Oven sometimes do not have enough cooking time to allow them to brown. If you prefer a deeper color, meat and poultry can be brushed with a 1-to-1 mixture of brown bouquet sauce and water. Meat and poultry may also be seared by the Microwave Oven Browning Skillet or under the broiler unit of a conventional oven or in a frying pan on a stove. This step should take place before cooking in Microwave Oven, and cooking time should be adjusted to allow for the conventional cooking.

Cakes and pastries may be browned by placing in a 425°F. oven for several minutes, if desired.

Thermometers
Meat and candy thermometers are made with vacuum seals and can explode if used in the Microwave Oven during cooking. Thermometers should be inserted in the foods after they have been removed from the oven. Quick-registering thermometers are now available which give the temperatures of the foods almost instantly.

Introduction

Standing Times Before Serving

Foods continue to cook after they are taken from the Microwave Oven and a standing period, at room temperature, is often desired. In small, less dense foods, this standing time is simply the time it takes to carry these foods to the table. In larger, more dense foods, a 15-to 30-minute standing time is usually advised. These times have been suggested in the individual recipes as needed. The temperatures of the foods will rise during this standing period, and this has been allowed for in the recipes. However, foods should be removed from the Microwave Oven slightly before they have finished cooking to allow for the cooking during the standing period.

Suggested Utensils

The following utensils were used in preparing the recipes in your Microwave Oven Cookbook. You may find, however, that all of these items are not essential for your purposes. For substitutions and other information, see "Utensils", page 2 .

All utensils are heat–resistant and non–metallic.

Bowls in 3 sizes (1½-pint, 1½-quart, 2½-quart)
Loaf pan (1¼-quart)
Deep casseroles, covered (1-quart, 1½-quart, 2-quart and 3-quart)
Shallow casseroles (1-quart, 1½-quart, 2-quart)
Skillets (6-inch and 9-inch with removable handles)
Square baking dishes (8- and 9-inch)
Round baking dishes (8- and 9-inch)
Pie pans (9- and 10-inch)
Custard cups (5-ounce to 12-ounce)
Serving platters

INGREDIENTS

Unless otherwise specified, all ingredients indicated are assumed to be taken directly from their storage places. For example, milk, butter and eggs are assumed to be fresh from the refrigerator — that is, chilled. Sugar and flour are considered to be from the cupboard, at room temperature.

Butter and margarine are interchangeable in all recipes.

Flour used in testing all recipes was all-purpose, unless otherwise specified.

Milk used is homogenized whole milk unless otherwise specified. For less rich dishes, substitute skim milk or non-fat milk. For richer dishes, undiluted evaporated milk, light cream or half and half may be used.

Sugar called for is granulated white sugar unless otherwise specified.

Eggs are large eggs unless otherwise specified.

WEIGHTS AND MEASURES

All measurements used in this cookbook are standard American measures.

Few drops	........less than ⅛ teaspoon
Few grains	........less than ⅛ teaspoon
1 tablespoon	......3 teaspoons
⅛ cup	..............2 tablespoons
¼ cup	..............4 tablespoons
⅓ cup	..............5 tablespoons plus 1 teaspoon
½ cup	..............8 tablespoons
⅔ cup	..............10 tablespoons plus 2 teaspoons
¾ cup	..............12 tablespoons
1 cup	.................16 tablespoons
1 jigger	..............1½ fluid ounces or 3 tablespoons
1 fluid ounce	......2 tablespoons
8 fluid ounces	......1 cup or ½ pint
1 quart	..............2 pints
1 gallon	..............4 quarts
16 ounces (dry)	...1 pound

Measure all dry ingredients by spooning ingredient into utensil and leveling off with the flat edge of a spatula.
Measure liquid ingredients in a "liquid" measuring cup holding the cup at eye level on a flat surface.

FOOD SUBSTITUTIONS

Baking powder (1 teaspoon)	...............¼ teaspoon baking soda plus ½ teaspoon cream of tartar
Chocolate (1 ounce)	........................1 square
	3 tablespoons cocoa plus 1 tablespoon shortening
Cream: light (1 cup)	........................⅞ cup milk plus 3 tablespoons butter
heavy (1 cup)	....................¾ cup milk plus ⅓ cup butter*
Eggs (1 large)	................................2 egg yolks plus 1 tablespoon water (baking)
	2 egg yolks (custards)
Flour (all purpose, 1 cup)	.................1 cup plus 2 tablespoons cake flour
	1 cup bread flour
Flour (for thickening, 1 tablespoon)	......½ tablespoon arrowroot
	½ tablespoon cornstarch
	½ tablespoon potato starch
Half and half (1 cup)	........................½ cup milk plus ½ cup cream
Herbs (1 tablespoon fresh)	...............¼ to ½ teaspoon dried herbs
Milk (1 cup)	....................................½ evaporated milk plus ½ cup water
	½ cup condensed milk plus ½ cup water**
	¼ cup powdered skim milk plus 1 cup water plus 2 tablespoons butter
1 cup (sour)	.................1 cup fresh milk plus 1 tablespoon vinegar or lemon juice
Stock (1 cup)	.................................1 envelope instant broth or 1 cube bouillon plus 1 cup water

*Cannot be whipped.
**Reduce sugar in recipe.

FOOD EQUIVALENTS

Bread crumbs	1 slice fresh bread—¾ cup soft crumbs
	3 to 4 slices toast—1 cup fine dry crumbs
Butter	¼ cup—4 tablespoons—½ stick
	½ cup—8 tablespoons—1 stick
	2 cups—1 pound—4 sticks
Cookie crumbs	10 to 15 cookies—1 cup fine crumbs
Cream	1 cup heavy—2 cups whipped
Eggs	4 large—1 cup
	6 to 7 yolks—½ cup
	4 to 6 whites—1 cup
Flour	1 pound—4 cups
Gelatine (unflavored)	1 tablespoon—1 envelope
Lemon	1 medium-sized—2 to 3 tablespoons juice
	1 medium-sized—1 tablespoon grated peel
Noodles	1 cup raw—4 cups cooked
Nuts	½ pound—1⅓ cups chopped
Onion	1 medium-sized—½ cup finely chopped
Orange	1 medium-sized—⅓ to ½ cup juice
	1 medium-sized—2 to 3 tablespoons grated peel
Potatoes	1 pound—3 medium-sized
	1 pound—2 cups mashed
Rice	1 cup raw—2 cups cooked
Spaghetti	8 ounces raw—4 cups cooked
Sugar (brown)	1 pound—2 cups firmly packed
(confectioners)	1 pound—4½ cups sifted
(granulated)	1 pound—2½ cups
Tomatoes	1 pound—3 medium-sized

WHAT TO DO BEFORE CALLING FOR SERVICE

Many times a service call can be avoided by checking a few simple things. The following conditions and problems are not caused by a defect in the unit itself. Therefore, please bear the following in mind.

CONDITION	CAUSE	REMEDY
1. Foods take longer to cook than time specified in cookbook.	1. Low Voltage at Receptacle. In this case, the output generated by the magnetron becomes low and cooking time becomes longer.	Use the Microwave Oven on a separate circuit. Make sure voltage to unit is adequate.
	2. Foods vary throughout the country and factors such as size and shape may cause cooking times to differ from those given. Factors that may affect cooking time include temperature of food at the beginning of cooking, volume of food, size and utensils.	This is not, in reality, a problem, therefore, please expect to cook a little longer. Remember in any case, it is better to undercook than to overcook.

CONDITION	CAUSE	REMEDY
2. Spark occurs inside the oven while cooking.	1. Using metallic ware and allowing it to touch the oven wall. METALLIC WARE 2. Ceramic ware trimmed in gold or silver.	Metal should only be used as specified in the utensil section of this cookbook. Dishes with metallic trim should not be used in the Microwave Oven.
3. Large pieces of meat not cooked evenly inside.	If meat is relatively large, microwaves will not reach the center of the meat causing the inside of the meat not to be cooked. Microwave penetration depends on the absorption ratio of the object. Usually the penetration of the microwaves into the food is approximately 1 inch from all sides. MICROWAVE 1 INCH	Utilize carry-over heating. Foods continue to cook after they are taken from the Microwave Oven and a standing period, at room temperature, is often desired. This standing time is usually 10—15 minute period. These times have been suggested in the individual recipes as needed.
4. The Microwave Oven not operate when timer is set for less than 2 minutes.	If the timer is set for less than 2 minutes, the unit may not turn on.	To set the timer for less than 2 minutes, turn the cook timer a little past the 2-minute position and then return to the desired time.
5. Food items explode	Because of the rapid cooking times, care must be taken to reduce pressure build-up from steam.	1. Baked potatoes need to be pierced. 2. Apples, tomatoes, etc. need a slit around circumference. 3. Cut slit in boil bags. 4. Loosen tight lids on bottles or containers. 5. Follow instructions for cooking eggs.

Defrosting Charts

Defrosting Charts

Your Microwave Oven makes defrosting quick and easy. It enables you to thaw foods in just a fraction of the time it would take conventionally. So you can plan more cooking around frozen foods. And last-minute meals are no problem. Take the food right out of the freezer. In minutes it's ready to cook. If foods have been frozen in non-metallic wrapping they may be placed directly into the oven cavity in their freezer wrappings. (Be certain to remove any metallic tie wraps.)

Just follow the chart on the following pages for best defrosting results. The shape and cut of meat and the package shape will alter the defrosting times to some extent. You may find that slight adjustments are necessary.

If "hot spots" (areas of the food that thaw faster than others) occur, they may be covered with small (1-inch-square) pieces of aluminum foil to slow down the heating process. It is sometimes advantageous to not completely thaw foods before cooking them. (For example, since fish cooks so quickly it is sometimes better to begin cooking it while it is still slightly frozen.) It may be necessary to increase the cooking times in the recipe to adjust for this.

Manual Defrost

Because foods heat so rapidly in Microwave Ovens, Manual Defrost must be done in stages, requiring rest periods. This allows the internal temperatures of the food to equalize so the food does not cook.
1. Place frozen food in oven in freezer wrappings (non-metallic).
2. Set timer (see chart for setting).
3. Press "Cook" button.
4. After ½ of defrosting time remove freezer wrappings and place food on a heat-resistant non-metallic plate or in a shallow non-metallic baking dish.
5. During remainder of defrosting time it may be necessary to rearrange food to make defrosting more even (see chart for instructions).
6. After defrosting, allow food to stand at room temperature for a few minutes so that the temperatures within the food can equalize.

Automotic Defrost

When you dial the defrosting recipe card, the oven automatically switches to a lower power with correct defrosting times on the recipe card. Automatic Defrost models should follow "Automatic Defrost" on the defrosting chart. To defrost:
1. Place frozen foods in oven in freezer wrappings (non-metallic).
2. Dial the defrosting recipe card.
3. Set the timer to register selection or see chart for correct defrosting time.
4. Press the "Cook" button.
5. After defrosting, allow food to stand at room temperature for a few minutes.
6. When defrosting is complete, turn the dial to the proper cooking recipe card.

GENERAL DEFROSTING HINTS

Foods fall into 3 categories for defrosting.
Using the following guide for general hints but check
the defrosting charts that follow for actual times.

Categories	Food Items	Hints
Quickies	Bread, cake, cookies, frozen fruit or vegetables, most precooked frozen foods	These foods are quick and easy to defrost. It will take just a few seconds or minutes of microwave exposure to bring them to serving or cooking temperature.
Easy	Hamburger patties, pork chops, steaks, ribs, chicken pieces, sea food	These foods are little more difficult but still require little attention when defrosting. Fish should not be fully defrosted in the Microwave Oven. It will defrost very rapidly at room temperature after some defrosting in the Microwave Oven.
More Difficult	Roast, turkey, duck, goose, ground beef	These foods require more attention when defrosting since they are thicker and bulkier than other foods. Require more standing and thawing time in addition to rotation during defrosting.

DEFROSTING CHART

Item	Amount	Manual Defrosting Times*	Manual Defrosting Method	Automatic Defrosting Method
Chops	2 pounds	3 (4) minutes + 2 (2½) minutes + 1 (1¼) minutes **Automatic Defrosting Times** 8 minutes	1. After the first rest period, unwrap and separate. 2. After the second rest period, rearrange chops so defrosted parts are towards center of plate and less defrosted parts are towards outside of plate. 3. Allow to stand several minutes for temperatures to equalize.	1. After 4 minutes unwrap and separate. 2. After additional 2 minutes turn chops over. 3. After additional 1 minute rearrange chops so defrosted parts are towards center of plate and less defrosted parts are towards outside of plate. 4. Allow to stand several minutes for temperatures to equalize.
Steaks, ¾-inch	1 pound	2 (2½) minutes + 30 (40) seconds + 30 (40) seconds **Automatic Defrosting Times** 4 minutes	1. After the first rest period, unwrap steak. 2. After the second rest period, turn steak over and turn plate ½ turn. 3. It may be necessary to cover narrow tail of a steak with aluminum foil to prevent cooking. 4. Allow to stand several minutes for temperatures to equalize.	1. After 3 minutes unwrap steak. 2. After additional 1 minute turn steak over. 3. It may be necessary to cover narrow tail of a steak with aluminum foil to prevent cooking. 4. Allow to stand several minutes for temperatures to equalize.
Steaks, ¾-inch	1½ pounds	2 (2½) minutes + 1 (1¼) minute + 30 (40) seconds **Automatic Defrosting Times** 5½ minutes	1. After the first rest period, unwrap steak. 2. After the second rest period, turn steak over and turn plate ½ turn. 3. It may be necessary to cover narrow tail of a steak with aluminum foil to prevent cooking. 4. Allow to stand several minutes for temperatures to equalize.	1. After 3 minutes unwrap steak. 2. After additional 1½ minutes turn steak over. 3. It may be necessary to cover narrow tail of a steak with aluminum foil to prevent cooking. 4. Allow to stand several minutes for temperatures to equalize.

*Plus sign + indicates oven "OFF" time equal to oven "ON" time for uniform defrosting.
*Parenthesis ( ) indicates 500 watt units.

Defrosting Charts

Item	Amount	Manual Defrosting Times*	Manual Defrosting Method	Automatic Defrosting Method
Ground Meat	1 pound	2 (2½) minutes + 30 (40) seconds + 30 (40) seconds + 30 (40) seconds **Automatic Defrosting Times** 5½ minutes	1. After the first rest period, unwrap meat. 2. After the second rest period, scrape off defrosted meat. 3. After the third rest period, scrape off defrosted part of meat again and crumble frozen part if possible. 4. Allow to stand several minutes for temperatures to equalize.	1. After 3½ minutes unwrap meat. 2. After additional 1 minute scrape off defrosted meat. 3. After additional ½ minute scrape off defrosted meat again and crumble frozen part if possible. 4. Allow to stand several minutes for temperatures to equalize.
Ribs	2 pounds	2 (2½) minutes + 1 (1¼) minute + 30 (40) seconds + 30 (40) seconds **Automatic Defrosting Times** 8 minutes	1. After the first rest period, unwrap and separate. 2. After the second rest period, turn ribs over and turn plate ½ turn. 3. After the third rest period, rearrange ribs so defrosted parts are towards center of plate and less defrosted parts are towards outside of plate. 4. Allow to stand several minutes for temperatures to equalize.	1. After 4 minutes unwrap and separate. 2. After additional 2 minutes turn ribs over. 3. After additional 1 minute rearrange ribs so defrosted parts are towards center of plate and less defrosted parts are towards outside of plate. 4. Allow to stand several minutes for temperatures to equalize.
Roasts	3 pounds	3 (4) minutes + 3 (4) minutes + 2 (2½) minutes + 1 (1¼) minute + 1 (1¼) minute **Automatic Defrosting Times** 14 minutes	1. After the first rest period, unwrap. 2. After the second rest period, turn roast ¼ turn. 3. After the third rest period, turn roast ¼ turn. 4. After the fourth rest period, turn roast ¼ turn. 5. It may be necessary to cover hot spots with aluminum foil. 6. Allow to stand several minutes for temperatures to equalize.	1. After 6 minutes unwrap. 2. After additional 2 minutes turn roast ¼ turn. 3. After additional 2 minutes turn roast ¼ turn. 4. After additional 2 minutes turn roast ¼ turn. 5. It may be necessary to cover hot spots with aluminum foil. 6. Allow to stand several minutes for temperatures to equalize.
Roasts	2 pounds	3 (4) minutes + 2 (2½) minutes + 2 (2½) minutes **Automatic Defrosting Times** 10 minutes	1. After the first rest period, unwrap. 2. After the second rest period, turn roast ½ turn. 3. It may be necessary to cover hot spots with aluminum foil. 4. Allow to stand several minutes for temperatures to equalize.	1. After 4 minutes unwrap. 2. After additional 2 minutes turn roast ⅓ turn. 3. After additional 2 minutes turn roast ⅓ turn. 4. It may be necessary to cover hot spots with aluminum foil. 5. Allow to stand several minutes for temperatures to equalize.

*Plus sign + indicates oven "OFF" time equal to oven "ON" time for uniform defrosting.
*Parenthesis ( ) indicates 500 watt units.

DEFROSTING CHART—continued

Item	Amount	Manual Defrosting Times*	Manual Defrosting Method	Automatic Defrosting Method
Chicken Breasts	1 pound	2 (2½) minutes + 1 (1¼) minute + 30 (40) seconds **Automatic Defrosting Times** 5 minutes	1. After the first rest period, unwrap and separate. 2. After the second rest period, rearrange chicken breasts so defrosted parts are towards center of plate and less defrosted parts are towards outside of plate. 3. Allow to stand several minutes for temperatures to equalize.	1. After 2½ minutes unwrap and separate. 2. After additional 1 minute turn skin-side-down. 3. After additional 1 minute rearrange chicken breasts so defrosted parts are towards center of plate and less defrosted parts are towards outside of plate. 4. Allow to stand several minutes for temperatures to equalize.
Chicken	3 pounds	3 (4) minutes + 2 (2½) minutes + 2 (2½) minutes + 1 (1¼) minute **Automatic Defrosting Times** 12 minutes	1. After the first rest period, unwrap. 2. After the second rest period, remove neck and giblets. 3. After the third rest period, turn chicken ½ turn. 4. It may be necessary to cover hot spots with aluminum foil. 5. Allow to stand several minutes for temperatures to equalize.	1. After 4 minutes unwrap. 2. After additional 2 minutes remove neck and giblets. 3. After additional 2 minutes turn chicken ⅓ turn. 4. After additional 2 minutes turn chicken ⅓ turn. 5. It may be necessary to cover hot spots with aluminum foil. 6. Allow to stand several minutes for temperatures to equalize.
Turkey, Whole	20 pounds	10 (13) minutes + 10 (13) minutes + 5 (6½) minutes + 5 (6½) minutes + 3 (4) minutes + 2 (2½) minutes + 2 (2½) minutes + 2 (2½) minutes **Automatic Defrosting Times** 30 minutes plus 15 minutes	1. After the first rest period, unwrap. 2. After the second rest period, remove neck and giblets. 3. After the third rest period, turn turkey ¼ turn. 4. After the fourth rest period, turn turkey ¼ turn. 5. After the fifth rest period, turn turkey ¼ turn. 6. It may be necessary to cover hot spots with aluminum foil. 7. After the sixth rest period, turn turkey ¼ turn. 8. Allow to stand several minutes for temperatures to equalize.	1. After 15 minutes unwrap. 2. After additional 15 minutes remove neck and giblets. 3. After additional 4 minutes turn turkey ¼ turn. 4. After additional 4 minutes turn turkey ¼ turn. 5. After additional 4 minutes turn turkey ¼ turn. 6. It may be necessary to cover hot spots with aluminum foil. 7. After additional 2 minutes turn turkey ¼ turn. 8. Allow to stand several minutes for temperatures to equalize.
Turkey Roast	4 pounds	10 (13) minutes + 5 (6½) minutes + 3 (4) minutes + 2 (2½) minutes + 1 (1¼) minute **Automatic Defrosting Times** 20 minutes	1. After the first rest period, unwrap. 2. After the second rest period, turn roast ¼ turn. 3. After the third rest period, turn roast ¼ turn. 4. After the fourth rest period, turn roast ¼ turn. 5. It may be necessary to cover hot spots with aluminum foil. 6. Allow to stand several minutes for temperatures to equalize.	1. After 8 minutes unwrap. 2. After additional 4 minutes turn roast ¼ turn. 3. After additional 4 minutes turn roast ¼ turn. 4. After additional 3 minutes turn roast ¼ turn. 5. It may be necessary to cover hot spots with aluminum foil. 6. After additional 2 minutes turn roast ¼ turn. 7. Allow to stand several minutes for temperatures to equalize.

*Plus sign + indicates oven "OFF" time equal to oven "ON" time for uniform defrosting.
*Parenthesis ( ) indicates 500 watt units.

Defrosting Charts

Item	Amount	Manual Defrosting Times*	Manual Defrosting Method	Automatic Defrosting Method
Duck or Goose	10 pounds	10 (13) minutes+ 5 (6½) minutes+ 2 (2½) minutes+ 1 (1¼) minute+ 1 (1¼) minute **Automatic Defrosting Times** 30 minutes	1. After the first rest period, unwrap. 2. After the second rest period, remove neck and giblets. 3. After the third rest period, turn duck ¼ turn. 4. After the fourth rest period, turn duck ¼ turn. 5. It may be necessary to cover hot spots with aluminum foil. 6. Allow to stand several minutes for temperatures to equalize.	1. After 15 minutes unwrap. 2. After additional 8 minutes remove neck and giblets. 3. After additional 3 minutes turn duck ¼ turn. 4. After additional 2 minutes turn duck ¼ turn. 5. It may be necessary to cover hot spots with aluminum foil. 6. After additional 1 minute turn duck ¼ turn. 7. Allow to stand several minutes for temperatures to equalize.
Fish Fillets	12 ounces	1 (1¼) minute+ 30 (40) seconds+ 30 (40) seconds+ **Automatic Defrosting Times** 3½ minutes	1. After the first rest period, unwrap and separate fillets. 2. After the second rest period, rearrange fillets so defrosted parts are toward center of plate and less defrosted parts are towards outside of plate. 3. Allow to stand several minutes for temperatures to equalize.	1. After 2½ minutes unwrap and separate fillets. 2. After additional ½ minute rearrange fillets so defrosted parts are towards center of plate and less defrosted parts are towards outside of plate. 3. Allow to stand several minutes for temperatures to equalize.
Lobster Tails	8 to 10 ounces	30 (40) seconds+ 30 (40) seconds+ 30 (40) seconds+ **Automatic Defrosting Times** 3 minutes	1. After the first rest period, unwrap. 2. After the second rest period, rearrange lobster tails so defrosted parts are towards center of plate and less defrosted parts are towards outside of plate. 3. Allow to stand several minutes for temperatures to equalize.	1. After 1 minute unwrap. 2. After additional 1 minute rearrange lobster tails so defrosted parts are towards center of plate and less defrosted parts are towards outside of plate. 3. Allow to stand several minutes for temperatures to equalize.
Shrimp	8 to 12 ounces	30 (40) seconds+ 30 (40) seconds+ 1 (1¼) minute **Automatic Defrosting Times** 3 minutes	1. After the first rest period, unwrap and separate. 2. After the second rest period, rearrange shirmp so defrosted parts are towards center of plate and less defrosted parts are towards outside of plate. 3. Allow to stand several minutes for temperatures to equalize.	1. After 1 minute unwrap and separate. 2. After additional 1 minute rearrange shrimp so defrosted parts are towards center of plate and less defrosted shrimp are towards outside of plate. 3. Allow to stand several minutes for temperatures to equalize.
Frozen Vegetables	10-ounce package	2 (2½) minutes+ 30 (40) seconds **Automatic Defrosting Times** 4 minutes	1. After the first rest period, unwrap and separate. 2. Allow to stand several minutes for temperatures to equalize.	1. After 3 minutes unwrap and separate. 2. Allow to stand several minutes for temperatures to equalize.

*Plus sign + indicates oven "OFF" time equal to oven "ON" time for uniform defrosting.
*Parenthesis ( ) indicates 500 watt units.

Special Recipes for Automatic Defrost and Delicate Food Cycle.

Special Recipes for Automatic Defrost and Delicate Food Cycle.

The recipes on the following pages are specially prepared for foods requiring more attention, cooking better at a lower power setting. Use the low power setting for delicate foods or the automatic defrost cycle depending on your oven model.
These settings will assure beautiful results on more delicate foods such as eggs, cheese dishes, various cakes, custards and meats requiring longer, slower cooking times.

Cooking times with the low power delicate food or automatic defrost cycles may be slightly longer than the same recipes provided in the other sections of this cookbook designed for full power cooking.
Refer to these full power recipes if you prefer a faster cooking time.

POACHED EGGS

2 cups water
½ teaspoon white vinegar
½ teaspoon salt
2 eggs

1. Combine water, vinegar and salt in a deep 1 quart non-metallic casserole.
2. Heat, uncovered, in Microwave Oven 1½ minutes on full power or until water mixture comes to a boil.
3. Carefully break eggs, 1 at a time, into the liquid.
4. Heat, covered with plastic wrap, in Microwave Oven on delicate food cycle for 3 minutes.
5. Let stand covered, 1 minute or until eggs reach desired degree of doneness.

Serves 1 to 2.

"FRIED" EGGS

½ tablespoon butter or margarine
2 eggs
Salt and pepper

1. Grease a heat-resistant non-metallic plate with the butter.
2. Carefully break eggs into plate. Sprinkle with salt and pepper.
3. With a toothpick carefully puncture membrane around egg yolk.
4. Heat, covered with plastic wrap, in Microwave Oven on delicate food cycle, 4 minutes or until eggs are almost cooked. Do not overcook as eggs will continue cooking while standing. Let eggs stand, covered, 1 minute to finish cooking.

Serves 2.

HAM QUICHE

3 eggs
½ cup light cream
¼ teaspoon ground nutmeg
½ teaspoon salt
⅛ teaspoon pepper
Few grains cayenne pepper
½ pound cooked ham, cut into thin strips
2 cups shredded Swiss cheese
1 baked 9-inch pastry shell (in a non-metallic pie pans)

1. In a medium-sized bowl beat eggs, cream, nutmeg, salt, pepper, and cayenne pepper until well mixed.
2. Stir in ham and cheese.
3. Pour mixture into baked pastry shell.
4. Heat, uncovered, in Microwave Oven, on delicate food cycle, for 10 minutes.
5. Move cooked edges toward center and heat an additional 10 to 14 minutes on delicate food cycle or until a knife inserted in center comes out clean.
6. Let stand at room temperature 3 to 4 minutes to finish cooking.

Serves 6 to 8.

Special Recipes for Automatic Defrost and Delicate Food Cycle.

SWEET CHOCOLATE SOUFFLÉ

6 eggs yolks
1 cup sugar
1 cup grated semi-sweet chocolate
6 egg whites, beaten

1. Prepare a 2-quart soufflé dish by forming a collar of wax paper around top of dish that extends about 3-inches above the dish.
2. In a medium size bowl beat egg yolks and sugar until lemoncolored. Add grated chocolate.
3. Beat egg whites and fold in chocolate mixture.
4. Fill a 9-inch glass cake dish with 1½ cups hot water. Set soufflé in pan of hot water. Bake in Microwave Oven on delicate food cycle for 9 to 12 minutes.
5. Serve immediately. Top with whipped cream.

Serves 4 to 6.

TUNA SOUFFLÉ

4 tablespoons butter or margarine
4 tablespoons flour
⅛ teaspoon pepper
½ teaspoon onion salt
¼ teaspoon salt
⅔ cup milk
4 egg yolks, well beaten
1 can (6½ to 7 oz.) tuna, drained and finely
  chopped
¼ cup shredded swiss cheese
8 egg whites
¼ teaspoon cream of tartar
2 tablespoons paprika

1. In a small-size heat resistant non-metallic bowl melt butter on delicate food cycle, 1½ minutes.
2. Stir in flour, salt, pepper and onion salt. Heat on delicate food cycle for 2 minutes or until mixture bubbles.
3. Blend in milk slowly. Heat uncovered, on delicate food cycle for 3 minutes, stirring after the first 1 minute or until mixture thickens and bubbles (sauce will be quite thick).
4. Beat mixture slowly into egg yolks. Stir in tuna and swiss cheese. Allow mixture to cool.
5. Prepare a 1½ quart soufflé dish by forming a collar of wax paper around top of dish that extends about 3-inchs above dish.
6. Beat egg whites with cream of tartar, until stiff but not dry.
7. Gently fold tuna mixture into egg whites. Pour into soufflé dish.
8. Sprinkle top with paprika.
9. Cook on delicate food cycle for 16 to 18 minutes, turning soufflé after 10 minutes of cooking. Soufflé should be fairly firm to the touch.

Serve at once.
Serves 4 to 6.

Note: Seafood soufflé: use 1 can (7¾ oz.) salmon or 1 can (7½ oz.) crab meat or 1 can (5 oz.) lobster, drained, boned and finely chopped in place of tuna.

HAM-MUSHROOM SOUFFLE

4 tablespoons butter or margarine
4 tablespoons flour
¼ teaspoon salt
⅛ teaspoon pepper
Dash of hot-pepper sauce
⅔ cup milk
4 egg yolks, well beaten
8 egg whites
⅔ cup ground, cooked ham
1 can (3 to 4 oz.) mushrooms, drained and finely
  chopped
2 tablespoons mincedaives
¼ teaspoon cream of tartar
2 tablespoons parmesan cheese
2 tablespoons paprika

1. In a small-size heat resistant non-metallic bowl melt butter on delicate food cycle ½ minute.
2. Stir in flour, salt, pepper, and hot pepper sauce, stirring until smooth.
3. Heat uncovered, on delicate food cycle for 2 minutes or until mixture bubbles.
4. Remove mixture from oven and blend in milk slowly.
5. Heat, uncovered, on delicate food cycle for 3 minutes stirring after the first 1½ minutes or until mixture thickens and bubbles. (sauce will be quite thick)
6. Beat mixture slowly into egg yolks: Stir in ham, mushrooms and chives. Allow mixture to cool.
7. Prepare a 1½ quart soufflé dish by forming a collar of wax paper around top of dish that extends about 3-inch above dish.
8. Beat egg whites with cream of tartar until stiff but not dry.
9. Gently fold ham mixture into egg whites. Pour into soufflé dish.
10. Sprinkle top with parmesan cheese, then with paprika.
11. Cook on delicate food cycle for 16 to 18 minutes, turning soufflé after 10 minutes of cooking. Souffllé should be fairly firm to the touch.

Serve at once.
Serves 4 to 6.

Tips: Chicken or turkey soufflé: Substitute ⅔ cup ground cooked chicken or turkey for ham.

Special Recipes for Automatic Defrost and Delicate Food Cycle.

BAKED CUSTARD

1¾ cups milk
¼ cup sugar
3 eggs
¼ teaspoon salt
½ teaspoon vanilla
⅛ teaspoon nutmeg

1. In a 4-cup measuring cup, measure 1¾ cups milk.
2. Add sugar, eggs, salt and vanilla to milk. Beat with mixer, until well combined.
3. Pour mixture into 5 to 6 oz. custard cups sprinkle with nutmeg.
4. Place custard cups in a circle formation on the glass shelf in the Microwave Oven.
5. Cook on delicate food cycle for 8 to 10 minutes or until custard starts to become firm.

Serves 5.

Tips: Custard may be cooked in a 1 quart casserole. Cooking time is 7 to 9 minutes.

POT ROAST

3-4 pounds chuck, blade or arm roast
2 tablespoons oil
1½ cups water
1 teaspoon flour
Salt and pepper

1. Lightly coat pot roast with flour.
2. On a conventional range, brown slowly all sides of the roast in 2 tablespoons of oil.
3. Remove from heat. Place roast in a non-metallic 4-quart, covered baking dish. Add remaining ingredients.
4. Cook on delicate food cycle or defrost cycle, covered, 1 to 1½ hours or until meat is tender. Turn roast over after half the cooking time.

Serves 5 to 6.

Tips: If desired, add small potatoes, pared and halved, small whole onions, and medium carrots, pared and cut into one-inch pieces.
Vegetables can be added without changing cooking time.

A 4-quart, glass, ceramic freezer to range top pan may be used to brown roast to eliminate transfer of roast to glass baking dish.

CORNED BEEF DINNER

3 pounds (whole) corned beef
3 cups water
2 bay leaves
1 clove garlic
½ cup chopped onion
2 potatoes, peeled and quartered
4 carrots, pared and sliced
4 cabbage wedges

1. In a 4-quart, covered, non-metallic, glass baking dish, combine beef, water, bay leaves, garlic and onion.
2. Cook on delicate food cycle or defrost cycle for one hour.
3. Add potatoes, carrots and cabbage. Cook 30 minutes on delicate food cycle or defrost cycle until vegetables are tender.

Serves 4 to 5.

COOKIES

Baked cookies (example: sugar cookies, oatmeal, pecan, etc) cook very evenly using the delicate food cycle.
Follow your favorite recipe for combining ingredients. Chill dough before baking.
Baking time on delicate food cycle:

1 cookie	1¼ to 1¾ minutes
3 cookies	2 to 2½ minutes
6 cookies	3½ to 4½ minutes
9 cookies	6½ to 7½ minutes

Bake cookies on waxed paper. Cookies are done when they lift freely from the waxed paper.
Allow cookies to cool on waxed paper and become firm before removing them.

Meal Planning

Meal Planning

Meal planning is made quick and easy with the help of your new Microwave Oven. This chapter is especially intended to give you hints on how to plan cooking times for full meals prepared in the Microwave Oven. Because microwave cookery is a new method of cooking, until you are more familiar with it, you might find that meals require a little more planning than when conventional cooking methods are employed. The little extra planning is well worth the cooking time saved with your Microwave Oven.

In order to make best use of this chapter, read through the menu, the directions for preparing the meal, and each of the recipes before beginning the meal. The asterisk (*) after a recipe title in the menu indicates that the recipe follows.

When first preparing these or any other meals in your Microwave Oven, you might want to allow yourself a little extra time, until you are completely at ease and familiar with your Microwave Oven. Foods can always be reheated in the Microwave Oven without losing their fresh-cooked flavor.

As you will discover, a certain amount of shuffling is required when cooking several foods at one time for a meal. Foods may be partially cooked and covered with aluminum foil to retain their heat. They may then be reheated or finished cooking at a later time. However, you must remember to *remove aluminum foil before returning foods to the Microwave Oven.*

Some foods need time to stand at room temperature to allow internal temperatures to equalize. This resting time can be used to good advantage for preparing side dishes, salads, and even setting the table.

You may find it more convenient at times to use conventional cooking methods for a part of a meal and the Microwave Oven for the remainder. Since the time saved in cooking foods that must be rehydrated is negligible, it's sometimes just as easy to cook these foods conventionally. Some examples of foods that are better cooked conventionally than in the Microwave Oven are rice, noodles, and other forms of pasta. However, the Microwave Oven is great for reheating these foods.

A chapter later in this book will show you how to convert conventional recipes to use in the Microwave Oven. Remember that it is always better to undercook foods than to overcook them since you can never "uncook" them.

Meal Planning

Stuffed Mushrooms*
Tossed Salad
Roast Loin of Pork with Apricot Glaze*
Succotash*
Boiled Parsley Potatoes*
Strawberry Cheesecake*

○ The Strawberry Cheesecake should be prepared in advance so that it has time to chill before serving.
○ The salad greens may also be prepared in advance so that there is less to do at mealtime. Do not put dressing on salad until just before serving.
○ The Stuffed Mushrooms may also be prepared in advance and heated just before serving.
○ In advance of dinner time, prepare potatoes up to Step 3. Reheat at serving time. Potatoes may be boiled conventionally and finished in Microwave Oven at serving time.
○ About 1½ hours before serving time, begin to prepare pork roast.
○ While roast is standing at room temperature, prepare Succotash and finish cooking potatoes.
○ Just before serving time, heat the Stuffed Mushrooms.
○ Put dressing on salad and serve the meal.

STUFFED MUSHROOMS

12 large fresh mushrooms
3 tablespoons butter or margarine
Salt and pepper
¼ cup butter or margarine
⅓ cup finely chopped onion
1 tablespoon flour
½ cup heavy cream
¼ cup chopped parsley
¼ cut grated Swiss cheese (optional)

1. Wipe mushrooms with a damp cloth. Carefully remove stems and set aside.
2. In a small heat-resistant non-metallic custard cup melt the 3 tablespoons of butter in Microwave Oven for 30 (40) seconds.
3. Brush mushroom caps with melted butter and place, hollow-side-up, in a shallow non-metallic baking dish. Sprinkle mushroom caps with salt and pepper.
4. Finely chop the reserved mushroom stems.
5. In a medium-size heat-resistant non-metallic bowl melt the ¼ cup of butter in Microwave Oven for 30 (40) seconds. Add onions and chopped mushroom stems; stir to combine.
6. Heat, uncovered, in Microwave Oven 3 (4) minutes or until onions and mushrooms are tender. Blend in flour until smooth.
7. Gradually stir in heavy cream until smooth.
8. Heat, uncovered, in Microwave Oven 3 (4) minutes or until thickened and smooth. Stir in chopped parsley.
9. Fill each mushroom cap with some of the mushroom mixture.
10. If desired, sprinkle a little grated Swiss cheese over each stuffed mushroom cap. (Refrigerate if not going to serve at this time.)
11. Heat, uncovered, in a non-metallic pie pan in Microwave Oven 3 (4) minutes just before serving. (If refrigerated, heating will take an additional 1 (1¼) minute.)
Serves 6.

ROAST LOIN OF PORK WITH APRICOT GLAZE

1 (12-ounce) package dried apricots
1 3-inch stick cinnamon
½ lemon, seeds removed
½ cup water
1 cup apple juice or apricot nectar
2 tablespoons orange juice
2 tablespoons honey
1 (6-pound) loin of pork roast with bone tips
  Frenched
Canned apricot halves (optional)

1. Remove twice as many dried apricot halves as there are bones on the roast and set aside. Place remaining dried apricots, cinnamon, the juice of the lemon half, the remainder of the lemon half cut into quarters, and the water in a medium-sized non-metallic bowl.
2. Heat, uncovered, in Microwave Oven 4 (5¼) minutes or until apricots are tender.
3. Remove cinnamon stick and lemon chunks. Add apple juice, orange juice and honey.
4. Heat, uncovered, in Microwave Oven 2 (2½) minutes.
5. Spread glaze over pork loin and heat, uncovered, in a shallow non-metallic baking dish in Microwave Oven about 1 (1¼) hours or 10 (13) minutes per pound or until a meat thermometer inserted in the thickest part of the meat registers 165°F. While roast cooks, turn it occasionally and baste meat with glaze.
6. Allow to stand wrapped in aluminum foil 15 minutes. *Do not place thermometer or aluminum foil in Microwave Oven.*
7. Before serving, place two of the reserved apricot halves on each bone tip. Press apricot halves together so they stay in place.
8. Garnish platter with canned apricot halves, if desired.

Serves 6.

SUCCOTASH

2 (10-ounce) packages frozen Fordhook lima beans, thawed (see chart Page 13)
2 (10-ounce) packages frozen whole kernel corn, thawed (see chart Page 13)
⅓ cup chopped canned pimiento
2 teaspoons salt
½ teaspoon sugar
¼ teaspoon pepper
6 tablespoons butter or margarine
½ cup light cream

1. Place lima beans and corn in a large heat-resistant non-metallic bowl.
2. Heat, covered, in Microwave Oven 10 (13) minutes or until vegetables are hot.
3. Add remaining ingredients and stir to combine. Heat, uncovered, in Microwave Oven 2 (2½) minutes or until heated through.

Serves 6.

BOILED PARSLEY POTATOES

6 medium-size potatoes, peeled and quartered
Water
½ teaspoon salt
⅓ cup butter or margarine
¼ cup finely chopped parsley

1. Place potatoes in water to cover in a deep 2-quart non-metallic casserole.
2. Add salt. Heat, covered, in Microwave Oven 20 (25) minutes or until fork-tender. Drain.
3. Add butter and parsley.
4. Heat, uncovered, in Microwave Oven 2 (2½) minutes.
Toss to thoroughly combine.

Serves 6.

STRAWBERRY CHEESECAKE

18 Zwieback crackers, crushed
3 tablespoons butter or margarine, softened
1 tablespoon sugar
2 (8-ounce) packages cream cheese, at room temperature
½ cup sugar
2 egg yolks
1 teaspoon grated lemon peel
1 tablespoon lemon juice
2 egg whites, stiffly beaten
1 cup commercial sour cream
1 tablespoon sugar
1 teaspoon vanilla extract
1 pint large strawberries, washed and hulled

1. If cheesecake is to be removed from pan, use a 9-inch "spring-form type" pan. (See Note.)
If cheesecake is not to be removed from pan, it can be made in a 9-inch round non-metallic baking dish. (The first piece may be difficult to remove from baking dish.)
2. Lightly grease the cooking utensil.
3. In a small bowl combine cracker crumbs, softened butter and the 1 tablespoon of sugar. Press into bottom of greased pan.
4. Heat, uncovered, in Microwave Oven 2 (2½) minutes. turning pan ½ turn after 1 (1¼) minute. Set aside.
5. In a large mixing bowl, beat cream cheese and the ½ cup of sugar together until light and fluffy. Add egg yolks, 1 at a time, beating well after each addition. Beat in lemon peel and juice.
6. Fold in stiffly beaten egg whites.
7. Pour into prepared cake pan; smooth with a spatula.
8. Heat, uncovered, in Microwave Oven 6 (8) minutes, rotating ⅓ turn after each 2 (2½) minutes.
9. In a small bowl combine sour cream, the 1 tablespoon sugar and the vanilla until well blended. Carefully spread over top of cheesecake.
10. Heat, uncovered, in Microwave Oven 1 (1¼) minute.
11. Arrange strawberries on cheesecake as desired and chill several hours before serving.

Serves 6.

Note: A 9-inch "spring-form type" pan can be made from a 4-inch deep section of a tube of plexiglass 9 inches in diameter. A 9-inch plexiglass circle can be used as the bottom. Use cellophane tape to seal outside of seam. (Any heat-resistant plastic can be used.)

*Parenthesis ( ) indicates 500 watt units.

Meal Planning

ITALIAN DINNER

Prosciutto and Melon
Tossed Salad
Chicken Breasts Parmesan*
Baked Ziti*
Italian Style Zucchini*
Rum Cake*

○ Prepare Prosciutto and Melon and Tossed Salad in advance and refrigerate until serving time.
○ Prepare Rum Cake in advance and allow to chill before serving.
○ Prepare Baked Ziti up to Step. 1. Cover and let stand.
○ Prepare Italian Style Zucchini up to Step 4. Cover and let stand.
○ Prepare Chicken Breasts Parmesan up to Step 6. Cover and let stand.
○ Finish cooking Baked Ziti and cover until serving time.
○ Finish cooking chicken breasts and cover until serving time.
○ While serving Prosciutto and Melon and the Tossed Salad, finish cooking the Zucchini.
○ Reheat any parts of the meal as necessary.

CHICKEN BREASTS PARMESAN

½ cup seasoned fine dry bread crumbs
¼ cup grated Parmesan cheese
1½ pounds boneless chicken breasts
1 egg, well beaten
2 tablspoons olive oil
1 cup shredded mozzarella cheese
1 (8-ounce) can tomato sauce
¼ teaspoon dried oregano leaves
Grated Parmesan cheese

1. On wax paper combine bread crumbs and the ½ cup grated Parmesan cheese. Dip chicken breasts first in egg and then in bread crumb mixture until well coated.
2. Heat oil in a non-metallic skillet over high heat on the top of a conventional stove. Quickly brown coated chicken pieces on both sides.
3. Sprinkle the shredded mozzarella cheese over the browned chicken.
4. In a small bowl combine tomato sauce and oregano leaves.
5. Spoon tomato sauce over chicken.
6. Heat, covered, in Microwave Oven 5 to 6 (6½ to 8) minutes or until sauce is bubbly and chicken is tender.
7. Sprinkle with grated Parmesan cheese and heat, uncovered, in Microwave Oven 30 (40) seconds or until cheese is melted.

Serves 4.

Tip: If a non-metallic skillet is not available, any skillet may be used and the browned chicken pieces may be transferred to a shallow non-metallic baking dish before Step 6.

BAKED ZITI

1 (8-ounce) package ziti (or other pasta product) cooked conventionally or according to spaghetti recipe on page 102
Italian Tomato Sauce (see recipe page 79)
½ cup shredded mozzarella cheese

1. In a deep 2-quart non-metallic casserole combine all ingredients.
2. Heat, covered, in Microwave Oven 5 to 8 (6½ to 10) minutes or until cheese has melted and sauce is bubbly.

Serves 4

ITALIAN STYLE ZUCCHINI

4 large zucchini
¼ cup water
2 tablespoons butter or margarine
2 tablespoons olive oil
1½ teaspoons salt
2 teaspoons chopped parsley
½ teaspoon dried basil leaves
½ teaspoon dried oregano leaves

1. Wash zucchini but do not peel. Cut zucchini into ¼-inch slices.
2. Place zucchini and water in a deep 1½-quart non-metallic casserole and heat, covered, in Microwave Oven 8 to 10 (10 to 13) minutes or until zucchini is crisp-tender.
3. Drain water, add butter and olive oil to zucchini.
4. Heat, uncovered, in Microwave Oven 2 (2½) minutes.
5. Add remaining ingredients and toss lightly. Return to Microwave Oven and heat, uncovered, an additional 2 to 3 (2½ to 4) minutes or until desired degree of doneness is reached.

Serves 4.

RUM CAKE

1 (18½-ounce) package devil's food cake mix
Ingredients as called for on cake package
3 egg whites, at room temperature
¼ teaspoon salt
6 tablespoons sugar
1 cup plus 2 tablespoons light corn syrup
2 teaspoons vanilla extract
Apricot preserves
Rum

1. Grease two 8-inch square non-metallic cake pans and set aside.
2. Prepare cake mix according to package directions,.
3. Pour ½ of batter into each prepared pan.
4. Heat each layer, uncovered, in Microwave Oven 7 (9) minutes, turning ¼ turn each 2 (2½) minutes.
5. Allow cake to cool 10 minutes before removing from pan.
6. While cakes are cooling prepare frosting.
7. In a small mixer bowl beat egg whites with salt until foamy. Add sugar 1 tablespoon at a time, beating until stiff peaks form.
8. Pour corn syrup into a 2-cup heat-resistant non-metallic measuring cup.
9. Heat, uncovered, in Microwave Oven 3 to 4 (4 to 5) minutes or until corn syrup comes to a boil.
10. Gradually pour boiling mixture over egg whites, beating constantly until frosting is cool and very stiff. Beat in vanilla.
11. Pour rum over the tops of both cake layers.
12. Spread apricot preserves over one of the cooled layers. Then spread some of the frosting on it.
13. Place second layer on top of first and spread entire cake with frosting.

Tips: Frosting will be neater if you place strips of wax paper under the bottom edges of the cake before frosting the sides. Remember to gently remove wax paper before serving cake.
Any leftover frosting can be used on cupcakes or stored in the refrigerator for later use.

ROAST CAPON DINNER

Vichyssoise
Roast Capon with Rye Bread Stuffing*
Cabbage Salad
Minted Fresh Peas*
Zesty Stewed Tomatoes*
Deep Dish Apple Pie*

○ Prepare and cook capon and stuffing.
○ While capon is cooking, prepare ingredients for Minted Fresh Peas and Zesty Stewed Tomatoes.
○ While capon is standing at room temperature after cooking, cook peas and tomatoes.
○ While peas and tomatoes are cooking, prepare Steps 1 and 3 of Deep Dish Apple Pie.
○ As you sit down to dinner, put apple mixture into the Microwave Oven according to Step 2 of apple pie.
○ While clearing the table, finish cooking pie.

ROAST CAPON WITH RYE BREAD STUFFING

1 (6-pound) capon or roasting chicken
4 tablespoons butter or margarine
½ cup finely chopped onion
½ cup finely chopped celery
1 teaspoon salt
¼ teaspoon pepper
½ teaspoon caraway seeds (optional)
1 envelope instant chicken broth or 1 cube chicken
  bouillon, crumbled
6 cups cubed day-old rye bread
¼ cup finely chopped parsley
½ cup boiling water
Salt and pepper

1. Wash and dry capon and set aside.
2. In a deep 2-quart non-metallic casserole melt butter in Microwave Oven 30 (40) seconds.
3. Add onion and celery and heat, uncovered, 4(5) minutes in Microwave Oven or until vegetables are tender.
4. Stir in the 1 teaspoon salt, the ¼ teaspoon pepper, the caraway seeds and chicken broth mix. Add rye bread and parsley; toss until well combined. Moisten bread mixture with ½ cup boiling water.
5. Rub inside cavity of capon with salt and pepper.
6. Stuff capon lightly with stuffing. Close body cavity with wooden skewers or sew with string.
7. Place bird, breast-side-up, in a shallow non-metallic baking dish. Use an inverted saucer as a a rack to keep capon out of pan drippings.
8. Heat, loosely covered with a paper towel, in Microwave Oven 36 (46) minutes (6 (8) minutes per pound) or until a meat thermometer inserted in the thickest part of the bird (not touching any bones) registers 160°F. *Do not place thermometer in Microwave Oven.*
9. Wrap in aluminum foil and allow to stand 15 minutes before carving. If it is necessary to reheat, *do not place aluminum foil in Microwave Oven.*
Serves 6.

Tip: Gravy, if desired, may be made according to recipe on page 78.

*Parenthesis (   ) indicates 500 watt units.

MINTED FRESH PEAS

8 large lettuce leaves
3 pounds peas, shelled
¾ teaspoon sugar
¾ teaspoon salt
⅛ teaspoon pepper
1½ teaspoons finely chopped fresh mint or ¼ teaspoon dried mint leaves
3 tablespoons butter or margarine

1. Wash lettuce leaves and line a deep 1½-quart non-metallic casserole with half of the moist lettuce leaves.
2. Top with peas.
3. Sprinkle with sugar, salt, pepper and mint and dot with butter.
4. Cover with remaining lettuce leaves.
5. Heat, covered tightly, in Microwave Oven 8 to 9 (10 to 11½) minutes or until peas are tender.
6. Carefully tilt cover to allow steam to escape. Then remove cover.
7. Remove lettuce leaves and toss peas well before serving.
Serves 6.

Tip: When tilting cover, tilt so that steam escapes away from you so that you don't get scalded.

Variations: ¼ teaspoon dried chervil or savory may be substituted for dried mint leaves.

ZESTY STEWED TOMATOES

3 tablespoons butter or margarine
¼ cup finely chopped onion
¼ cup finely chopped green pepper
6 large tomatoes, peeled and quartered
¾ teaspoon salt
⅛ teaspoon pepper
½ teaspoon sugar
⅛ teaspoon garlic salt
½ teaspoon dried oregano leaves

1. In a deep 2-quart non-metallic casserole melt butter in Microwave Oven 30 (40) seconds.
2. Add onion and green pepper, and heat, uncovered, in Microwave Oven 3 (4) minutes or until lightly browned.
3. Add remaining ingredients and stir to combine.
4. Heat, covered, in Microwave Oven 5 to 6 (6½ to 8) minutes or until tomatoes are very tender. Stir occasionally.
5. Serve hot or cold.
Serves 6.

DEEP DISH APPLE PIE

5 cups peeled and sliced tart apples
½ cup sugar
3 tablespoons water
½ teaspoon ground cinnamon, allspice, or cloves, or a combination of these spices
1 cup butter milk biscuit mix
2 tablespoons sugar
½ cup milk
Whipped cream (optional)

1. In a deep 2-quart non-metallic casserole combine apples, sugar, water and the ½ teaspoon of spice.
2. Heat, covered, 4 (5) minutes or until apples are almost tender.
3. While apples are cooking, prepare topping. Combine biscuit mix, sugar and milk, stirring with a fork until just moistened.
4. Drop by spoonfuls on hot apple mixture.
5. Heat, covered, 5 (6½) minutes or until topping is no longer doughy underneath.
6. If desired, serve with dollops of whipped cream.
Serves 6.

GREEK DINNER

Greek Lemon Soup*
Greek Salad*
Moussaka*
Tomato Sauce for Moussaka*
Spinach Pie*
Pita and Butter
Caramel Custard*

○ The Caramel Custard should be prepared in advance so that it has time to chill before serving.
○ The Spinach Pie can be prepared up to Step 10.
○ About 1½ hours before serving begin to prepare the Mousssaka. It will be necessary to reserve a portion of the tomato paste used in the Moussaka for the Tomato Sauce.
○ While Moussaka is cooking, Tomato Sauce for Moussaka can be prepared.
○ The ingredients for the Greek Lemon Soup can be gathered, prepared and combined while the Moussaka is being prepared.
○ Reheat the Tomato Sauce for Moussaka just before serving.
○ Cook Greek Lemon Soup.
○ While the soup and salad are being eaten, the Spinach Pie can be baked.
○ If desired, pita, a Greek bread, can be warmed in the Microwave Oven on a paper or cloth napkin for 30 seconds to 1 minute (40 sec. to 1¼ min.). Do not heat for too long as pita may become tough and rubbery.

GREEK LEMON SOUP

2 (10½-ounce) cans condensed chicken rice soup
2 soup cans water
1 egg, well beaten
2 medium-sized lemons

1. In a medium-sized heat-resistant non-metallic bowl combine the chicken rice soup and water. Heat, covered, in Microwave Oven 6 to 8 (8 to 10) minutes or until soup is very hot.
2. Gradually, a very little at a time, add some of the hot soup mixture to the well-beaten egg; stir until completely combined. Return the egg-soup mixture to the hot soup; stir to combine.
3. Heat, uncovered, in Microwave Oven 2 (2½) minutes or until soup thickens slightly. While the soup is heating slice one of the two lemons into thin circles. Squeeze the juice from the other lemon.
4. Just before serving, add the lemon slices and juice to the soup. Heat, uncovered, in Microwave Oven 2 (2½) minutes.

Serves 6.

Greek Dinner

MOUSSAKA

4 or 5 (7 to 8 inch) eggplants, washed
1 tablespoon salt
2 tablespoons olive oil
2 pounds lean ground lamb
Vegetable oil
⅔ cup finely chopped onion
1 (8-ounce) can sliced mushrooms, drained
1 teaspoon salt
½ teaspoon dried thyme leaves

1 teaspoon dried rosemary leaves
1 clove garlic, peeled and crushed
⅔ cup beef stock or broth
1½ teaspoons cornstarch
3 tablespoons tomato paste (save rest for sauce, recipe at right)
3 eggs, slightly beaten

1. Remove green caps from eggplants and slice eggplants in half lengthwise. Make deep slashes in eggplant pulp, but do not cut through skins.
2. Sprinkle eggplant halves with the 1 tablespoon salt and allow to stand ½ hour.
3. Squeeze moisture out of eggplants. Brush cut surfaces with the 2 tablespoons of olive oil.
4. Heat 4 eggplant halves at a time in Microwave Oven 7 (9) minutes or until tender.
5. Scoop flesh out of eggplant, being careful not to rip skins. Set skins aside. Chop eggplant flesh coarsely. Place in a medium-sized heat-resistant non-metallic bowl and heat, uncovered, in Microwave Oven 4 (5¼) minutes or until tender. Stir occasionally.
6. In a large heat-resistant non-metallic bowl, crumble the lamb. Heat, uncovered, in Microwave Oven 5 (6½) minutes, stirring frequently to break up pieces until meat is no longer pink.
7. Liberally oil a deep 2-quart non-metallic casserole. Line casserole with the reserved eggplant skins. Arrange with purple sides toward the outside and wide ends of the eggplant skins at the top of the casserole.
8. Drain the lamb juices and discard. Add chopped eggplant, onion, mushrooms, the 1 teaspoon salt, thyme, rosemary and garlic to the cooked lamb; stir to combine well. Heat, uncovered, in Microwave Oven 5 (6½) minutes.
9. In a small heat-resistant non-metallic bowl combine beef stock and cornstarch. Heat, uncovered, in Microwave Oven 1 (1¼) minute or until thickened and clear; stir occasionally. Add, with remaining ingredients, to lamb mixture.
10. Pour mixture into eggplant-skin-lined casserole. Fold skins over filling. Heat, covered, with a plate, in Microwave Oven 7 to 9 (9 to 11½) minutes or until a knife inserted in the mixture comes out clean.
11. Invert onto serving platter.

Serves 6.

*Parenthesis (   ) indicates 500 watt units.

Meal Planning

TOMATO SAUCE FOR MOUSSAKA

3 tablespoons vegetable oil
½ cup finely chopped onion
1 clove garlic, peeled and crushed
1 (15-ounce) can tomato sauce
1 (6-ounce) can tomato paste, minus 3 tablespoons
2 teaspoons sugar
½ teaspoon dried thyme leaves
½ teaspoon dried rosemary leaves
½ teaspoon salt
¼ teaspoon pepper

1. Place oil and onion in a deep 1½-quart casserole; heat, uncovered, in Microwave Oven 3 (4) minutes.
2. Add remaining ingredients; stir to combine well. Heat, covered, in Microwave Oven 6 (8) minutes or until sauce bubbles.

Serves 6.

GREEK SALAD

8 cups torn lettuce, washed and drained
2 tomatoes, washed and cut into 8 wedges each
1 (8-ounce) can pitted ripe olives
½ cup crumbled feta cheese
Oil and vinegar dressing

1. Lightly toss lettuce, tomatoes, olives and feta cheese in a salad bowl.
2. Just before serving time, pour oil and vinegar dressing on salad.

Serves 6.

SPINACH PIE

½ pound phyllo or strudel pastry leaves
¼ cup butter or margarine
½ cup coarsely chopped onion
3 (10-ounce) packages frozen chopped spinach, thawed (see chart page 13)
3 eggs, well beaten
½ pound feta cheese
¼ cup chopped parsley
1 teaspoon pepper
¾ cup butter or margarine

1. Bring pastry to room temperature.
2. In a medium-sized heat-resistant non-metallic bowl melt butter in Microwave Oven 30 (40) seconds. Add onion and heat, uncovered, in Microwave Oven 3 (4) minutes or until tender.
3. Press all moisture out of spinach and blot dry.
4. Combine spinach, onion, eggs, cheese, parsley, salt and pepper in a large bowl; stir until well blended.

5. Brush a 9-inch square non-metallic baking dish lightly with some of the ¾ cup melted butter.
6. In the bottom of the baking dish layer 8 pastry leaves, one by one, brushing the top of each with some of the melted butter.
7. Spread evenly with spinach mixture.
8. Repeat the layering process with 8 more leaves.
9. Trim off uneven edges of pastry. Cut through the pastry layer to form squares.
10. Pour any remaining butter over the top. Bake in Microwave Oven, uncovered, 8 (10) minutes, turning ½ turn after 4 (5) minutes.

Serves 6.

Tip: Any remaining pastry leaves may be frozen for future use.

CARAMEL CUSTARD

1 cup sugar
3 eggs
5 egg yolks
2 (13-ounce) cans evaporated milk
¾ cup sugar
2 teaspoons vanilla extract

1. Place the 1 cup sugar in an 8-inch round non-metallic baking dish. Heat, uncovered, in Microwave Oven 4 (5) minutes.
2. Stir and heat sugar an additional 4 (5) minutes, stirring very frequently with a rubber spatula until sugar melts and turns a light brown.
3. Rotate pan until completely coated with caramel.
4. In a large bowl combine remaining ingredients until well blended.
5. Pour egg mixture into caramel-coated pan. Heat, uncovered, in Microwave Oven 3 (4) minutes. Move cooked portions of mixture toward the center of the pan with a rubber spatula.
6. Return to Microwave Oven and heat, uncovered, an additional 3 (4) minutes; move cooked portions to center again.
7. Heat, uncovered, in Microwave Oven 4 (5) minutes longer, turning ½ turn after 2 (2½) minutes.
8. Insert a knife 1 inch from the outside edge. If knife comes out clean, custard is done. If not, return to oven for an additional minute of cooking. Cool custard slightly and invert onto a platter while caramel is still warm or the caramel will stick to the pan. Chill before serving.

Serves 6.

Tip: Unused egg white can be frozen in the compartments of an ice cube tray and then stored in a plastic bag for later use.

OVEN-FRIED CHICKEN DINNER

Curried Pear Halves*
Lettuce and Tomato Salad
Oven-fried Chicken*
Glazed Belgian Carrots*
Duchess Potatoes*
Brownies à la Mode*

○ Brownies may be prepared in advance and reheated at serving time.

○ The Duchess Potatoes may be prepared in advance up to Step 3. If preferred, they may be boiled conventionally and finished in Microwave Oven at serving time.

○ About 1 hour before serving time, cook carrots but do not glaze. Allow them to stand, covered with aluminum foil, until serving time.

○ Prepare Oven-fried Chicken up to Step 6 and cover with aluminum foil.

○ Just before serving time, while chicken is standing at room temperature, prepare Curried Pear Halves.

○ While pear halves and Lettuce and Tomato Salad are being served, allow chicken to finish cooking.
Do not put aluminum foil in Microwave Oven.

○ While chicken is standing at room temperature, finish cooking Glazed Belgian Carrots and Duchess Potatoes.

○ While dishes are being cleared, reheat brownies for serving. If ice cream is too hard to scoop, it may be heated in Microwave Oven for 30 to 60 (40 to 75) seconds, depending upon size of container.

CURRIED PEAR HALVES

1 (29-ounce) can pear halves
⅓ cup butter or margarine
¾ cup firmly packed dark brown sugar
1 to 2 teaspoons curry powder
Commercial sour cream (optional)

1. Drain pear halves and reserve ⅓ cup of the liquid.
2. Place pear halves in a shallow non-metallic baking dish.
3. In a small heat-resistant non-metallic bowl, melt butter in Microwave Oven 30 (40) seconds.
4. Stir in reserved pear liquid, brown sugar and curry powder to taste.
5. Spread curry mixture over pears and heat, uncovered, in Microwave Oven 5 (6½) minutes or until heated through.
6. Serve warm with dollops of sour cream, if desired.

Serves 4 to 6.

OVEN-FRIED CHICKEN

2 (2½-pound) broiler-fryer chickens, cut up
2 cups seasoned bread crumbs, cornflake crumbs, cracker crumbs or packaged coating mix
2 teaspoons paprika
⅔ cup milk

1. Wash chickens and pat dry.
2. Combine desired crumb coating with paprika.
3. Coat each piece of chicken with milk, then crumb mixture.
4. Place coated chicken pieces in a shallow non-metallic baking dish with the larger pieces along the outside edges of the pan and the smaller pieces in the center.
5. Heat, uncovered, in Microwave Oven for 20 (25) minutes.
6. Turn and heat, uncovered, an additional 10 (13) minutes or until chicken is fork-tender.
7. Let chicken stand, covered, for 5 minutes.
8. Serve either hot or cold.

Serves 4 to 6.

GLAZED BELGIAN CARROTS

2 bunches small Belgian carrots
¼ cup water
½ teaspoon salt
6 tablespoons butter
2 tablespoons honey
¼ to ½ teaspoon ground ginger

1. Wash and peel carrots.
2. Place carrots, water and salt in a deep 1½-quart non-metallic casserole.
3. Heat, covered, in Microwave Oven 9 to 10 (11½ to 13) minutes or until just about fork-tender. Stir occasionally.
4. Add butter, honey and ginger to taste.
5. Heat, uncovered, in Microwave Oven 2 (2½) minutes, stirring occasionally to glaze carrots.
6. Let stand, covered, 3 minutes to finish cooking. If carrots are not tender enough, return to Microwave Oven for an additional 1 to 2 (1¼ to 2½) minutes.

Serves 4 to 6.

Tip: If Belgian carrots are not available, regular carrots may be used if cut into thirds.

*Parenthesis ( ) indicates 500 watt units.

DUCHESS POTATOES

6 medium-sized potatoes, peeled and cut into large cubes
Water
1 teaspoon salt
1 egg, slightly beaten
¼ cup milk or light cream
4 tablespoons butter or margarine, softened
1 teaspoon salt
⅛ teaspoon pepper
Paprika

1. In a deep 2-quart non-metallic casserole place potatoes and water to cover. Sprinkle with the 1 teaspoon salt.
2. Heat, covered, in Microwave Oven 10 to 12 (13 to 15½) minutes or until fork-tender.
3. Partially mash potatoes with a potato masher.
4. Add egg, milk, butter, the 1 teaspoon salt and the pepper.
5. Beat with an electric mixer until smooth.
6. Place in a heat-resistant non-metallic serving dish and sprinkle with paprika.
7. Heat, uncovered, in Microwave Oven 4 (5) minutes.

Serves 4 to 6.

BROWNIES À LA MODE

¾ cup unsifted flour
1 cup sugar
7 tablespoons unsweetened cocoa
½ teaspoon baking powder
¾ teaspoon salt
⅔ cup butter or margarine, at room temperature
2 eggs
1 teaspoon vanilla extract
1 tablespoon dark corn syrup
Vanilla ice cream

1. Grease an 8-inch square non-metallic baking dish and set aside.
2. Sift together flour, sugar, cocoa, baking powder and salt into the large bowl of an electric mixer. Add remaining ingredients and beat until smooth.
3. Pour batter into the prepared baking dish.
4. Heat, uncovered, in Microwave Oven 6 (8) minutes; turn ¼ turn after each 1½ (2) minutes of cooking time.
5. Test for doneness with a toothpick; if not done, return to Microwave Oven for an additional minute.
6. Allow to cool slightly and cut into squares for serving.
7. Place a scoop of vanilla ice cream on each serving.

Tip: If brownies are prepared in advance, they may be reheated at serving time for 1 (1¼) minute in Microwave Oven. Brownie batter may be prepared in advance and baked at serving time.

A SIMPLE LUNCHEON

Egg Drop Soup*
Cheeseburgers*
Cherry Tomatoes
Assorted Relishes
Pimientos Stuffed with Corn*
Easy Rice Pudding*

○ Prepare Egg Drop Soup up to Step 6.
○ While soup is standing at room temperature, prepare Cheeseburgers.
○ Prepare Easy Rice Pudding up to Step 2.
○ Prepare Pimientos Stuffed with Corn.
○ Reheat Egg Drop Soup, garnish and serve.
○ While serving Cheeseburgers and stuffed pimientos, cook Easy Rice Pudding.

EGG DROP SOUP

6 cups water
1 (3½-ounce) package chicken noodle soup mix (2 envelopes)
2 eggs, well beaten
1 tablespoon soy sauce (optional)
Chinese fried noodles

1. Pour water into a deep 2-quart non-metallic casserole and heat, covered, in Microwave Oven 8 (10) minutes or until boiling.

2. Add noodle soup mix and heat, covered, 4 (5¼) minutes.
3. Allow to stand 4 to 5 minutes or until noodles and chicken are tender.
4. Pour beaten eggs in soup mixture and heat, uncovered, 2 to 3 (2½ to 4) minutes or until egg is cooked. Stir frequently to make eggs form thin strings.
5. If desired, stir in soy sauce.
6. Garnish with fried noodles.

Serves 6.

Cheeseburger

CHEESEBURGERS

1½ pounds lean ground beef
Salt
Brown bouquet sauce (optional)
Water (optional)
6 hamburger buns
6 slices cheese

1. Form beef into 6 patties about ½ inch thick.
2. Sprinkle with salt and brush patties with a 1-to-1 mixture of brown bouquet sauce and water, if a deep brown color is desired.
3. Arrange patties in a circle in a paper-towel-lined shallow non-metallic baking dish. Do not place any patties in center of circle. Heat, covered with paper toweling, in Microwave Oven 5 (6½) minutes.
4. Turn and brush again with brown bouquet mixture, if desired.
5. Heat, covered with paper toweling, an additional minute. Cheeseburgers will be rare. Heat an additional 1-2 minutes for medium or well-done.
6. Place 1 patty each on a hamburger bun and top each hamburger with a slice of cheese. Arrange hamburgers on a heat-resistant non-metallic serving platter and heat, uncovered, in Microwave Oven 2 (2½) minutes or until cheese has melted.

Serves 6.

PIMIENTOS STUFFED WITH CORN

1 (12-ounce) can corn
1 cup soft bread crumbs
1 tablespoon chili sauce
3 tablespoons melted butter or margarine
Salt and pepper
6 whole canned pimientos, well drained

1. Combine the corn, bread crumbs, chili sauce, butter and salt and pepper to taste in a small bowl.
2. Stuff the pimientos with the corn mixture and place in a shallow non-metallic baking dish.
3. Heat, uncovered, in Microwave Oven 4 (5) minutes or until heated through.
Serves 6.

EASY RICE PUDDING

1 (3-ounce) package vanilla pudding and pie filling mix (not instant)
2½ cups milk
½ cup seedless raisins
½ cup quick cooking rice

1. In a deep 1-quart non-metallic casserole combine all ingredients.
2. Heat, uncovered, in Microwave Oven 6 (8) minutes or until mixture boils. Stir occasionally during last 3 (4) minutes of cooking time.
3. Serve either hot or chilled.

Serves 6.

*Parenthesis ( ) indicates 500 watt units.

FRENCH LUNCHEON

Potage Mongol*
Stuffed Fillets of Sole with Mushroom Sauce*
Artichoke Hearts Vinaigrette*
Relish Tray*
Peach Halves with Raspberry Sauce*

○ Prepare Peach Halves with Raspberry Sauce in advance. This dessert may be served chilled or reheated at serving time.
○ The Relish Tray may also be prepared in advance and refrigerated.
○ Prepare Potage Mongol up to Step 2.
○ Prepare Artichoke Hearts Vinaigrette. They may be served chilled or reheated at serving time.
○ Prepare Stuffed Fillets of Sole with Mushroom Sauce up to Step 5. Have remainder of ingredients ready.
○ Heat Potage Mongol.
○ Prepare sauce for fish as soup is cooking. Heat sauce and fish while soup is being eaten.
○ If necessary or desired, reheat artichokes.
○ As entree dishes are being cleared, reheat peaches and sauce, if desired.

POTAGE MONGOL

1 (10½-ounce) can condensed tomato soup
1 (10½-ounce) can condensed green pea soup
1½ soup cans water
¼ cup dry sherry

1. In a deep 2½-quart non-metallic casserole or heat-resistant non-metallic soup tureen combine the tomato soup, pea soup and water; stir until smooth.
2. Heat, covered, in Microwave Oven 8 to 10 (10 to 13) minutes or until soup bubbles. Stir several times during heating.
3. Before serving, stir in sherry.

Serves 6.

French Luncheon

RELISH TRAY

Carrots
Celery sticks
Pimiento-stuffed Spanish olives

1. To make carrot curls, wash and peel carrots.
2. With a vegetable parer cut lengthwise into paper-thin slices. Roll carrot around finger, then slip carrot off finger and fasten curls with toothpicks.
3. Chill in a bowl of ice water.
4. Remove picks before arranging, as desired, in relish tray with celery sticks and olives.

STUFFED FILLETS OF SOLE WITH MUSHROOM SAUCE

Butter or margarine
2½ pounds salmon-stuffed sole fillets (see Note)
Salt and pepper
¼ cup finely chopped onion
1 cup dry white wine
⅓ cup butter or margarine
1 (4-ounce) can mushroom slices
4 tablespoons flour
1½ cups light cream
Paprika

1. Butter a shallow non-metallic baking dish lightly.
2. Place stuffed fish fillets in baking dish.
3. Sprinkle with salt and pepper to taste. Sprinkle with onions and pour wine over fish.
4. Heat, covered with clear plastic wrap, in Microwave Oven 7 to 8 (9 to 10) minutes or until fish flakes easily. Baste fish with wine and onions several times during cooking. Set dish of poached fish aside.
5. In a medium-sized heat-resistant non-metallic bowl melt the ⅓ cup butter in Microwave Oven 45 (60) seconds.

(Continued on next page)

6. Add mushroom slices and heat, uncovered, in Microwave Oven 2 (2½) minutes.
7. Blend in flour until smooth.
8. Gradually add cream, stirring until smooth.
9. Return sauce to Microwave Oven and heat, uncovered, 4 to 5 (5 to 6½) minutes or until thickened and smooth.
10. Add ½ cup fish liquid from baking dish to mushroom sauce and stir until well blended.
11. Place fish fillets on a heat-resistant non-metallic serving platter.
12. Spoon mushroom sauce over fish.
13. Heat, uncovered, in Microwave Oven 2 to 3 (2½ to 4) minutes or until heated through.
14. Sprinkle with paprika just before serving.

Serves 6.

Note: Many fish markets sell sole pre-stuffed with salmon. However, if this is not available, you can roll a piece of fresh salmon (about 1 inch in diameter and 4 inches long) in a small fillet of sole. Fasten each roll with a toothpick or wooden skewer. Unstuffed sole can also be used for this recipe. It is advisable to roll sole fillets even though they may not be stuffed.

Variations: Any fish fillets may be used in place of sole. Shrimp, lobster, crabmeat, scallops or other fish may be used in place of salmon.

ARTICHOKE HEARTS VINAIGRETTE

2 (14-ounce) cans artichoke hearts
¼ cup butter or margarine
Flour
⅓ cup butter or margarine, melted
Vinaigrette Dressing (see recipe at right)

1. Drain liquid from artichoke hearts and discard.
2. In a small heat-resistant non-metallic bowl melt the ¼ cup butter in Microwave Oven 30 (40) seconds.
3. Dip artichoke hearts in melted butter and then coat lightly with flour.
4. Place the ⅓ cup melted butter in a 10-inch non-metallic pie pan or non-metallic skillet.
5. Place flour-coated artichokes in melted butter and heat, uncovered, in Microwave Oven 6 (8) minutes. Turn artichoke hearts as needed to brown lightly.
6. While artichoke hearts are cooking, prepare Vinaigrette Dressing.
7. Just before serving, pour dressing over sautéed artichoke hearts.

Serves 6.

VINAIGRETTE DRESSING

¼ cup wine vinegar
¼ cup olive oil
¼ cup finely chopped parsley
2 tablespoons finely chopped chives
1 tablespoon finely chopped canned pimiento
1 teaspoon salt
⅛ teaspoon pepper

1. Combine all ingredients in a small bowl. Stir until well blended.

Makes 1 cup.

PEACH HALVES WITH RASPBERRY SAUCE

1 cup water
½ cup sugar
6 large fresh peaches, peeled, halved and pitted
1 pint fresh raspberries, washed and hulled
¼ cup sugar
¼ cup water

1. In a large heat-resistant non-metallic bowl combine the 1 cup of water and the ½ cup of sugar.
2. Heat, covered, in Microwave Oven 5 (6½) minutes, stirring occasionally.
3. Add peach halves and heat, covered, in Microwave Oven an additional 4 (5) minutes, basting peaches frequently.
4. In a medium-sized non-metallic bowl combine remaining ingredients.
5. Heat, covered, in Microwave Oven 3 (4) minutes or until berries are soft.
6. To serve, arrange two peach halves on each dessert plate and spoon some of the raspberry sauce over them.
7. Serve either warm or chilled.

Serves 6.

Tip: If serving this dish chilled, refrigerate peaches and raspberries separately.

Variations: Canned peach halves may be used. When using canned peach halves, begin with Step 4. If desired, pears, apricots or other fruit may be substituted for peaches. Other berries may be used for the sauce.

*Parenthesis ( ) indicates 500 watt units.

Meal Planning

BRUNCH

Bloody Mary Cocktails
Baked Apples with Mincemeat Stuffing*
Welsh Rarebit on Toast Points with Ham*
Sautéed String Beans*
Chocolate Cake with Fudge Icing*

○ Prepare Chocolate Cake in advance so it has time to chill.
○ Prepare Baked Apples, Welsh Rarebit and Sautéed String Beans, but do not cook at this time.
○ About 20 (25) minutes before serving time, heat Baked Apples in Microwave Oven.
○ Heat Welsh Rarebit and set aside, covered with aluminum foil, until serving time.
○ Just before serving, heat string beans.
○ If necessary, reheat Welsh Rarebit just before serving. *Do not put aluminum foil in Microwave Oven.*

BAKED APPLES WITH MINCEMEAT STUFFING

6 medium-sized baking apples
3 tablespoons butter or margarine
6 tablespoons mincemeat

1. Wash and core apples. Do not peel.
2. Place apples in a shallow non-metallic baking dish.
3. Place ½ tablespoon of butter and 1 tablespoon of mincemeat in the center of each apple.
4. Heat, uncovered, in Microwave Oven 7 to 8 (9 to 10) minutes or until apples are almost tender.
5. Allow to stand, covered, about 5 minutes.

Serves 6.

Variations: If desired, raisins, nuts, chutney or preserves can be substituted for mincemeat.

WELSH RAREBIT

3 eggs
1 (12-ounce) can beer or ale
3 cups cubed Cheddar chesse (about 1 pound)
3 tablespoons butter or margarine
1½ teaspoon dry mustard
1½ teaspoon Worcestershire sauce
⅛ teaspoon Tabasco sauce
12 toast triangles (from 6 pieces of bread)
6 slices of ham, cut into triangles the size of
  the bread triangles

1. In a deep 1½-quart non-metallic casserole beat eggs until well blended. Stir in remaining ingredient except toast and ham.
2. Heat, uncovered, in Microwave Oven 6 to 7 (8 to 9) minutes or until cheese has melted and mixture has thickened. Stir mixture about once every minute.
3. Beat with a rotary beater or electric mixer until very smooth.
4. Serve on individual plates Spoon rarebit over 2 toast triangles that have been topped with ham triangles.

Serves 6.

SAUTÉED STRING BEANS

4 tablespoons butter or margarine
2 (17-ounce) cans whole string beans, drained
¼ teaspoon dried savory leaves, crushed
⅛ teaspoon dried oregano leaves, crushed
½ teaspoon salt
⅛ teaspoon pepper

1. In a shallow non-metallic baking dish, melt butter in Microwave Oven 30 (40) seconds.
2. Add string beans and heat uncovered, in Microwave Oven 4 (5) minutes or until heated through.
3. Add remaining ingredients and toss lightly.

Serves 6.

CHOCOLATE CAKE WITH FUDGE ICING

1 (2-layer) package chocolate cake mix
Ingredients as called for on cake package
Fudge Icing (recipe below)

1. Prepare cake mix, as directed on package, in a large heat-resistant non-metallic mixing bowl.
2. Press a glass, right-side-up, through batter to form a tube shape.
3. Heat, uncovered, in Microwave Oven 8 to 9 (10 to 11½) minutes or until a wooden skewer inserted in the center comes out clean and batter around glass no longer looks doughy.
4. Let cool 30 minutes.
5. Remove glass by twisting slightly and invert cake onto serving plate. While cake is cooling, prepare Fudge Icing.

FUDGE ICING

1 cup evaporated milk
3 eggs
1 cup sugar
½ cup butter or margarine
1 teaspoon vanilla
2 (1-ounce) squares semisweet chocolate

(Continued on next page)

1. Beat eggs and milk in a deep 1-quart non-metallic casserole until well combined. Stir in sugar and butter.
2. Heat, uncovered, in Microwave Oven 5 (6½) minutes, stirring occasionally, until mixture thickens and boils.

3. Stir in vanilla and chocolate until chocolate has melted.
4. Cool to spreading consistency. Use to frost cake completely. Any remaining frosting may be refrigerated for use at a later time.

BREAKFAST

Fresh Orange Juice
Baked Grapefruit (see recipe page 123)
Poached Eggs for 4*
Canadian Bacon*
Toast and Butter
Coffee

○ Prepare coffee and toast conventionally. They can both be reheated in the Microwave Oven at serving time
○ with no loss of their fresh-cooked flavor.
○ Prepare Baked Grapefruit up to Step 4.
○ Prepare Step 1 of the Poached Eggs for 4.
○ While water is heating, arrange Canadian Bacon on a paper towel-lined paper plate.
○ Poach eggs.
○ While eggs are standing at room temperature, heat Canadian Bacon.
○ Bake grapefruit according to recipe on page 123.
○ If necessary, just before serving reheat toast and coffee in Microwave Oven.

POACHED EGGS FOR 4

2 quarts hot water
2 teaspoons salt
½ teaspoon white vinegar
8 eggs

1. Heat water, salt and vinegar in a deep 2½-quart non-metallic casserole until boiling (about 6 (8) minutes).
2. Carefully break eggs into boiling water, 1 at a time.
3. Heat, covered, in Microwave Oven 4 (5) minutes or until almost done.
4. Allow eggs to stand at room temperature 3 to 4 (4 to 5) minutes to finish cooking.
5. If necessary, return to Microwave Oven for 30 seconds to 1 minute (40 sec. to 1¼ min.) additional cooking to reach desired degree of doneness.

Serves 4.

CANADIAN BACON

12¼-inch slices Canadian bacon

1. Arrange bacon slices in a single layer on a paper-towel-lined paper plate.
2. Heat, covered loosely with wax paper or paper toweling, in Microwave Oven 6 (8) minutes or until the edges of the meat begin to sizzle, and bacon is well heated. Pork products should always be cooked to well done.

Breakfast

TO REHEAT BUTTERED TOAST

1. Place conventionally toasted bread in Microwave Oven in a single layer on a paper towel or cloth-lined paper plate and heat, uncovered, in Microwave Oven according to the chart below. The times are approximate, as they are dependent upon the temperature of the toast when placed in the Microwave Oven. *Do not overheat the toast* as it will become tough and dehydrated. It is better to heat for the

(Continued on next page)
*Parenthesis (   ) indicates 500 watt units.

minimum amount of time, rather than risk overheating toast.

1 slice	15 to 30 (20 to 40) seconds
2 slices	30 to 45 (40 to 60) seconds
4 slices	1 to 1¼ (1¼ to 2) minutes

TO REHEAT COFFEE

1. Place coffee in individual heat-resistant non-metallic mugs or cups or a heat-resistant non-metallic carafe and heat in Microwave Oven until hot. *Do not boil.* If coffee is allowed to boil, it may become strong and bitter. (See beverage heating chart page 61.)

A SIMPLE BREAKFAST

Orange Ambrosia*
Cooked Ham*
Oatmeal*
Hot Lemonade*

○ Prepare ingredients for Orange Ambrosia.

○ Prepare Oatmeal.

○ While Oatmeal is standing at room temperature, heat Orange Ambrosia.

○ Prepare Cooked Ham.

○ Prepare ingredients for Hot Lemonade.

○ While Orange Ambrosia is being eaten, heat Hot Lemonade.

○ If necessary, reheat Oatmeal just before serving.

ORANGE AMBROSIA

4 large oranges, peeled, pitted and sectioned
1 medium-sized banana, peeled and sliced
½ cup shredded coconut

1. Combine all ingredients in a medium-sized heat-resistant non-metallic bowl. Stir to combine.
2. Heat, uncovered, in Microwave Oven 3 (4) minutes or until heated through.
3. Serve either hot or cold.

Serves 4.

Tip: Oranges may be prepared the night before and covered tightly to save time in the morning.

COOKED HAM

4 slices ham (¼-inch thick and 4 x 5-inch)

1. Place ham in a single layer on a heat-resistant non-metallic serving platter.
2. Heat, covered with a paper towel, 4 (5) minutes or until edges begin to sizzle.

Serves 4.

OATMEAL

3 cups water
1⅓ cup quick-cooking rolled oats

¼ teaspoon salt
Butter
Cream or milk
Sugar

1. In a deep 1-quart non-metallic casserole combine water, oats and salt; stir to combine.
2. Heat, uncovered, in Microwave Oven 4½ (6) minutes or until mixture boils; stir occasionally.
3. Let stand, covered, 3 to 5 minutes before serving. Serve with butter, cream and sugar to taste.
4. Reheat if necessary.

Serves 4.

HOT LEMONADE

6 to 8 tablespoons sugar
½ cup lemon juice
Water
Lemon slices

1. Dissolve sugar in lemon juice in a 1-quart heat-resistant non-metallic measuring cup.
2. Add water to measure 1 quart.
3. Heat, uncovered, in Microwave Oven 6 (8) minutes or until mixture comes to a boil.
4. Pour into individual mugs and garnish with lemon slices.

Serves 4.

DINNER NO. 1

Fresh Artichokes Vinaigrette*
Crown Roast of Lamb with Corn Bread Stuffing*
Mint Sauce*
Tomatoes Parmesan*
Asparagus Salad*
Strawberry Shortcake*

○ Prepare Fresh Artichokes Vinaigrette up to Step 7, in advance, to allow for chilling, if desired.
○ Prepare Mint Sauce and allow to stand.
○ About 1½ hours before serving time, prepare Crown Roast of Lamb with Corn Bread Stuffing.
○ While the Crown Roast is cooking, prepare Steps 1 and 2 of the Strawberry Shortcake.
○ Prepare the Asparagus Salad and refrigerate until serving time.
○ While the Crown Roast is standing at room temperature, prepare Vinaigrette Dressing.
○ Prepare Tomatoes Parmesan up to Step 6 and the Strawberry Shortcake up to Step 9.
○ Just before serving time, cook Tomatoes Parmesan.
○ While clearing the dishes, cook Strawberry Shortcake and assemble.

FRESH ARTICHOKES VINAIGRETTE

4 large globe artichokes
1 cup water
2 tablespoons vinegar
1 tablespoon whole pickling spices
Vinaigrette Dressing (see recipe page 32)

Dinner No. 1

1. Wash artichokes carefully and drain. Slice off ⅓ of upper tip of each artichoke with a sharp knife. With a kitchen shears trim off the thorny ends of the leaves. The stems should be cut off even with the base of the artichoke.
2. Combine water, vinegar and pickling spices in a deep 3-quart non-metallic casserole.
3. Heat, uncovered, in Microwave Oven 3 (4) minutes or until mixture comes to a boil.
4. Place artichokes upright in casserole.
5. Heat, covered, in Microwave Oven 12 to 15 (15½ to 20) minutes, turning casserole after each 3 (4) minutes of cooking time.
6. Cook until bases are tender when pierced with a fork and lower leaves pull away easily.
7. While artichokes are cooking, prepare Vinaigrette Dressing according to the recipe on page 32.
8. Dip leaves into Vinaigrette Dressing. Artichokes and dressing may be served either hot or cold.

Serves 8.

Tip: If desired, the leaves may be removed and arranged on a platter before serving. The fuzzy choke should be removed and the heart cut for serving.

*Parenthesis (   ) indicates 500 watt units.

CROWN ROAST OF LAMB WITH CORN BREAD STUFFING

1 (4 to 5-pound) shaped and tied crown roast of
   lamb, with bone tips Frenched and trimmings
   ground
½ cup butter or margarine
½ cup finely chopped onion
¾ cup finely chopped celery
1 teaspoon salt
¼ teaspoon pepper
1 teaspoon dried rubbed sage
⅛ teaspoon garlic powder
2 cups crumbled corn bread, freshly prepared

1. Remove ground lamb from crown roast and
crumble it into a medium-sized heat-resistant
non-metallic bowl.
2. Heat, uncovered, in Microwave Oven, stirring
frequently, for 5 (6½) minutes. Drain fat and set meat
aside.
3. In a small heat-resistant non-metallic bowl melt
butter in Microwave Oven 1 (1¼) minute.
4. Add onion and celery and heat, uncovered, in
Microwave Oven 4 (5) minutes or until vegetables
are tender.
5. Stir in salt, pepper, sage and garlic powder.
6. Add vegetable mixture and corn bread to cooked
lamb. Toss to combine thoroughly.
7. Place roast in a shallow non-metallic baking dish.
Spoon stuffing into center of crown roast.
8. Heat, uncovered, in Microwave Oven 25 (32)
minutes or until a meat thermometer inserted in the
meat between 2 ribs registers 165°F. Turn meat twice
during cooking. *Do not place thermometer in
Microwave Oven.*
9. Cover meat with aluminum foil and allow to
stand at room temperature 20 to 30 (25 to 40) minutes
or until internal temperature reaches 175° to 180°F.
10. If necessary or desired, the crown roast may be
returned to the Microwave Oven for longer cooking.
*Do not place aluminum foil or meat thermometer in
Microwave Oven.*
11. Place paper frills on bone tips before serving.

Serves 8.

MINT SAUCE

1 cup malt vinegar or white vinegar
½ cup sugar
1 cup chopped fresh mint leaves

1. In a small heat-resistant non-metallic bowl heat
vinegar and sugar in Microwave Oven 2 (2½) minutes
or until mixture comes to a boil.
2. Pour hot mixture over mint leaves and allow to
stand at least 1 hour.
3. If desired, more sugar may be added to make a
sweeter sauce.

Makes 2 cups sauce.

TOMATOES PARMESAN

4 large ripe tomatoes
¼ cup butter or margarine
½ cup grated Parmesan cheese
¼ cup finely chopped parsley
1 tablespoon dried oregano leaves

1. Wash tomatoes and pat dry. Cut tomatoes in half
crosswise.
2. Place cut-side-up in a shallow non-metallic baking
dish.
3. Dot each tomato half with about ½ tablespoon
butter.
4. In a small bowl combine remaining ingredients.
5. Top each tomato half with some of the cheese
mixture.
6. Heat, uncovered, in Microwave Oven 5 to 6 (6½ to 8)
minutes or until tomatoes are soft and topping
begins to melt.
7. Do not overcook.

Serves 8.

Variation: If desired, dry seasoned bread crumbs
may be substituted for all or part of the Parmesan
cheese.

ASPARAGUS SALAD

3 (17-ounce) cans whole white asparagus, vertically
   packed
Lettuce leaves
Homemade mayonnaise, or commercial mayonnaise
   thinned with light cream
2 hard-cooked eggs, sieved

1. Drain asparagus, trying to keep spears whole.
2. Place lettuce leaves on 8 salad plates and arrange
asparagus on lettuce leaves.
3. Place a spoonful of mayonnaise over asparagus.
4. Garnish with hard-cooked egg.
5. Chill before serving.

Serves 8.

STRAWBERRY SHORTCAKE

2 pints fresh strawberries
¾ cup sugar
2 cups unsifted flour
3 tablespoons sugar
3 teaspoons baking powder
1 teaspoon salt
½ cup shortening
⅓ cup light cream
1 egg, slightly beaten
Butter or margarine
Sweetened whipped cream

1. Wash and hull strawberries.
2. Slice strawberries into a medium-sized bowl and
sprinkle with the ¾ cup sugar and toss lightly to coat

(Continued on next page)

berries. Refrigerate for 30 to 60 minutes (40 minutes to 1¼ hours)

3. Sift flour, the 3 tablespoons sugar, baking powder and salt together into a large bowl.

4. Cut in shortening with a pastry blender or two knives until mixture resembles corn meal.

5. In a small bowl combine light cream and egg.

6. Stir cream mixture into flour mixture with a fork until mixture is moistened.

7. Turn dough out onto a lightly floured board and knead gently about 5 times.

8. Press mixture into the bottom of a 9-inch round non-metallic baking dish.

9. Heat, uncovered, in Microwave Oven 6 to 7 (8 to 9) minutes or until shortcake tests done with a toothpick. Turn pan ¼ turn after each 1½ (2) minutes of cooking time.

10. Split shortcake with a knife while it is still warm and spread with butter.

11. Fill and top with reserved strawberries.

12. Serve warm with dollops of whipped cream.

Serves 8.

DINNER NO. 2

Fruit Soup*
Tossed Salad
Chicken Tetrazzini*
Sunshine Asparagus*
Butterscotch Fondue*

○ Prepare Fruit Soup in advance and allow to chill before serving.

○ Cook spaghetti for Chicken Tetrazzini conventionally or according to recipe on page 102.

○ Prepare Chicken Tetrazzini up to Step 6. Cover and let stand.

○ Prepare Sunshine Asparagus and cover until serving time.

○ Finish cooking Chicken Tetrazzini. Reheat Sunshine Asparagus, if necessary, just before serving.

○ While Chicken Tetrazzini is cooking, prepare Butterscotch Fondue up to Step 2.

○ While clearing the dinner dishes, heat Butterscotch Fondue.

FRUIT SOUP

2 (10-ounce) packages frozen raspberries, in pouches
2 chicken bouillon cubes or 2 envelopes instant
  chicken broth
1¼ cups boiling water
½ cup pineapple juice
2 tablespoons sugar
½ cup commercial sour cream

1. To thaw raspberries, place pouches in Microwave Oven and heat, uncovered, 1(1¼) minute. Allow to stand 1 minute and then heat an additional 1(1¼) minute. Allow to stand 1 minute to distribute the heat. If not completely thawed, heat an additional minute.

2. Pour thawed berries and juice into the container of a blender and blend until smooth. Berries may also be pressed through a sieve or food mill.

3. In a large heat-resistant non-metallic bowl combine chicken bouillon, water, pineapple juice and sugar; stir until dissolved.

4. Heat, uncovered, in Microwave Oven 2 (3) minutes. Stir in raspberries.

5. Chill several hours or overnight.

6. Serve garnished with a dollop of sour cream.

Serves 4 to 6.

SUNSHINE ASPARAGUS

¼ cup dry white wine
3 tablespoons finely chopped onion
1 tablespoon lemon juice
¾ cup mayonnaise
2 hard-cooked eggs, finely chopped
2 (10-ounce) packages frozen asparagus, cooked
  (see chart page 110)
Paprika (optional)

1. In a small heat-resistant non-metallic bowl pour wine over onion and heat, uncovered, in Microwave Oven 2 (3) minutes or until onion is tender.

2. Stir in lemon juice and mayonnaise.

3. Heat, uncovered, in Microwave Oven 2 (3) minutes or until mixture comes to a boil.

4. Gently stir in eggs.

5. Spoon sauce over cooked asparagus.

6. If desired, sprinkle with paprika.

Serves 4 to 6.

*Parenthesis ( ) indicates 500 watt units

CHICKEN TETRAZZINI

¼ cup butter or margarine
¼ cup flour
½ teaspoon salt
¼ teaspoon pepper
1 chicken bouillon cube, crumbled, or 1 envelope instant chicken broth
1 cup boiling water
1 cup heavy cream
2 tablespoons sherry
1 (8-ounce) package spaghetti, cooked and drained (see recipe page 102)
2 (7-ounce) cans cooked boned chicken or 2 cups cubed cooked chicken
1 (4-ounce) can sliced mushrooms
½ cup grated Parmesan cheese

1. Melt butter in a large heat-resistant non-metallic bowl in Microwave Oven 30 (40) seconds.
2. Blend in flour, salt, pepper and crumbled buillon cube.
3. Gradually stir in boiling water and cream.
4. Heat, uncovered, in Microwave Oven 4 (5) minutes or until thickened and smooth, stirring frequently.
5. Stir in sherry, spaghetti, chicken and mushrooms.
6. Pour mixture into a deep 2-quart non-metallic casserole.
7. Sprinkle with grated cheese and heat, uncovered, in Microwave Oven 4 (5) minutes or until heated through.

Serves 4 to 6.

BUTTERSCOTCH FONDUE

2 (6-ounce) packages butterscotch pieces
¼ cup butter or margarine
½ cup hot water
½ cup light corn syrup
1 teaspoon vanilla extract
Few grains salt
Ladyfingers, split
Marshmallows
Banana chunks, sprinkled with lemon juice

1. Combine butterscotch, butter and hot water in a deep 1-quart non-metallic casserole or non-metallic fondue pot.
2. Heat, uncovered, in Microwave Oven 5 (6½) minutes or until butterscotch is melted. Stir frequently.
3. Add corn syrup, vanilla and salt; stir to blend.
4. Set fondue pot over low heat.
5. Arrange ladyfingers, marshmallows and banana chunks on a platter.
6. Place a ladyfinger, marshmallow or banana chunk on a fondue fork and dip it into the butterscotch mixture.

Serves 4 to 6.

Variation: You may use nearly any kind of cake or fruit and many kinds of candy in place of ladyfingers, marshmallows and banana chunks. Use your imagination!

Tip: Any remaining sauce may be stored in a tightly covered jar in the refrigerator to be used over ice cream or cake.

DINNER NO. 3

Clam Chowder*
Tomato Salad
Trout Almondine*
Herbed Mashed Potatoes*
Buttered Peas and Carrots
Grasshopper Pie*

○ Prepare Grasshopper Pie in advance and chill before serving.
○ Prepare Herbed Mashed Potatoes and cover to keep warm. If necessary they may be reheated just before serving time.
○ Prepare almonds for Trout Almondine.
○ Prepare Clam Chowder.
○ Prepare Peas and Carrots from frozen packages according to directions on pages 111 and 112 or prepare conventionally.
○ While serving the Clam Chowder and Tomato Salad, cook the trout for the Trout Almondine.
○ Reheat Herbed Mashed Potatoes, if necessary.
○ Finish cooking the Trout Almondine while clearing the salad dishes.

CLAM CHOWDER

3 slices raw bacon, diced
1 (8-ounce) can minced clams, undrained
1½ cups peeled and cubed potatoes
⅓ cup finely chopped onion
1 medium-sized carrot, diced
2 tablespoons flour
1 cup milk
½ cup light cream
1 teaspoon salt
⅛ teaspoon pepper
¼ teaspoon thyme

1. Place bacon in a deep 2-quart non-metallic casserole.
2. Heat, covered with a paper towel, in Microwave Oven 2 (3) minutes or until bacon is crisp.
3. Remove cooked bacon with a slotted spoon. Crumble bacon and set aside. Reserve drippings in casserole.
4. Drain liquid from clams and add to bacon drippings. Set clams aside.
5. Add potatoes, onion and carrot to casserole.
6. Heat, covered, in Microwave Oven 8 (10) minutes or until vegetables are tender; stir occasionally.
7. Blend flour into vegetable mixture.
8. Gradually stir in milk until smooth.
9. Heat, uncovered, in Microwave Oven 2 (3) minutes or until thickened and smooth.
10. Stir in cream, salt, pepper, thyme and reserved clams.
11. Heat, uncovered, in Microwave Oven 2 (3) minutes or until heated through.
12. Garnish with crumbled bacon before serving.

Serves 4.

TROUT ALMONDINE

⅓ cup butter or margarine
½ cup slivered blanched almonds
4 (8-ounce) trout
4 tablespoons butter or margarine
1½ teaspoons lemon juice
Salt and pepper

1. In a small heat-resistant non-metallic bowl melt the ⅓ cup butter in Microwave Oven 30 (40) seconds.
2. Add almonds and heat, uncovered, in Microwave Oven 4 (5) minutes or until lightly browned; stir occasionally. Set almonds aside.
3. Arrange fish in a shallow 2-quart non-metallic baking dish.
4. Place 1 tablespoon of butter on each fish and sprinkle with lemon juice and salt and pepper to taste.
5. Heat, covered with wax paper, 5 to 7 (6½ to 9) minutes or until fish flakes easily with a fork.
6. Spoon browned almonds over fish and heat, uncovered, in Microwave Oven 2 (3) minutes or until heated through.
Serves 4.

HERBED MASHED POTATOES

1½ cups hot water
½ teaspoon salt
⅛ teaspoon pepper
3 tablespoons butter or margarine
½ cup milk or light cream
1½ cups instant mashed potato flakes
⅓ cup sour cream
¼ cup finely chopped parsley
3 tablespoons snipped chives
1 egg, slightly beaten

1. Combine water, salt, pepper and butter in a deep 1½-quart non-metallic casserole.
2. Heat, uncovered, in Microwave Oven 2 to 3 (3 to 4) minutes or until mixture boils.
3. Add milk.
4. Stir in potato flakes with a fork.
5. Stir in remaining ingredients until well blended.
6. Heat, uncovered, in Microwave Oven 3 (4) minutes or until heated through.

Serves 4.

GRASSHOPPER PIE

¼ cup butter or margarine
1½ cups chocolate cookie crumbs
3 tablespoons sugar
3 cups miniature marshmallows
½ cup milk or light cream
3 tablespoons creme de cocoa
3 tablespoons green creme de menthe
1 cup chilled heavy cream, whipped
chocolate curls

1. In a 9-inch non-metallic pie pan melt butter in Microwave Oven 1 (1¼) minute.
2. Combine cookie crumbs and sugar in a small bowl until well blended.
3. Stir cookie mixture into butter.
4. Press mixture onto bottom and sides of pie pan.
5. Heat, uncovered, in Microwave Oven 2 (3) minutes or until crust has a crunchy texture. Allow to cool while preparing filling.
6. In a large heat-resistant non-metallic bowl combine marshmallows and milk.
7. Heat, uncovered, in Microwave Oven 2 (3) minutes or until marshmallows begin to puff. Stir to blend. If not completely melted return to Microwave Oven for additional 10 to 15 (13 to 20) seconds.
8. Stir in creme de cocoa and creme de menthe.
9. Chill until thickened but not set, about 20 minutes.
10. Fold in whipped cream.
11. Pour mixture into crust.
12. Refrigerate at least 4 hours.
13. Serve garnished with chocolate curls.

Serves 8.

*Parenthesis ( ) indicates 500 watt units.

DINNER NO. 4

Roast Turkey with Gravy*
Stuffin' Muffins*
Sweet Potato Casserole*
Fresh Broccoli*
Acorn Squash with Cranberry Filling*
Pumpkin Pie*

○ Prepare Pumpkin Pie in advance and allow to cool.

○ Defrost turkey, if necessary, in Microwave Oven at least 2½ to 3 (3¼ to 4) hours before the meal is to be served. For defrosting instructions see page 12.

○ While defrosting the turkey it is advisable to arrange the ingredients for the remaining recipes.

○ Cook turkey. Prepare other recipes up to the cooking points.

○ While the turkey is standing at room temperature, cook Acorn Squash.

○ Cook Sweet Potato Casserole and keep covered until serving time.

○ Cook Stuffin' Muffins and keep them covered until serving time.

○ Cook Fresh Broccoli.

○ Prepare gravy and reheat any parts of the dinner as necessary.

Dinner No. 4

STUFFIN' MUFFINS

½ cup butter or margarine
½ cup finely chopped onion
½ cup finely chopped celery
1 (4-ounce) can mushroom stems and pieces, drained
1 teaspoon dried rubbed sage
1 cup chicken broth
1 (8-ounce) package seasoned bread stuffing
Butter or margarine

1. In a medium-sized heat-resistant non-metallic bowl melt the ½ cup butter in Microwave Oven 1 (1¼) minute.
2. Add onion, celery and mushrooms and heat, uncovered, in Microwave Oven 5 (6½) minutes or until vegetables are tender.
3. Sprinkle sage over vegetable mixture.
4. Add chicken broth and stir to combine.
5. Heat, uncovered, in Microwave Oven 3 (4) minutes.
6. Add bread stuffing and toss lightly.
7. Lightly grease 8 small custard or coffee cups with butter.
8. Divide stuffing among cups.
9. Just before serving, heat, uncovered, in Microwave Oven 8 (10) minutes or until heated through.

Serves 8.

ROAST TURKEY WITH GRAVY

1 (12-ounce) turkey
Salt and pepper
6 tablespoons flour
Salt and pepper
Chicken broth

1. If turkey is frozen it may be defrosted in the Microwave Oven as directed on page 12, or it may be defrosted by placing it in the refrigerator overnight or until thawed.
2. Wash turkey and sprinkle inside cavity with salt and pepper.
3. Tie legs together. Tie wings and legs to body.
4. Invert a heat-resistant non-metallic saucer or small

(Continued on next page)

casserole cover in a shallow non-metallic baking dish.

5. Place turkey breast-side-down on saucer.
6. Heat, uncovered, for half of cooking time, 3 (4) minutes per pound (a total of 36 (48) minutes).
7. Turn turkey breast-side-up and continue cooking covered with a paper towel for the remaining half of the cooking time, 3 (4) additional minutes per pound.
8. Insert a meat thermometer into fleshy portion of turkey, not touching any bones. It should register 160°F. *Do not place thermometer in Microwave Oven.*
9. If temperature is not 160°F return turkey to Microwave Oven for an additional few minutes until correct temperature is reached.
10. Let turkey stand covered with aluminum foil at room temperature 20 to 30 minutes to finish cooking. The internal temperature of the turkey should be 170°F after standing.
11. While turkey is standing at room temperature, prepare the gravy. Turkey should be removed from roasting pan.
12. Pour pan drippings into a bowl, leaving the residue in the pan.
13. Allow fat to rise to the top. Skim off about 6 tablespoons of fat. Reserve pan drippings. (If there is not enough fat, add butter or margarine to make 6 tablespoons total. Discard any excess fat.)
14. Return fat to baking dish.
15. Blend in flour and salt and pepper to taste.
16. Heat, uncovered, in Microwave Oven 4 (5) minutes or until lightly browned.
17. Measure remaining pan drippings and add enough chicken broth to measure 3 cups.
18. Gradually stir liquid into flour mixture until smooth, scraping sides of pan to loosen any particles that stick to the pan.
19. Heat, uncovered, in Microwave Oven 5 to 6 (6½ to 8) minutes or until thickened and smooth. Stir gravy every minute during cooking.

Serves 12 to 16.

Tip: If a fresh turkey is used, begin with Step 2.

SWEET POTATO CASSEROLE

2 (16-ounce) cans sweet potatoes
1 (14-ounce) can pineapple tidbits, undrained
4 tablespoons butter or margarine
4 tablespoons firmly packed dark brown sugar
1½ cups miniature marshmallows
Butter or margarine

1. Drain potatoes and discard liquid. Drain pineapple and set pineapple and juice aside.
2. In a small heat-resistant non-metallic bowl melt butter in Microwave Oven 30 (40) seconds.
3. Place potatoes in a medium-sized bowl and mash with a potato masher or fork.
4. Add melted butter and brown sugar. Stir until well combined.
5. Stir in pineapple juice until desired consistency is reached. Fold in pineapple tidbits and marsh-

mallows. Butter a shallow 1½-quart non-metallic casserole and spoon potato mixture into casserole.
6. Heat, uncovered, in Microwave Oven 5 to 6 (6½ to 8) minutes or until potato mixture is heated through and marshmallows begin to melt.

Serves 8.

FRESH BROCCOLI

2 pounds fresh broccoli
⅓ cup water
Butter or margarine
Salt and pepper

1. Wash broccoli and drain.
2. Split stems of broccoli so stalks are uniform in size.
3. Arrange stalks with the stems toward the outside of a deep 2-quart non-metallic casserole.
4. Add water and heat, covered, in Microwave Oven 9 to 10 (11½ to 13) minutes or until tender.
5. Serve dotted with butter and seasoned with salt and pepper to taste.

Serves 6 to 8.

ACORN SQUASH WITH CRANBERRY FILLING

4 small acorn squash
Salt
8 tablespoons butter or margarine
8 tablespoons honey
1 (17-ounce) can whole-berry cranberry sauce

1. Wash and dry squash.
2. Place squash in Microwave Oven and heat, uncovered, 15 (20) minutes or until they feel soft to the touch.
3. Let stand 5 minutes.
4. Cut in half and remove seeds.
5. Place cut-side-up in a shallow non-metallic baking dish.
6. Sprinkle with salt. Place 1 tablespoon of butter and 1 tablespoon of honey in each half.
7. Heat, uncovered, in Microwave Oven 4 (5) minutes or until butter has melted.
8. With a brush or spoon spread honey-butter mixture over cut surfaces of squash.
9. Place a spoonful of cranberry sauce in each squash half. If warmed cranberry sauce is desired, return filled squash halves to the Microwave Oven for 6 (8) minutes or until cranberry sauce is hot.

Serves 8.

PUMPKIN PIE

2 eggs
½ cup sugar
½ cup firmly packed dark brown sugar
1 tablespoon flour
½ teaspoon salt

(Continued on next page)

*Parenthesis (   ) indicates 500 watt units.

1 teaspoon ground cinnamon
¼ teaspoon ground nutmeg
¼ teaspoon ground ginger
¼ teaspoon ground allspice
1 (16-ounce) can cooked pumpkin
1 (14-ounce) can evaporated milk
1 baked 9-inch pastry shell (in a non-metallic pie pan)

1. In a large mixing bowl combine all ingredients, except pastry shell, and beat until well combined.
2. Pour pumpkin mixture into pastry shell. If there is too much filling for the shell, the remaining filling may be cooked in custard cups.

3. Heat, uncovered, in Microwave Oven 4 (5) minutes or until edges begin to set.
4. Carefully move the cooked portions toward the center.
5. Heat, uncovered, in Microwave Oven an additional 6 (8) minutes or until a knife inserted in the center comes out clean. Cool before serving.

Serves 8.

Variation: Heat 3 or 4 custard cups of filling, uncovered, 3 to 4 (4 to 5) minutes or until a knife inserted in the centers comes out clean.

DINNER NO. 5

Roast Goose*
Cinnamon Apples*
Green Beans Almondine*
Mashed Turnips and Potatoes*
Pineapple and Cranberry Sauce Tray
Candy Cane Cake*
Fruitcake*

○ In advance of the dinner prepare Fruitcake and Candy Cane Cake. Fruitcake may be prepared up to three weeks in advance. Wrap cake in a piece of brandy-soaked cheesecloth and store in a tightly covered tin in a cool place. This storage time will allow the Fruitcake to mellow. The Candy Cane Cake may be made up to 2 days in advance if stored in the refrigerator.

○ If using a frozen goose, defrost according to directions on page 13, at least 3 to 3½ (4 to 4½) hours before meal is to be served.

○ Prepare Pineapple and Cranberry Sauce Tray and place in refrigerator until serving time.

○ Prepare Cinnamon Apples about 3 hours before serving time.

○ Cook goose.

○ While goose is cooking, prepare vegetables for cooking. If desired the turnips and potatoes may be cooked conventionally at this time. They may be cooked in the Microwave Oven after the goose has finished cooking.

○ Prepare Green Beans Almondine and Mashed Turnips and Potatoes while goose is standing at room temperature.

Dinner No. 5

CINNAMON APPLES

4 medium-sized apples
2 (1⅝-ounce) jars red cinnamon candies
½ cup sugar
2 cups water
Red food coloring (optional)

1. Wash, peel and quarter apples, remove seeds.
2. Combine remaining ingredients in a large heat-resistant non-metallic bowl.
3. Heat, uncovered, in Microwave Oven 5 (6½) minutes or until cinnamon candies melt.
4. Place apple quarters in cinnamon mixture and allow to stand 1 hour or until apples turn desired shade of red. (Caution: Mixture will stain hands.)
5. Heat apples, uncovered, in Microwave Oven 3 (4) minutes or until they begin to become tender. Do not allow apples to lose their shape.
6. Stuff cavity of goose with apples and garnish serving tray with them.
7. Apples may be served chilled if desired.

Serves 6.

ROAST GOOSE

1 (8½-pound) goose

1. If goose is frozen, defrost in Microwave Oven as directed on page 13, or goose may be defrosted by placing it in the refrigerator overnight or until thawed.
2. Remove neck and giblets from the body cavity and use as desired. Invert a heat-resistant non-metallic saucer or a small casserole cover in a shallow non-metallic baking dish. Tie legs together. Tie wings and legs to body.
3. Place the goose breast-side-down on the saucer.
4. Heat, uncovered, in Microwave Oven 6 (8) minutes per pound. Turn goose over. Pour out excess pan drippings as they accumulate.
5. Heat goose, uncovered, an additional 3 (4) minutes per pound or until a meat thermometer inserted into the center of the breast registers 160°F.
Do not place thermometer in the Microwave Oven.
6. Allow to stand covered 20 (25) minutes before serving.

Serves 6.

GREEN BEANS ALMONDINE

2 pounds fresh green beans
½ cup water
3 tablespoons butter or margarine
⅓ cup slivered blanched almonds
1 teaspoon salt
¼ teaspoon pepper
¼ teaspoon ground nutmeg (optional)

1. Wash beans and cut off ends. Place in a deep 2-quart non-metallic casserole with water.
2. Heat, covered, in Microwave Oven 10 to 12 (13 to 15½) minutes or until beans are crisp-tender. Drain beans.
3. Add remaining ingredients to drained green beans.
4. Stir to combine. Heat, uncovered, in Microwave Oven 3 (4) minutes or until butter has melted and beans are tender.

Serves 6.

MASHED TURNIPS AND POTATOES

1 pound yellow turnips or rutabagas
1 pound small potatoes
Water
¼ cup butter or margarine
1 teaspoon salt
¼ teaspoon pepper
¼ teaspoon ground nutmeg (optional)
¼ to ½ cup heavy cream
⅓ cup finely chopped parsley (optional)

1. Wash and pare turnips and potatoes. Cut into small cubes.
2. Place turnips and potatoes in a deep 3-quart non-metallic casserole.
3. Add water to cover vegetables.
4. Heat, covered, in Microwave Oven 15 to 18 (20 to 23) minutes or until vegetables are fork-tender. Drain excess water.
5. With a potato masher or fork, mash turnips and potatoes until almost smooth.
6. With a rotary beater or electric mixer beat vegetables, butter, salt, pepper, and nutmeg until fluffy.
7. Stir in heavy cream gradually until desired consistency is reached.
8. If desired, stir in parsley.

Serves 6.

CANDY CANE CAKE

1 (14-ounce) package hot roll mix
Ingredients as called for on package label
2 cups drained finely chopped maraschino cherries
1 cup slivered blanched almonds
Melted butter or margarine

1. Prepare hot roll mix according to package directions.
2. Allow to raise as package directs.
3. Divide dough into 2 equal parts. Roll each part into a 15x6 inch rectangle; place each on a wax paper-covered piece of cardboard.
4. With scissors, make 2-inch cuts at ½-inch intervals on long sides of dough rectangles.
5. In a small bowl combine cherries and almonds and spread ½ of mixture down center of each rectangle.
6. Crisscross strips over filling. Stretch dough to 22 inches and curve to form a candy cane.
7. Heat each cane, uncovered, in Microwave Oven 5 to 6 (6½ to 8) minutes or until no longer "doughy".
8. While warm, brush with melted butter.
9. If desired, decorate with a ribbon bow.

Tip: You may want to brown cakes for a few minutes under the broiler of a conventional oven.

*Parenthesis ( ) indicates 500 watt units.

FRUITCAKE

¾ **cup unsifted flour**
¾ **teaspoon salt**
¾ **teaspoon baking powder**
¾ **teaspoon ground nutmeg**
¾ **teaspoon ground allspice**
1¾ **cups diced green candied cherries**
1¾ **cups diced red candied cherries**
6 **cups coarsely chopped walnuts**
¾ **cup butter or margarine, at room temperature**
6 **tablespoons firmly packed dark brown sugar**
3 **tablespoons honey**
6 **eggs**
6 **tablespoons brandy**

1. Sift flour, salt, baking powder, nutmeg and all spice together. Set aside.
2. In a large bowl combine candied cherries and walnuts and set aside.
3. In another large bowl cream butter until light and fluffy. Gradually beat in sugar and honey. Beat in eggs one at a time.
4. Add flour mixture and beat until smooth.
5. Beat in brandy.
6. Fold in nut mixture.
7. Pour batter into a deep straight-sided 1½-quart non-metallic casserole. Heat, covered with a piece of greased wax paper, in Microwave Oven 6 to 8 (8 to 10) minutes or until a cake tester comes out clean when inserted in the center of the cake.
8. Let cake stand at room temperature for 20 minutes before turning out of pan.
9. If desired, a glaze may be prepared from confectioners' sugar and water.

*Parenthesis (   ) indicates 500 watt units.

Cooking for Company

Cooking for Company

This chapter is designed to help you cook for company using your Microwave Oven. The speed and ease of using the Microwave Oven will not only give you more time to spend with your guests but also let you relax and enjoy your own party.

With the techniques and skills you have acquired from using the Meal Planning Chapter, you will now be ready to tackle almost anything. The meals planned in this chapter range from a casual dinner for company to an intimate dinner for 2—from a simple weekend lunch to a more elaborate ladies' luncheon. The possibilities are limitless.

Again, we suggest reading through the menu, the directions for preparing the meal and each of the recipes before beginning the meal.

DINNER FOR THE BOSS

Coquilles St. Jacques*
Coq au Vin*
Zucchini*
New Potatoes*
French Bread
Floating Island Custard*

○ Prepare custard for Floating Island Custard in advance and refrigerate.

○ About an hour before serving time, prepare New Potatoes and keep covered until ready to serve. If necessary, reheat just before serving. If preferred, potatoes may be cooked conventionally and reheated in Microwave Oven at serving time.

○ Prepare Coq au Vin up to Step 9. Cover and set aside.

○ Prepare Coquilles St. Jacques up to Step 13. Cover and set aside.

○ Prepare Zucchini and keep covered until serving time.

○ Finish cooking Coquilles St. Jacques and serve.

○ While serving Coquilles St. Jacques, finish cooking Coq au Vin.

○ Prepare meringue for the Floating Island Custard and assemble just before serving.

COQUILLES ST. JACQUES

½ pound bay scallops
1 tablespoon butter or margarine
1 tablespoon finely chopped onion
1½ teaspoons lemons juice
¼ teaspoon salt
Few leaves dried marjoram, crushed
Dash paprika
6 tablespoons white wine
1 (4-ounce) can mushroom stems and pieces, drained
3 tablespoons butter or margarine
2 tablespoons flour
½ cup heavy cream
1 teaspoon finely chopped parsley

1. Wash scallops and remove any shell particles; drain.
2. In a deep 1½ quart non-metallic casserole place the 1 tablespoon butter and the onion.
3. Heat, uncovered, in Microwave Oven 1 (1¼) minute or until onion is tender.
4. Add scallops, lemon juice, salt, marjoram paprika and wine. Stir to combine.
5. Heat, covered, in Microwave Oven 3 (4) minutes.
6. Add mushrooms and heat, covered, in Microwave Oven 1 (1¼) minute or until scallops are tender. Do not overcook scallops as they will become tough.
7. Drain liquid, reserve and set scallops and liquid aside.
8. Melt the 3 tablespoons of butter in a small heat-resistant non-metallic bowl in Microwave Oven 30 (40) seconds.
9. Blend in flour.
10. Gradually stir in reserved scallop liquid and cream.
11. Heat, uncovered, in Microwave Oven 2 (2½) minutes or until thickened and smooth.
12. Stir in parsley.
13. Combine reserved scallop mixture and sauce.

Spoon mixture into 4 serving shells or small non-metallic ramekins.
14. Heat, uncovered, in Microwave Oven 3 (4) minutes.
15. If browning is desired, place under broiler of a conventional oven several minutes or until lightly browned.

Serves 4.

COQ AU VIN

2 (2½-pound) broiler-fryer chickens, cut into serving pieces
4 tablespoons flour
2 teaspoons salt
½ teaspoon pepper
6 tablespoons butter or margarine
12 small white onions
4 tablespoons brandy
1 clove garlic, peeled
1 bay leaf
1 stalk celery, cut into 4 pieces
3 cups red wine
1 pound fresh mushrooms, thinly sliced

1. Wash chickens and pat dry.
2. Combine flour, salt and pepper. Coat chicken pieces with flour mixture.
3. Melt butter in a skillet, using a conventional stove. Lightly brown chicken pieces on all sides.
4. Place browned chicken pieces in a deep 3-quart non-metallic casserole.
5. Brown onions lightly in skillet and set aside.
6. Pour brandy into skillet, scraping pan to loosen any browned particles.
7. Add brandy mixture to chicken in casserole. Add garlic, bay leaf, celery and red wine.
8. Heat, covered, in Microwave Oven 10 (13) minutes, stirring occasionally.
9. Add mushrooms and heat, uncovered, an additional

(Continued on next page)
*Parenthesis ( ) indicates 500 watt units.

4 (5) minutes or until chicken and onions are tender.
10. Remove garlic, bay leaf and celery pieces.
11. If sauce is not thick enough, it may be thickened with a little flour mixed with cold water. Heat, uncovered, in Microwave Oven an extra 1 to 2 minutes if flour mixture is added.

Serves 4 to 6.

Tip: If casserole to be used is flameproof, it may be used in place of skillet to brown chicken and onions.

ZUCCHINI

2 pounds small fresh zucchini
⅓ cup water
½ teaspoon salt
4 tablespoons butter or margarine
3 tablespoons finely chopped parsley

1. Wash zucchini, do not peel. Cut into ¼-inch slices.
2. Place zucchini and water in a deep 2-quart non-metallic casserole. Cover. Heat in Microwave Oven 7 to 8 (9 to 10) minutes or until tender.
3. Add remaining ingredients and stir to combine.
4. Heat, uncovered, in Microwave Oven for an additional 2 (2½) minutes.

Serves 4.

NEW POTATOES

2 pounds small new potatoes
Water
1 teaspoon salt
4 tablespoons butter or margarine, melted
1 tablespoon freshly snipped dill (optional)

1. Scrub potatoes but do not peel.
2. Place potatoes and water to cover in a deep

2-quart non-metallic casserole.
3. Heat, covered, in Microwave Oven 12 to 14 (15 to 18) minutes or until fork-tender.
4. Add remaining ingredients and toss well to combine.

Serves 4 to 6.

FLOATING ISLAND CUSTARD

2 egg yolks, at room temperature
¼ cup sugar
1½ teaspoon cornstarch
1½ cups milk
½ teaspoon vanilla extract
2 egg whites, at room temperature
4 tablespoons sugar
½ teaspoon vanilla extract
1 pint fresh strawberries, washed, hulled and halved

1. Place egg yolks, the ¼ cup sugar and the cornstarch in a medium-sized, heat-resistant non-metallic bowl; mix well. Gradually stir in milk.
2. Heat, uncovered, in Microwave Oven 4 (5) minutes or until mixture just about boils. *Do not allow to boil.* Stir mixture occasionally during last half of cooking.
3. Add the ½ teaspoon vanilla and chill until ready to serve.
4. Just before serving time, beat egg whites until stiff but not dry. Beat in the 4 tablespoons of sugar, 1 tablespoon at a time, until mixture forms stiff peaks. Beat in the ½ teaspoon vanilla.
5. Divide the strawberries among four heat-resistant non-metallic dessert dishes. Pour chilled custard over berries. Place a dollop of egg white mixture in each dessert dish.
6. Place desserts in Microwave Oven and heat, uncovered, 45 seconds to 1 minute (1 to 1¼ min.) or until meringue puffs are set.

Serves 4.

CASUAL DINNER FOR COMPANY

**Chilled Melon
Shrimp Creole***
Rice*
Broccoli in Lemon Sauce*
Cherry Cobbler*

○ Prepare Broccoli in Lemon Sauce up to Step 3. Cover until serving time. Gather remaining ingredients.
○ Prepare Rice.
○ While Rice is standing at room temperature, gather ingredients for Shrimp Creole.
○ Prepare Shrimp Creole and lemon sauce for broccoli
○ Prepare Cherry Cobbler up to Step 5.
○ While clearing dishes, bake Cherry Cobbler.

SHRIMP CREOLE

3 tablespoons butter or margarine
¾ cup finely chopped green pepper
1 cup finely chopped onion
¾ cup finely chopped celery
2 tablespoons flour
2 tablespoons parsley flakes
1 (15-ounce) can tomatoes
1 teaspoon sugar
⅛ to ¼ teaspoon Tabasco sauce
Few leaves dried thyme
1 teaspoon salt
⅛ teaspoon pepper
1 (10-ounce) package frozen raw shrimp, shelled
   and thawed (see chart page 13)
Cooked rice (see recipe below)

1. Melt butter in a deep 3-quart non-metallic casserole
30 (40) seconds in Microwave Oven.
2. Add green pepper, onion and celery.
3. Heat, uncovered, in Microwave Oven 4 (5)
minutes or until vegetables are crisp-tender. Stir
occasionally.
4. Add flour and parsley flakes and stir until well
blended.
5. Stir in tomatoes and heat, uncovered, in Microwave
Oven 3 (4) minutes.
6. Add remaining ingredients and stir to blend.
7. Heat, covered, in Microwave Oven 5 (6½) minutes
or until shrimp are pink and tender. Do not overcook
as shrimp will become tough. Let stand 3 to 5
minutes before serving. Serve over rice (see recipe
below).
Serves 4.

RICE

2 cups water
1 cup long grain rice
1 tablespoon butter
1 teaspoon salt

1. Combine all ingredients in a deep 3-quart
non-metallic casserole.
2. Heat, covered, in Microwave Oven 12 to 13 (15½ to 17)
minutes.
3. Allow rice to stand at room temperature 4 to 5
minutes, covered.
4. Fluff with a fork before serving.
5. If necessary rice may be returned to Microwave
Oven for a few minutes additional cooking.
Serves 4.

BROCCOLI IN LEMON SAUCE

2 (10-ounce) packages frozen broccoli spears
2 tablespoons butter or margarine
2 tablespoons flour
½ cup milk
1 teaspoon lemon peel
1 tablespoon lemon juice
½ teaspoon salt
¼ teaspoon ground ginger

1. Cook broccoli in a shallow non-metallic baking
dish according to chart on page 110.
2. Drain and set aside.
3. In a small heat-resistant non-metallic bowl melt
butter in Microwave Oven 30 (40) seconds.
4. Blend in flour until smooth.
5. Gradually stir in milk.
6. Heat, uncovered, in Microwave Oven 2 (2½)
minutes or until thickened and smooth. Carefully stir
in remaining ingredients.
7. Spoon sauce over drained broccoli spears and
heat, uncovered, in Microwave Oven 1 to 2 minutes
or until heated through.
Serves 4 to 6.

CHERRY COBBLER

1 (17-ounce) can cherry pie filling
1 teaspoon lemon juice
½ cup butter or margarine
⅓ cup firmly packed dark brown sugar
1 cup unsifted flour
¾ teaspoon ground cinnamon
¼ teaspoon ground allspice
⅔ cup coarsely chopped nuts
Vanilla ice cream

1. Combine cherry pie filling and lemon juice in
a shallow 1-quart non-metallic casserole.
2. In a small heat-resistant non-metallic bowl melt
butter in Microwave Oven 30 (40) seconds. Combine
butter, brown sugar, flour, cinnamon, allspice and
chopped nuts with a fork until crumbly.
3. Sprinkle topping over cherry filling.
4. Heat, uncovered, in Microwave Oven 5 to 6 (6½ to 8)
minutes or until cobbler is bubbly. Serve with
scoops of ice cream.
Serves 4 to 6.

Tip: If ice cream is too hard to scoop it may be heated
in Microwave Oven 30 to 60 (40 to 75) seconds
depending on size of container.

Dinner for the Boss Page 48

*Parenthesis (   ) indicates 500 watt units.

Cooking for Company

SUNDAY DINNER

Onion Soup*
Rolled Rib Roast*
Baked Sweet Potatoes*
Creamed Spinach*
Banana Ambrosia*

○ Prepare Onion Soup up to Step 5 and cover until serving time. The French bread and cheese can be added just before serving.
○ Prepare roast beef.
○ While Rolled Rib Roast is standing at room temperature, bake sweet potatoes and prepare Creamed Spinach.
○ Just before serving time, reheat Onion Soup and add French bread and cheese.
○ Prepare Banana Ambrosia up to Step 4.
○ While clearing the dinner dishes, heat the Banana Ambrosia.

ONION SOUP

¼ cup butter or margarine
3 cups thinly sliced onion
¾ teaspoon salt
¼ teaspoon pepper
6 envelopes instant beef broth or 6 cubes beef
  bouillon, crumbled
6 cups hot water
⅛ to ¼ teaspoon brown bouquet sauce
6 2-inch rounds toasted French bread
Parmesan cheese

1. Place butter in a 3-quart non-metallic casserole and melt in Microwave Oven 30 (40) seconds.
2. Add onions and heat, uncovered, in Microwave Oven 4 (5) minutes or until lightly browned, stirring occasionally.
3. Add salt, pepper, instant beef broth, water and brown bouquet sauce.
4. Heat, uncovered, in Microwave Oven 25 (32) minutes, stirring occasionally.
5. Pour into heat-resistant non-metallic soup bowls and float a round of French bread in each bowl. Sprinkle liberally with Parmesan cheese.
6. Heat, uncovered, in Microwave Oven 3 to 4 (4 to 5) minutes or until cheese has melted.

Serves 6.

ROLLED RIB ROAST

1 (4-pound) rolled rib roast
Peeled garlic cloves (optional)
Pepper (optional)
Salt (optional)

1. Place a heat-resistant non-metallic saucer or small casserole cover in the bottom of a shallow non-metallic baking dish. (The saucer is used to keep the meat out of the fat while it is cooking.)
2. Place meat fat-side-down on the saucer. If desired, rub beef with garlic and pepper before cooking.
3. Heat, uncovered, in Microwave Oven 6 (8)

minutes per pound for rare, 7 (9) minutes per pound for medium and 8 (10) minutes per pound for well-done.
4. After half of the cooking time, drain pan juices and reserve if gravy is to be made. Turn meat over and cover loosely with waxed paper or paper toweling. Continue to cook.
5. Let roast stand covered with aluminum foil 15 to 30 minutes or until desired internal temperature is reached. *Do not place thermometer or aluminum foil in Microwave Oven.* The internal temperature after standing should be 130-140°F for rare, 150-160°F for medium and 170°F for well-done.
6. If necessary, return roast to Microwave Oven for a few minutes additional cooking until desired internal temperature is reached.
7. Salt meat after cooking, if desired.

Serves 6.

BAKED SWEET POTATOES

Fresh sweet potatoes

1. Select sweet potatoes for uniform shape and size. Scrub potatoes well and pierce each potato with the tines of a fork.
2. Arrange potatoes on paper toweling leaving at least 1 inch between them.
3. Bake according to the following chart, turning potatoes after half of the cooking time.
4. Check for doneness, as cooking times vary according to variety and shape of the potatoes.

Quantity	Total Cooking Time	
1 sweet potato	3—4 (4—5)	minutes
2 sweet potatoes	6—7 (8—9)	minutes
4 sweet potatoes	12—15 (15½—20)	minutes
6 sweet potatoes	20—25 (25-32)	minutes

Tip: Potatoes should be arranged in rows or in a circle with as much space as possible between them. If potatoes are placed in a ring never place a potato in the center as the one in the center may not cook.

CREAMED SPINACH

¼ cup butter or margarine
½ cup finely chopped onion
2 (10-ounce) packages frozen chopped spinach
½ teaspoon salt
⅛ teaspoon pepper
¼ teaspoon nutmeg
2 (3-ounce) packages cream cheese, at room temperature
Milk (optional)

1. In a small heat-resistant non-metallic bowl melt butter in Microwave Oven 30 (40) seconds.
2. Add onion and heat, uncovered, in Microwave Oven 4 (5) minutes or until onion is lightly browned. Stir occasionally.
3. Cook spinach according to the chart on page 112 Drain well.
4. Combine browned onion, spinach, salt, pepper, nutmeg and cream cheese in a shallow 1½-quart non-metallic casserole. If desired, add milk to make a thinner mixture.
5. Heat, uncovered, in Microwave Oven 5 to 6 (6½ to 8) minutes or until heated through.

Serves 6.

BANANA AMBROSIA

3 tablespoons butter or margarine
6 large ripe bananas, peeled and quartered lengthwise
The juice of 1 orange
1 orange, peeled, pitted and diced
3 tablespoons brown sugar, firmly packed
½ cup shredded coconut

1. Melt butter in a shallow non-metallic baking dish in Microwave Oven 30 (40) seconds.
2. Place bananas in baking dish and coat well with butter.
3. In a small bowl combine the orange juice and pieces and brown sugar until well blended. Spoon over bananas.
4. Heat, uncovered, in Microwave Oven 4 (5) minutes or until bananas are soft and glazed.
5. Just before serving, sprinkle with coconut.
6. Serve either hot or cold.

Serves 6.

INTIMATE DINNER FOR 2

Oyster Stew*
Steamed Lobster*
Lemon Butter*
Wilted Spinach Salad*
Rice Pilaf*
Chocolate Fondue*

○ Wash spinach for salad and refrigerate until serving time.
○ Prepare Rice Pilaf and keep covered until serving time. If necessary, reheat just before serving.
○ Prepare lobsters and cook.
○ While lobsters are cooking, prepare ingredients for Oyster Stew.
○ Prepare Chocolate Fondue up to Step 2.
○ Cook Oyster Stew.
○ Cook bacon for Wilted Spinach Salad and gather remainder of ingredients for the dressing.
○ Serve Oyster Stew.
○ Just before serving, complete dressing for Willted Spinach Salad. If necessary, reheat Rice Pilaf.
○ Heat Chocolate Fondue while clearing dinner dishes.

OYSTER STEW

2 tablespoons butter or margarine
1 (8-ounce) can oysters or ½ pint shucked oysters
Milk
½ teaspoon salt
⅛ teaspoon celery salt
Few grains cayenne pepper
Paprika

1. Melt butter in a deep 1-quart non-metallic casserole in Microwave Oven 30 (40) seconds.
2. While butter is melting, drain oysters and reserve liquor.

3. Add drained oysters to butter and heat, covered, in Microwave Oven 2 (2½) minutes or until edges are curled.
4. Pour oyster liquor into a 2-cup heat-resistant non-metallic measuring cup and add enough milk to measure 1½ cups.
5. Add milk mixture to oysters with salt, celery salt and cayenne pepper.
6. Heat, covered, in Microwave Oven 3 (4) minutes or until serving temperature is reached.
7. Sprinkle with paprika and serve in soup bowls with crackers.

Serves 2.

*Parenthesis ( ) indicates 500 watt units.

STEAMED LOBSTER

½ cup water
½ teaspoon salt
1 lemon, sliced
2 (1-pound) live lobsters, pegged

1. In a 3-quart non-metallic casserole place water, salt and lemon.
2. Heat, uncovered, in Microwave Oven 2 (2½) minutes or until water boils.
3. Place live lobsters head first into boiling water; this will render them immobile.
4. Heat, covered, in Microwave Oven 12 (15½) minutes.
5. Let stand, covered, 4 minutes to finish cooking.
6. Drain. With a sharp heavy knife split tail, and if meat is still translucent in center, heat, covered, about 1 minute longer or until meat is no longer translucent. Continue to cut up the center towards the head. Remove the stomach and the intestinal tract. The green liver and the red roe are considered to be delicacies. Serve with Lemon Butter (see recipe below).

Serves 2.

LEMON BUTTER

¼ pound butter or margarine
1 tablespoon lemon juice
⅛ teaspoon pepper

1. Place all ingredients in a small heat-resistant non-metallic bowl and heat, uncovered, in Microwave Oven 1 (1¼) minute or until butter is melted.
2. Stir to combine.
3. Any leftover butter may be refrigerated and used at a later date over fish, vegetables or seafood.

WILTED SPINACH SALAD

1 pound fresh spinach
6 slices raw bacon
3 tablespooons finely chopped onion
¼ teaspoon pepper
2 tablespoons sugar
⅓ cup wine vinegar
⅓ cup water
3 tablespoons finely chopped canned pimiento

1. Wash spinach very carefully, and remove any thick stems and bruised leaves. Drain well and place in a salad bowl.
2. Place bacon slices in a 9-inch non-metallic pie pan.
3. Heat, covered with a paper towel, in Microwave Oven 5 (6½) minutes or until crisp. Remove bacon slices, crumble and set aside.
4. Add finely chopped onion to bacon fat and heat, uncovered, in Microwave Oven 2 (2½) minutes or until lightly browned.
5. To make dressing, add remaining ingredients and

heat, uncovered, in Microwave Oven 3 (4) minutes or until mixture comes to a boil.
6. Just before serving, pour boiling dressing over spinach. Add crumbled bacon and toss well. Serve immediately.

Serves 2.

RICE PILAF

2 tablespoons butter or margarine
½ cup long grain rice
2 tablespoons finely chopped onion
2 tablespoons finely chopped parsley
2 tablespoons finely chopped celery
1 (4-ounce) can mushroom slices, drained
⅓ cup condensed chicken broth
⅛ teaspoon salt
⅓ cup water

1. In a deep 1-quart non-metallic casserole combine butter, rice, onion, parsley and celery.
2. Heat, uncovered, in Microwave Oven 3 (4) minutes.
3. Add remaining ingredients and heat, covered, in Microwave Oven 10 (13) minutes or until rice is almost tender. Stir occasionally.
4. Allow to stand 5 minutes to finish cooking.

Serves 2.

CHOCOLATE FONDUE

1 (6-ounce) package semisweet chocolate pieces
2 tablespoons butter or margarine
¼ cup hot water
¼ cup light corn syrup
1 teaspoon vanilla extract
Few grains salt
Ladyfingers, split
Marshmallows

1. Combine chocolate, butter, water and corn syrup in a deep 1-quart non-metallic casserole or a small non-metallic fondue pot.
2. Heat, uncovered, in Microwave Oven 3 (4) minutes or until chocolate is melted. Stir frequently.
3. Add vanilla and salt; stir to blend.
4. Set fondue pot on stand over low heat.
5. Arrange ladyfingers and marshmallows on a platter.
6. Place a ladyfinger or a marshmallow on a fondue fork and dip it into the chocolate mixture.

Serves 2.

Variation: You may use nearly any kind of cake or fruit and many kinds of candy in place of ladyfingers and marshmallows. Use your imagination!

Tip: Any remaining sauce may be placed in a tightly covered jar and stored in the refrigerator to be used over ice cream or cake.

*Parenthesis ( ) indicates 500 watt units.

LADIES' LUNCHEON

Hot Gazpacho*
Chicken à la King in Puff Pastry Shells*
Tossed Salad*
Pickled Beets*
Glazed Orange Cake*

○ The Glazed Orange Cake should be prepared in advance and chilled to allow the glaze to set.
○ Prepare Pickled Beets in advance and refrigerate to marinate.
○ If preparing your own puff pastry shells, they should be prepared in advance and reheated before filling at serving time.
○ The salad may be prepared, in advance, up to Step 2. Keep salad greens refrigerated until serving time to keep crisp.
○ Prepare Hot Gazpacho and finish Chicken à la King.

HOT GAZPACHO

3 cups tomato juice or vegetable juice cocktail
2 beef bouillon cubes, crumbled, or 2 envelopes instant beef broth
2 medium-sized ripe tomatoes, peeled and chopped
¼ cup chopped green pepper
¼ cup chopped onion
¼ cup wine vinegar or cider vinegar
2 tablespoons olive oil
1 teaspoon salt
1 teaspoon Worcestershire sauce
Few drops Tabasco sauce, to taste
1 clove garlic, peeled and crushed
Flavored croutons
Chopped tomato
Chopped cucumber
Chopped onion
Chopped green pepper

1. Place tomato juice in a non-metallic soup tureen or a deep 2½-quart non-metallic casserole and heat, uncovered, in Microwave Oven 6 (8) minutes or until boiling.
2. Stir in bouillon cubes until dissolved. Add the 2 chopped tomatoes, the ¼ cup green pepper, the ¼ cup onion, vinegar, oil, salt, Worcestershire sauce, Tabasco sauce and garlic.
3. Heat, uncovered, in Microwave Oven 2 (2½) minutes.
4. Serve accompanied by croutons and chopped tomato, cucumber, onion and green pepper.
5. Serve either hot or cold.

Serves 8.

CHICKEN À LA KING

3 tablespoons butter or margarine
5 tablespoons flour
1 teaspoon salt
⅛ teaspoon pepper
1¾ cups chicken stock
3 cups cubed cooked chicken
1 (4-ounce) can mushroom stems and pieces, drained
¼ cup finely chopped canned pimiento
8 puff pastry shells

1. In a deep 2-quart non-metallic casserole melt butter in Microwave Oven 30 (40) seconds.
2. Blend in flour, salt and pepper.
3. Gradually stir in chicken stock.
4. Heat, uncovered, in Microwave Oven 4 (5) minutes or until thickened and smooth. Stir occasionally.
5. Add remaining ingredients except pastry shells and heat, uncovered, in Microwave Oven 3 (4) minutes or until heated through.
6. Heat pastry shells on a heat-resistant non-metallic serving platter in Microwave Oven 2 (2½) minutes or until heated through. Fill each with some of the chicken mixture.

Serves 8.

Ladies' Luncheon

TOSSED SALAD

2 quarts loosely packed torn lettuce leaves (about one large head)
1 medium-sized cucumber, peeled and thinly sliced
1 medium-sized red onion, thinly sliced and separated into rings
2 medium-sized ripe tomatoes, quartered
Salad dressing

1. In a salad bowl, lightly toss lettuce, cucumber, onion rings and tomato quarters.
2. Add your favorite dressing and toss again gently.

Serves 8.

PICKLED BEETS

2 (17-ounce) cans sliced beets, undrained
2 teaspoons whole pickling spices
⅔ cup sugar
⅔ cup white vinegar

1. Drain beets and reserve ⅔ cup liquid.
2. Tie pickling spices in a piece of cheesecloth.
3. Combine beets, reserved liquid, sugar, vinegar and cheesecloth bag in a deep 2-quart non-metallic casserole.
4. Heat, covered, in Microwave Oven 7 to 8 (9 to 10) minutes or until mixture boils. Stir occasionally.
5. Chill to marinate.
6. Remove pickling spices before serving.

Serves 8.

GLAZED ORANGE CAKE

2 egg whites, at room temperature
½ cup sugar
2¼ cup unsifted cake flour
1 cup sugar
3 teaspoons baking powder
1 teaspoon salt
⅓ cup vegetable oil
1 cup orange juice
2 egg yolks
Orange Glaze (recipe below)

1. In the small bowl of an electric mixer, beat egg whites until foamy. Beat in the ½ cup sugar, 1 tablespoon at a time, beating until stiff and glossy. Set meringue aside.
2. Place flour, the 1 cup sugar, baking powder, salt, oil and half of the orange juice into a large heat-resistant non-metallic bowl; beat 1 minute at high speed, scraping sides of bowl constantly.
3. Add remaining orange juice and egg yolks; beat an additional 1 minute at high speed, scraping sides of bowl constantly.
4. Gently fold in meringue.
5. Press a glass, right-side-up, through batter to form a tube shape.
6. Heat, uncovered, in Microwave Oven 8 to 9 (10 to 11½) minutes or until a wooden skewer inserted in the center comes out clean and batter around glass no longer looks doughy.
7. Let cool 30 minutes.
8. Remove glass by twisting slightly.
9. Invert cake onto serving plate. Spread cake with Orange Glaze.
10. Chill cake to allow glaze to set.

ORANGE GLAZE

1 cup confectioner's sugar
½ teaspoon grated orange peel
1 teaspoon orange juice
About 2 tablespoons water
1 drop red food coloring
2 drops yellow food coloring

1. Combine all ingredients and beat until smooth.

FALL FOOTBALL LUNCH

Tomato Soup*
Sloppy Joes*
Assorted Pickles
Cinnamon Applesauce*
Warmed Donuts*

○ This is an easy-to-prepare Fall Lunch that can be adapted to serve any number of guests. The recipes that follow are planned for 8. Cooking times should be altered according to recipe size. The Sloppy Joe filling freezes well, so any leftovers can be stored for use at future date.
○ Prepare Sloppy Joe filling up to Step 4.
○ Prepare Tomato Soup and serve. While serving soup, finish cooking Sloppy Joe filling.
○ While Sloppy Joes are being served, cook Cinnamon Applesauce.
○ Donuts may be warmed just before serving time.

*Parenthesis ( ) indicates 500 watt units.

TOMATO SOUP

3 (10½-ounce) cans condensed tomato soup
3 soup cans water
Grated Parmesan cheese

1. In a non-metallic soup tureen or a deep 3-quart non-metallic casserole combine condensed soup and water.
2. Heat, covered, in Microwave Oven 8 to 10 (10 to 13) minutes or until heated through.
3. Soup can also be prepared in individual mugs. Divide condensed soup and water evenly between mugs.
4. Heat, covered with clear plastic wrap, in Microwave Oven according to the following chart.

Quantity	Total Cooking Time
2 to 3 mugs	3 to 4 (4 to 5) minutes
4 to 6 mugs	6 to 8 (8 to 10) minutes

5. Garnish soup with a sprinkling of grated Parmesan cheese.

Serves 8.

Tip: By heating soup in mugs you can heat only the amount of soup needed at one time.

SLOPPY JOES

2 tablespoons vegetable oil
2 pounds lean ground beef round
2 teaspoons salt
¼ teaspoon pepper
6 to 8 teaspoons chili powder
1 (15-ounce) can tomato sauce
1 pound frankfurters, sliced into ¼-inch rounds
Hamburger buns

1. In a deep 3-quart non-metallic casserole heat oil in Microwave Oven 2 (2½) minutes.
2. Crumble meat into hot oil and heat, uncovered, 6 (8) minutes, breaking up the meat particles frequently. Cook until all red has gone out of meat.
3. Drain off excess fat.
4. Stir in salt, pepper chili powder and tomato sauce.
5. Heat, uncovered, in Microwave Oven 4 (5) minutes or until heated through.
6. Add frankfurter rounds and heat, uncovered, an additional 4 (5) minutes, or until frankfurters are hot.
7. Spoon Sloppy Joe mixture over hamburger buns. (Buns may be toasted conventionally, if desired.)

Serves 8.

CINNAMON APPLESAUCE

8 to 10 medium-sized apples, peeled and quartered
½ cup water
½ to 1 cup sugar, to taste
¼ cup cinnamon candies

1. In a deep 3-quart non-metallic casserole combine apples, water, sugar and cinnamon candies.

2. Heat, covered, 8 to 10 (10 to 13) minutes or until apples are soft. Stir occasionally.
3. Let stand a few minutes to finish cooking.
4. Apples may be rubbed through a food mill or pureed in a blender if a smooth applesauce is desired.

Serves 8.

WARMED DONUTS

1. Place desired number of donuts on a heat-resistant non-metallic plate lined with a cloth or paper towel.
2. Heat, uncovered, in Microwave Oven according to the chart below.

Quantity	Total Cooking Time
1 donut	10 seconds
3 donuts	20 (25) seconds
5 donuts	30 (40) seconds
7 donuts	40 (50) seconds
9 donuts	50 (60) seconds
11 donuts	1 (1¼) minute

Fall Football Lunch
Page 56

BRUNCH FOR 6

Hot Bull Shots*
Omelets for 6*
Cheddar Cheese Sauce*
Western Topping*
Bacon for 6*
Sausage for 6*
Sour Cream Coffee Cake*

○ Prepare Sour Cream Coffee Cake in advance and warm it at serving time, if desired.
○ Gather and measure ingredients for Omelets, Cheddar Cheese Sauce and Western Topping.
○ Heat bacon and sausage in Microwave Oven until almost cooked. Wrap in aluminum foil to keep them hot.
○ Prepare and serve Hot Bull Shots.
○ Prepare Cheddar Cheese Sauce and Western Topping and place on hot tray until serving time.
○ If necessary, or if hot tray is not available, sauce and topping may be reheated, as desired.
○ Prepare Omelets and arrange on heated platter and place on hot tray to keep warm. If necessary, or if hot tray is not available, Omelets may be prepared as needed or prepared and reheated before serving.
○ Finish cooking the bacon and sausage. *Do not place aluminum foil in Micowave Oven.*

HOT BULL SHOTS

2 medium-sized cucumbers
3 (10½-ounce) cans condensed beef broth
1½ soup cans water
Few drops Tabasco sauce, to taste
1¼ cups vodka

1. Wash cucumber but do not peel.
2. In a heat-resistant non-metallic punch bowl combine beef broth, water and Tabasco sauce.
3. Heat, uncovered, in Microwave Oven 7 to 8 (9 to 10) minutes or until heated through. Stir occasionally.
4. While broth mixture is heating, prepare cucumbers for garnishing. With the tines of a table fork, score through the skin (at even intervals) of one cucumber. Slice the scored cucumber thinly. The other cucumber should be cut in half crosswise and then cut into long thin wedges.
5. Add vodka to the hot broth mixture.
6. Place cucumber slices in punch bowl and garnish each glass with a cucumber wedge.

Serves 6.

OMELETS FOR 6

12 eggs
¾ cup milk
¾ teaspoon salt
⅛ teaspoon pepper
6 tablespoons butter or margarine

1. In a large bowl combine eggs, milk, salt and pepper until thoroughly blended.
2. Melt 1 tablespoon of the butter in a 9-inch non-metallic pie pan in Microwave Oven 30 (40) seconds.
3. Add about ⅓ cup of egg mixture (or enough to cover bottom of pie pan).

4. Cover tightly with plastic wrap and heat in Microwave Oven 1 (1¼) minute.
5. With a fork, move cooked egg to center.
6. Cover with plastic wrap and heat in Microwave Oven 1 minute longer.
7. Fold omelet in half and place on heated platter.
8. Repeat process with remaining mixture. If desired, omelets may be returned to the Microwave Oven for a few minutes before serving to reach serving temperature and desired degree of doneness.

Serves 6.

WESTERN TOPPING

4 tablespoons butter or margarine
1 cup finely chopped onion
1½ cups finely diced green pepper
2 cups ¼-inch cubes of boiled ham
¼ teaspoon pepper

1. In a deep 1½-quart non-metallic casserole melt butter in Microwave Oven 30 (40) seconds.
2. Add remaining ingredients and heat, uncovered, in Microwave Oven 4 (5) minutes, stirring occasionally, until onion and green pepper are tender.
3. Spoon over omelets.
Serves 6.

CHEDDAR CHEESE SAUCE

6 tablespoons butter or margarine
4 tablespoons flour
½ teaspoon salt
⅛ teaspoon pepper
3 cups milk
2¼ cups shredded Cheddar cheese
2 eggs, slightly beaten

(Continued on next page)

*Parenthesis ( ) indicates 500 watt units.

1. In a deep 2-quart non-metallic casserole melt butter in Microwave Oven 30 (40) seconds. Blend in flour, salt and pepper.
2. Gradually stir in milk until smooth.
3. Heat, uncovered, in Microwave Oven 2 (2½) minutes.
4. Stir and heat, uncovered, an additional 2 (2½) minutes or until slightly thickened.
5. Add cheese and stir until cheese has melted.
6. Very gradually add a small amount of the hot cheese mixture to the beaten eggs.
7. Add cheese-egg mixture to hot cheese mixture and heat, uncovered, in Microwave Oven 2 (2½) minutes or until thickened and smooth. Stir frequently.
8. Spoon over omelets.

Serves 6.

BACON FOR 6

12 slices of bacon

1. Place 2 layers of paper toweling in a shallow non-metallic baking dish.
2. Lay strips of bacon on paper towel. (If desired, bacon may be cooked in 2 layers with paper toweling between.) Cover bacon with another piece of paper toweling to prevent spattering.
3. Heat in Microwave Oven 6 to 6½ (8 to 8½) minutes or until desired degree of crispness is reached.

Serves 6.

Tip: The paper toweling is used to absorb the bacon grease as it forms. If the bacon grease is desired for cooking, the layers of paper toweling underneath may be eliminated. However, bacon should still be covered lightly with a single piece of paper toweling. Drain bacon strips and blot on paper toweling.

SAUSAGE FOR 6

1 pound precooked frozen breakfast sausage links

1. Place 2 layers of paper toweling in a shallow non-metallic baking dish.
2. Arrange sausage links on paper towel. Cover with another piece of paper toweling to prevent spattering.
3. Heat in Microwave Oven 4 (5) minutes. Turn sausages and heat, covered with paper toweling, an additional 3 (4) minutes or until desired degree of doneness is reached. (Pork should always be cooked to well done. If non-precooked sausage links are used, increase total cooking time by 2 to 3 (2½ to 4) minutes.

Serves 6.

SOUR CREAM COFFEE CAKE

½ cup butter or margarine, at room temperature
1 cup sugar
2 eggs
1 cup commercial sour cream
1 teaspoon vanilla extract
2 cups unsifted flour
1 teaspoon baking soda
½ teaspoon baking powder
½ teaspoon salt
½ cup firmly packed dark brown sugar
¾ cup coarsely broken nuts
1 teaspoon ground cinnamon

1. In the large bowl of an electric mixer cream butter until soft. Add sugar gradually and beat until light and fluffy. Add eggs, one at a time; beat until thoroughly combined. Beat in sour cream and vanilla.
2. Sift flour, baking soda, baking powder and salt together.
3. Add flour mixture to sour cream mixture, beating until smooth.
4. Pour batter into a 9-inch square non-metallic baking dish and heat, uncovered, in Microwave Oven 3 (4) minutes, turning dish ½ turn after 1½ (2) minutes.
5. While cake is baking, combine remaining ingredients in a small bowl.
6. Sprinkle topping mixture over cake and heat, uncovered, an additional 3 to 5 (4 to 6½) minutes, turning dish ½ turn after each 1½ (2) minutes.
7. Test for doneness with a toothpick. Serve warm.

Brunch for 6
Page 58

*Parenthesis (   ) indicates 500 watt units.

Beverages

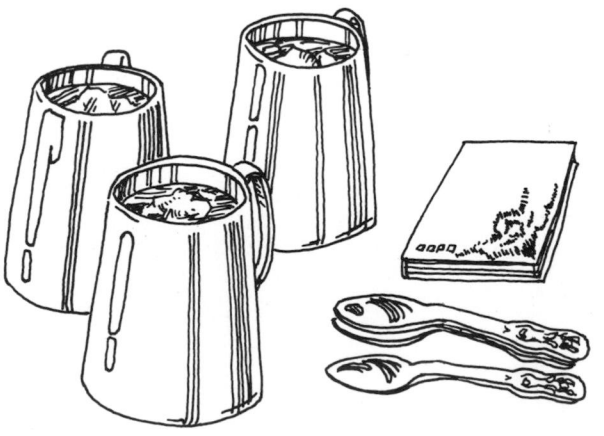

Beverages

Brewing or reheating beverages can be a fast and easy task with your Microwave Oven. Beverages almost always can be prepared and served in the same container, since microwaves are not absorbed by ceramics, glass or plastics. The liquid is hot; mugs and cups stay cool enough to handle. And microwave cooking is fast: water will boil in about 2 to 3(2½ to 4) minutes per cup. However, times are given in ranges dependent upon the type of cookware and temperature of the liquid used. Milk may boil over quickly, so be sure to leave extra room in mugs and cups when preparing beverages with milk. (For best results milk should not be allowed to boil.)

Heat-resistant non-metallic cups and mugs of ceramics, glass and plastics may be used in the following recipes. Do not use cups or mugs with glued-on handles.

This chapter includes recipes for everyday beverages such as tea and coffee, as well as festive drinks like Irish Coffee and Hot Buttered Rum. The chart below lists heating times for a number of servings.

Mugs or cups	Total Cooking Time
1	1½ to 2½ (2 to 3¼) minutes
2	3 to 3½ (4 to 4½) minutes
3	4 to 4½ (5 to 6) minutes
4	5 to 5½ (6½ to 7) minutes
5	6½ to 7 (8½ to 9) minutes
6	7½ to 8½ (9½ to 10½) minutes
7	9 to 9½ (11½ to 12) minutes
8	10 to 11 (13 to 14) minutes
9	12 to 13 (15½ to 17) minutes
10	13 to 14 (17 to 18) minutes

INSTANT COFFEE

¾ cup cold water
Instant coffee

1. Pour water into a heat-resistant non-metallic mug or cup.
2. Add desired amount of instant coffee. Stir.
3. Heat, uncovered, in Microwave Oven 1½ to 2½ (2 to 3¼) minutes.

Serves 1.

TEA

¾ cup cold water
1 tea bag or 1 teaspoon loose tea in tea ball

1. Pour water into a heat-resistant non-metallic mug or cup.
2. Submerge tea bag in water.
3. Heat, uncovered, in Microwave Oven 1½ to 2½ (2 to 3¼) minutes.
4. Allow to steep 1 to 2 minutes or until desired strength is reached.

Serves 1.

HOT COCOA

2 teaspoons unsweetened cocoa
1 teaspoon sugar
1 tablespoon cold water
¾ cup milk

1. Combine cocoa, sugar and water in a heat-resistant non-metallic mug or cup.
2. Heat, uncovered, in Microwave Oven 30 (40) seconds.
3. Stir in milk and heat, uncovered, in Microwave Oven 1½ to 2½ (2 to 3¼) minutes or until hot. Do not allow milk to boil.

Serves 1.

HOT CHOCOLATE MILK

1 to 2 tablespoons chocolate syrup
½ teaspoon vanilla extract
¾ cup milk

1. Combine chocolate syrup and vanilla in a heat-resistant non-metallic mug or cup.
2. Stir in milk and heat, uncovered, in Microwave Oven 1½ to 2½ (2 to 3¼) minutes or until hot. Do not allow milk to boil.

Serves 1.

HOT MOCHA MILK

1 to 2 tablespoons chocolate syrup
½ teaspoon instant coffee
⅛ teaspoon ground cinnamon
¾ cup milk
Whipped cream

1. Combine chocolate syrup, instant coffee and cinnamon in a heat-resistant non-metallic mug or cup.
2. Stir in milk and heat, uncovered, in Microwave Oven 1½ to 2½ (2 to 3¼) minutes or until hot. Do not allow milk to boil.
3. Garnish with a dollop of whipped cream.

Serves 1.

HOT MULLED CIDER

¼ cup apple cider or juice
1 to 2 whole cloves
1-inch cinnamon stick
Whipped cream
Nutmeg

1. Combine apple cider, whole cloves and cinnamon in a heat-resistant non-metallic mug, cup or glass.
2. Heat, uncovered, in Microwave Oven 2 to 3 (2½ to 4) minutes.
3. Garnish with a dollop of whipped cream and a sprinkling of nutmeg.

Serves 1.

Hot Mulled Cider

*Parenthesis (   ) indicates 500 watt units.

Beverages

IRISH COFFEE

1 teaspoon sugar
¾ to 1 cup strong black coffee
1 jigger (1½-ounces) Irish whiskey
Whipped cream

1. Dissolve sugar in black coffee in an Irish Coffee glass(*do not use a glass with metallic trim*) or a heat-resistant non-metallic glass, cup or mug.
2. Heat, uncovered, in Microwave Oven 1½ to 2½ (2 to 3¼) minutes or until hot.
3. Stir in Irish whiskey.
4. Carefully float a spoonful of whipped cream on top.

Serves 1.

HOT BUTTERED RUM

1 tablespoon brown sugar
1 tablespoon water
⅔ cup apple cider, milk or water
1 1-inch piece cinnamon stick
1 jigger (1½-ounces) rum
1 teaspoon butter or margarine
Ground nutmeg

1. Dissolve sugar in water and apple cider in a heat-resistant non-metallic mug or cup. Add cinnamon stick.
2. Heat, uncovered, in Microwave Oven 1½ to 2½ (2 to 3¼) minutes or until it comes to a boil.
3. Stir in rum.
4. Top with butter and a sprinkling of ground nutmeg.

Serves 1.

TOM AND JERRYS

¾ cup milk or water
2 tablespoons butter or margarine
2 egg whites
1 tablespoon sugar
2 egg yolks, slightly beaten
¼ teaspoon vanilla extract
3 ounces brandy
3 ounces dark rum
Ground nutmeg

1. Combine the milk and butter in a 2-cup heat-resistant non-metallic measuring cup.
2. Heat, uncovered, in Microwave Oven 1½ (2) minutes or until butter melts and milk is hot.

3. Beat egg whites until soft peaks form. Beat in sugar until stiff and glossy.
4. Beat egg yolks and vanilla into egg whites.
5. Slowly pour milk mixture into egg mixture, beating contantly. Add brandy and rum, beating constantly.
6. Heat, uncovered, in Microwave Oven 1 to 2 (1¼ to 3) minutes or until heated through.
7. Beat mixture until frothy.
8. Serve hot with a sprinkling of nutmeg.

Serves 3.

WITCHES' BREW

2 quarts apple cider
Juice of 2 oranges
Juice of 2 lemons
1 teaspoon ground cinnamon
¼ teaspoon ground cloves
Cinnamon sticks (optional)
Ground nutmeg (optional)

1. Combine apple cider, orange and lemon juices, ground cinnamon and cloves in a heat-resistant non-metallic pitcher or punch bowl.
2. Heat, uncovered, in Microwave Oven 8 to 10 (10 to 13) minutes or until almost boiling.
3. Serve with cinnamon sticks and a sprinkling of nutmeg, if desired.

Serves 8 to 10.

ICED TEA

1 quart water
5 tea bags
Ice cubes
Sugar (optional)
Lemon juice (optional)

1. Pour water into a 1-quart heat-resistant non-metallic measuring cup or a small heat-resistant non-metallic bowl.
2. Add tea bags and heat, uncovered, in Microwave Oven 8 to 9 (10 to 11½) minutes or until water boils.
3. Carefully pour hot tea over ice in a pitcher or individual glasses.
4. Sweeten and add lemon juice to taste.

Serves 4 to 5.

*Parenthesis (   ) indicates 500 watt units.

Appetizers and Hors d'Oeuvres

Appetizers and Hors d'Oeuvres

You can be a guest at your own party when appetizers and hors d'oeuvres are served quick, fresh and piping hot from your Microwave Oven. You can reduce last-minute kitchen scurrying by preparing these recipes ahead of time for heating just before serving. A heat-resistant non-metallic serving platter will go from the Microwave Oven to your table in just minutes. Little Cheese Sandwiches, Hawaiian Kabobs or any of the recipes here are quick enough to whip up for unexpected company or quick snacks anytime.

For best results, always arrange appetizers in a single layer for more even heating. You will find breads turn out crisper when they are heated on paper toweling or cloth napkins that absorb any extra moisture.

CHICKEN LIVERS IN BACON

Chicken livers
Bacon strips

1. Cut chicken livers into 1-inch pieces. Pierce chicken livers in several places to allow steam to escape.
2. Cut bacon strips into thirds. Wrap each piece of chicken liver in bacon and secure with a toothpick.
3. Arrange chicken livers, 10 at a time, on a paper plate that has been covered with a double thickness of paper toweling.
4. Heat, covered with a piece of paper toweling, in Microwave Oven 5 (6½) minutes or until liver is cooked and bacon is crisp. Turn plate after 2½ (3¼) minutes.
5. Serve hot.

Variations: Olives, shrimp, pineapple chunks, water chestnuts, walnuts or hard-cooked egg wedges can be substituted for the chicken livers.

Tip: If the chicken livers are not pierced in enough places, livers may pop during cooking. If popping occurs, pierce again with a toothpick.

Chicken Livers in Bacon

FANTAIL FRANKS

Cocktail frankfurters or regular-sized frankfurters cut into thirds

1. Make a ¾-inch crosswise slit in each end of each frankfurter.
2. Arrange a maximum of 16 frankfurter pieces on a large heat-resistant non-metallic platter.
3. Heat, uncovered, in Microwave Oven 3 (4) minutes.
4. Turn platter and heat, uncovered, in Microwave Oven 2 (2½) minutes or until frankfurters are heated through and the ends have curled.
5. Serve hot.

Variation: Let frankfurters stand in Barbecue Sauce several hours or overnight in refrigerator before cooking.

Fantail Franks

HAWAIIAN KABOBS

Canned pineapple chunks, undrained
Boiled ham, cut into ½-inch cubes
Soy sauce

1. Drain pineapple chunks and reserve juice. Cut pineapple chunks in half.
2. On a toothpick, arrange 2 pineapple chunks and 1 ham cube, alternating ham with pineapple. Repeat for as many kabobs as desired.
3. Combine reserved pineapple juice and soy sauce, 3 parts pineapple juice to 1 part soy sauce.
4. Brush juice mixture liberally over kabobs. Arrange kabobs on a large heat-resistant non-metallic serving platter, no more than 30 at a time.
5. Heat, uncovered, in Microwave Oven 2 (2½) minutes.
6. Turn and brush kabobs again with pineapple juice mixture. Heat, uncovered, in Microwave Oven an additional 2 (2½) minutes or until heated through.
7. Serve hot or cold.

CHEESE-STUFFED FRANKFURTERS

Cocktail frankfurters or regular-sized frankfurters cut into thirds
Mustard
Cheese slices (American, Cheddar or Swiss)

1. Make a slit down the center of each frankfurter leaving about ¼-inch on each end uncut. Cut almost all the way through the frankfurter, making a pocket.

(Continued on next page)
*Parenthesis ( ) indicates 500 watt units.

2. Spread a little mustard in each slit. Insert small strips of cheese in each pocket. Fasten pocket closed with a toothpick.
3. Arrange a maximum of 16 frankfurter pieces on a large heat-resistant non-metallic platter.
4. Heat, uncovered, in Microwave Oven 2 to 4 (3 to 5) minutes or until frankfurters are heated through and cheese begins to melt.
5. Serve hot.

Variations: Olive, water chestnut, or dill pickle slices or pickle relish may be substituted for the cheese.

LITTLE CHEESE SANDWICHES

Bread slices (white, rye or whole wheat)
Cheese slices (American, muenster, Cheddar or mozzarella)
Garnishes (cooked bacon, pepperoni strips, olive slices, pimiento slivers, mushroom slices or green pepper slices)

1. Toast bread conventionally. Place a slice of cheese on each piece of toast. Arrange 6 slices of toast at a time on a large heat-resistant non-metallic serving platter that has been covered with a paper or cloth napkin.
2. Heat, uncovered, in Microwave Oven 1½ (2) minutes, turning bread slices ½ turn after 45 (60) seconds.
3. Arrange desired garnishes on cheese.
4. Return sandwiches to Microwave Oven and heat, uncovered 15 to 30 (20 to 40) seconds or until garnishes are hot and cheese is melted.
5. Cut each sandwich into individual hors d'oeuvres as desired.
6. Serve hot.

HOT CRAB MEAT CANAPES

1 (6½-ounce) can crab meat
½ cup mayonnaise
1 teaspoon lemon juice
Few grains cayenne pepper
Crackers or Melba toast
Paprika

1. Rinse and drain crab meat, remove any ligament, cartilage or shell. Shred crab meat with a fork.
2. Combine crab meat, mayonnaise, lemon juice and cayenne pepper to taste in a bowl; stir to blend.
3. Spread about 1 teaspoon of crab mixture on each cracker and sprinkle with paprika.
4. Arrange 24 canapes on a large heat-resistant non-metallic serving platter.
5. Heat, uncovered, in Microwave Oven 3 to 3½ (4 to 4½) minutes or until heated through.
6. Serve hot.

Tip: If desired 12 canapes may be heated at a time for 1½ to 2 (2 to 2½) minutes.

MINIATURE PIZZA

English muffins
Tomato sauce
Mozzarella cheese slices, diced
Dried oregano leaves
Grated Romano or Parmesan cheese
Garnishes (anchovy fillets, pepperoni slices, sausage slices or mushroom slices)

1. Split and toast English muffins conventionally.
2. Spread a heaping teaspoon of tomato sauce on each toasted English muffin half. Arrange mozzarella cheese pieces on muffin halves.
3. Place 6 muffin halves at a time on a heat-resistant non-metallic serving platter that has been covered with a paper or cloth napkin.
4. Heat, uncovered, in Microwave Oven 1 (1¼) minutes or until cheese begins to melt and become bubbly.
5. Spread a little additional tomato sauce on each muffin half. Sprinkle with oregano and grated cheese.
6. Arrange garnish on tops of pizzas as desired and heat, uncovered, in Microwave Oven 30 to 45 (40 to 60) seconds or until cheese is completely melted and garnishes are hot.
7. Cut each pizza into individual hors d'oeuvres as desired.
8. Serve hot.

HOT ROQUEFORT CANAPES

1 (3-ounce) package cream cheese
¼ cup Roquefort cheese, crumbled
¼ cup finely chopped walnuts
¼ teaspoon dry mustard
½ teaspoon Worcestershire sauce
Crackers or Melba toast
Chopped walnuts

1. Place cream cheese in a small heat-resistant non-metallic bowl and heat, uncovered, in Microwave Oven 30 (40) seconds or until cheese is soft.
2. Add Roquefort cheese, chopped walnuts, mustard and Worcestershire sauce; stir to blend.
3. Spread cheese mixture on crackers. Arrange a maximum of 10 canapes on a large paper plate, or heat-resistant non-metallic serving platter lined with a paper or cloth napkin.
4. Heat, uncovered, in Microwave Oven 45 seconds to 1 minute (1 to 1¼ min.) or until cheese begins to melt.
5. Top with a piece of walnut and serve hot.

Variation: Blue cheese, sharp Cheddar cheese or any strong-flavored cheese may be substituted for the Roquefort cheese.

Little Cheese Sandwiches and Miniature Pizza   Page 67

HAM ROLL-UPS

1 pound thinly sliced boiled ham
1 pound thinly sliced American cheese
2 tablespoons prepared brown mustard

1. Spread each slice of ham with a little mustard.
2. Place a slice of cheese on each slice of ham and roll from the short end so that the cheese is completely encased in the ham.
3. Cut roll-ups in quarters crosswise and secure loose ends of ham with toothpicks.
4. Arrange 20 roll-ups in a single layer on a heat-resistant non-metallic serving platter.
5. Heat, uncovered, in Microwave Oven 3 to 4 (4 to 5) minutes until cheese begins to melt and ham is hot. Turn platter several times during cooking.
6. Repeat with remaining roll-ups.

Variation: Any cheese slices may be substituted for American cheese.

*Parenthesis (   ) indicates 500 watt units.

SWEDISH MEATBALLS

¼ cup butter or margarine
1 cup finely chopped onion
3 eggs
1⅓ cups milk
1½ teaspoons ground allspice
½ teaspoon ground nutmeg
1 tablespoon salt
2 cups soft bread crumbs
3 pounds lean ground beef round
1 envelope instant beef broth or 1 cube beef bouillon
1 cup boiling water
4 tablespoons flour
2 cups light cream or milk

1. Melt butter in a large heat-resistant non-metallic bowl in Microwave Oven 30 (40) seconds.
2. Add onions and heat, uncovered, in Microwave Oven 3 (4) minutes or until onions are lightly browned. Set aside.
3. In a small bowl mix eggs and milk until well blended.
4. Add egg mixture, allspice, nutmeg, salt, and bread crumbs to cooked onions. Stir to combine.
5. Crumble meat into mixture.
6. Mix with hands or kitchen fork until thoroughly combined.
7. Form meat mixture into 1-inch balls.
8. Heat meatballs in a single layer in a shallow 1-quart non-metallic casserole in Microwave Oven 5 to 6 (6½ to 8) minutes or until almost done. Turn meatballs occasionally during cooking.
9. While meatballs are cooking, combine beef bouillon and water in a small bowl and set aside.
10. Repeat the cooking process with the remaining meatballs.
11. Reserve any meat juices that collect in the bottom of the baking dish. Skim off excess fat and discard. Pour meat juices into a deep 2½-quart non-metallic casserole and stir in flour. Stir in reversed beef broth.
12. Heat, uncovered, in Microwave Oven 2 (2½) minutes or until slightly thickened.
13. Gradually stir in cream.
14. Heat, uncovered, in Microwave Oven 4 (5) minutes or until thickened and smooth. Stir occasionally.
15. Place meatballs in sauce. If necessary, meatballs and sauce may be reheated to bring them to serving temperature.

Variation: Any ground meat or combination of meats may be substituted for all or a portion of the ground beef.

HERBED DRUMSTICKS

½ cup butter or margarine
1 teaspoon dried tarragon leaves
2 teaspoons chopped chives
2 tablespoons chopped parsley
Salt and pepper
12 chicken drumsticks

1. In a shallow non-metallic baking dish melt butter in Microwave Oven 1 (1¼) minute.
2. Add herbs, salt and pepper to taste; stir to combine.
3. Place drumsticks in baking dish and toss gently to coat well with butter mixture.
4. Heat, uncovered, in Microwave Oven 7 to 8 (9 to 10) minutes or until chicken is done. Turn occasionally.

Serves 4 to 6.

Variation: If desired, drumsticks can be partially cooked over charcoal, then transferred to the Microwave Oven.

MARINATED CHICKEN WINGS

1 cup dry sherry
½ cup soy sauce
¼ teaspoon garlic powder
1 teaspoon ground ginger
48 chicken wings

1. In a large bowl combine sherry, soy sauce, garlic powder and ginger and set aside.
2. Disjoint chicken wings into 3 parts each. Discard the tip end or save to use for soup stock at a later date.
3. Marinate chicken pieces in sherry mixture in the refrigerator at least 3 hours but not longer than 24 hours.
4. Arrange 20 pieces at a time in a single layer on a heat-resistant non-metallic serving platter.
5. Heat, uncovered, in Microwave Oven 5 to 6 (6½ to 8) minutes or until chicken is well cooked.
6. Turn chicken pieces over after 3 minutes.
7. Repeat with remaining chicken pieces as needed.

Tip: Uncooked chicken pieces can either be stored in refrigerator for 2 to 3 days or may be frozen for 3 months. Cooked pieces may be reheated.

*Parenthesis ( ) indicates 500 watt units.

Soups

Soups made in the Microwave Oven retain their fresh flavor because cooking times are greatly decreased. One serving or many, soups can be prepared and served in the same container, so there are fewer dishes to clean. Quick microwave cooking and defrosting make it possible to freeze a portion for later use. You'll find recipes in this section for hot hearty soups like Quick Corn Chowder. Cold Borscht and Cherry Soup.

Soups may be heated in any heat-resistant non-metallic vessel devoid of metal decoration and glued-on handles. Be sure to allow enough room for soups to expand during cooking, especially in recipes containing milk.

Quick Corn Chowder Page 73

CANNED CONDENSED SOUPS

**1 (10 to 12-ounce) can condensed soup
Water or milk**

1. Place soup in a deep 1½-quart non-metallic casserole.
2. Add water or milk as label directs, stirring until smooth.
3. Heat, uncovered, in Microwave Oven 6 to 8 (8 to 10) minutes or until soup bubbles. Stir several times during heating.

Serves 2 to 3.

CANNED NON-CONDENSED SOUPS

1 (10 to 19-ounce) can non-condensed soup

1. Place soup in a deep 1½-quart non-metallic casserole.
2. Heat, uncovered, in Microwave Oven 5 to 8 (6½ to 10) minutes or until soup bubbles. Stir several times during heating. The heating time will depend on the size of the can.

Serves 2 to 4.

INDIVIDUAL SERVINGS OF DEHYDRATED SOUP

**¾ cup water
1 envelope dehydrated soup mix (for one serving)**

1. Pour water into a heat-resistant non-metallic mug, cup or bowl.
2. Heat, uncovered, in Microwave Oven 1 to 2 (1¼ to 3) minutes or until water reaches a full rolling boil.
3. Stir in soup mix.

Serves 1.

FROZEN NON-CONDENSED SOUPS

1 to 4 cups, frozen

1. Place soup in a deep non-metallic casserole large enough to prevent any boil-over.
2. Heat, uncovered, in Microwave Oven 5 to 12 (6½ to 15½) minutes or until soup bubbles. Stir several times during last half of heating.

Serves 1 to 5.

Tip: The type and amount of soup as well as its bulk will determine the defrosting and heating times.

REHEATING SOUPS

1 to 4 cups soup

1. Place soup in a deep non-metallic casserole large enough to prevent any boil-over.
2. Heat, uncovered, in Microwave Oven 3 to 8 (4 to 10) minutes or until soup bubbles. Stir several times during heating.

Serves 1 to 5.

Tip: The type and amount of soup will determine the heating time.

CREAM OF PEA SOUP

**2 tablespoons butter or margarine
1 tablespoon finely chopped onion
2 cups canned or cooked peas
½ teaspoon salt
1 teaspoon sugar
2 cups water
1 cup light cream
¼ teaspoon garlic salt
¼ teaspoon pepper**

1. Place butter and onion in a deep 2½-quart non-metallic casserole.
2. Heat, uncovered, in Microwave Oven 3 (4) minutes. Turn casserole ½ turn after 1½ (2) minutes. Stir mixture occasionally.
3. Add peas, salt, sugar and water. Heat, uncovered, in Microwave Oven 3 (4) minutes.
4. Press mixture through a sieve or food mill or blend in a blender until smooth.
5. Add light cream and heat, uncovered, in Microwave Oven 3 to 5 (4 to 6½) minutes or until heated through. Stir occasionally.
6. Add remaining ingredients and heat, uncovered, in Microwave Oven 1 (1¼) minute longer or until soup bubbles.
7. Allow soup to stand 2 to 3 minutes before serving.

Serves 6.

Cream of Pea Soup

*Parenthesis ( ) indicates 500 watt units.

VEGETABLE SOUP

3 slices raw bacon, diced
¼ cup finely chopped onion
1 cup finely chopped celery
1 cup thinly sliced carrots
1 cup potatoes cut into ¼-inch cubes
3 tablespoons flour
3 cups vegetable juice cocktail or tomato juice
1 cup water
½ teaspoon thyme
1 cube beef bouillon, crumbled or 1 envelope instant
  beef broth
Salt and pepper
1 (8½-ounce) can peas, drained

1. Place bacon and onion in a deep 2½-quart
non-metallic casserole.
2. Heat, covered with paper toweling, in Microwave
Oven 3 (4) minutes. Turn casserole ½ turn after 1½
(2) minutes. Stir mixture occasionally.
3. Add celery, carrots and potatoes. Heat, covered,
in Microwave Oven 8 (10) minutes or until vegetables
are tender. Stir mixture and turn casserole
occasionally.
4. Blend in flour.
5. Gradually stir in vegetable juice cocktail, water,
thyme, bouillon cube and salt and pepper to taste.
6. Heat, uncovered, in Microwave Oven 10 (13)
minutes, stirring occasionally.
7. Add peas and heat, uncovered, in Microwave
Oven an additional 2 (2½) minutes or until soup
bubbles and peas are hot.
8. Allow soup to stand 2 to 3 minutes before serving.
Serves 6 to 8.

Vegetable Soup

QUICK CORN CHOWDER

3 slices raw bacon, diced
¼ cup finely chopped onion
1 (16-ounce) can cream-style corn
¼ cup hot water
1 cup milk

½ teaspoon salt
¼ teaspoon pepper
Finely chopped fresh parsley

1. Place bacon and onion in a deep 2-quart
non-metallic casserole.
2. Heat, covered with paper toweling, in Microwave
Oven 3 (4) minutes. Turn casserole ½ turn after
1½ (2) minutes. Stir mixture occasionally.
3. Add remaining ingredients, except parsley. Stir
to combine.
4. Heat, uncovered, in Microwave Oven 4 to 5 (5 to 6½)
minutes or until soup is heated through. Stir
occasionally.
5. Allow soup to stand 2 to 3 minutes before serving.
6. Garnish with parsley.

Serves 4 to 5.

BORSCHT

1 to 1½ pounds beets
1 quart water
1½ teaspoon salt
¼ teaspoon pepper
2 tablespoons sugar
⅓ cup lemon juice
Commercial sour cream

1. Wash, scrape and coarsely grate beets.
2. Place beets, water, salt, pepper, sugar and lemon
juice in a deep 2-quart non-metallic casserole.
3. Heat, covered, in Microwave Oven 10 to 12 (13 to 15½)
minutes or until beets are tender.
4. Chill soup several hours or overnight.
5. Serve cold garnished with dollops of sour cream.

Serves 8 to 10.

CHERRY SOUP

1 quart fresh sweet cherries, pitted
1 quart water
¼ cup sugar
1 cup claret wine
4-inch cinnamon stick
Juice of 1 lemon
2 tablespoons cornstarch
¼ cup water
2 egg yolks, well beaten

1. In a deep 3-quart non-metallic casserole combine
cherries, the 1 quart water, the sugar, wine,
cinnamon and lemon juice. Stir to combine.
2. Heat, covered, in Microwave Oven 15 (20) minutes
or until cherries are tender.
3. In a small bowl combine cornstarch and the
¼ cup water. Stir into hot cherry mixture.
4. Heat, uncovered, in Microwave Oven 4 (5)
minutes or until thickened and smooth.
5. Pour soup very gradually over egg yolks,
stirring constantly.
6. Refrigerate 6 hours or overnight. Serve cold.
Serves 8 to 10.

*Parenthesis (   ) indicates 500 watt units.

Sauces

Sauces

In this chapter we've put together a variety of your favorite sauces that you can cook up in just minutes. You'll find cherry sauce, butterscotch sauce, barbecue sauce. We've even included brown gravy and strawberry jam plus more. Beautiful, versatile sauces for every occasion.

Sticking and scorching are no longer a problem When cooking sauces in your Microwave Oven. Sauces must be watched during cooking, however, because cooking times will vary depending upon the type of cookware and the temperature of the ingredients used.

CHERRY SAUCE

1 (17-ounce) can dark sweet cherries, undrained (pitted or unpitted)
1 tablespoon cornstarch
1½ teaspoons lemon juice
1 teaspoon grated lemon peel

1. Drain cherry juice into a deep 1-quart non-metallic casserole. Set cherries aside. Blend cornstarch into cherry juice until smooth.
2. Heat, uncovered, in Microwave Oven 4 (5) minutes or until thickened and clear. Stir occasionally.
3. Add cherries, lemon juice and lemon peel to thickened cherry juice. Stir to combine.
4. Heat, uncovered, in Microwave Oven 1 (1¼) minute or until sauce bubbles and cherries are hot.
5. Spoon over ice cream or cake.

Makes 2 cups.

Variations: If desired, sauce may be made from canned blueberries, strawberries, raspberries, pineapple or diced peaches.

Cherries Jubilee: Heat ¼ cup brandy in Microwave Oven in a heat-resistant non-metallic long-handled dish or spoon 20 (25) seconds. Ignite brandy and pour over Cherry Sauce. Spoon over ice cream.

Tip: If a heat-resistant non-metallic long-handled spoon is not available, brandy may be heated in any heat-resistant non-metallic vessel and transferred to a long-handled ladle before igniting.

BUTTERSCOTCH SAUCE

⅓ cup light cream
1½ cups firmly packed dark brown sugar
3 tablespoons butter or margarine
1 teaspoon vanilla extract

1. In a deep 1-quart non-metallic casserole combine light cream, brown sugar and butter.
2. Heat, uncovered, in Microwave Oven 4 (5) minutes, stirring occasionally. Stir in vanilla.
3. Serve over ice cream, cake or pudding.

Makes 2 cups.

CHOCOLATE FUDGE SAUCE

1 (6-ounce) package semisweet chocolate pieces
1 tablespoon butter or margarine
¼ cup hot water
¼ cup sugar
¼ cup light corn syrup
Few grains salt
1 teaspoon vanilla extract

1. In a 2-cup non-metallic measuring cup melt chocolate pieces with butter and water in Microwave

Oven 4 (5) minutes. Stir frequently.
2. Add sugar, corn syrup, salt and vanilla; stir until well blended.
3. Heat, uncovered, in Microwave Oven 30 seconds to 1 minute (40 sec. to 1¼ min.) or until smooth and thickened.
4. Serve over ice cream, cake or pudding.

Makes 1½ cups.

LEMON SAUCE

½ cup sugar
1 tablespoon cornstarch
1 cup water
2 tablespoons butter or margarine
1 teaspoon grated lemon peel
2 tablespoons lemon juice
Few grains salt
Yellow food coloring (optional)

1. In a deep 1-quart non-metallic casserole combine sugar and cornstarch. Gradually add water, stirring until smooth.
2. Heat, uncovered, in Microwave Oven 2 (2½) minutes, stirring frequently, until sauce is thickened and smooth.
3. Add butter, lemon peel, lemon juice and salt. If desired, add food coloring, a drop at a time, until desired color is reached.
4. Serve over cake, fruit or pudding.

Makes 1 cup.

Variation: Orange Sauce: Substitute 1 cup plus 2 tablespoons orange juice for water and lemon juice. Grated orange peel may be substituted for lemon peel.

MEDIUM WHITE SAUCE

2 tablespoons butter or margarine
2 tablespoons flour
½ teaspoon salt
1 cup milk

1. In a deep 1-quart non-metallic casserole melt butter in Microwave Oven 30 (40) seconds.
2. Blend in flour and salt until smooth.
3. Gradually, stirring constantly, add milk.
4. Heat, uncovered, in Microwave Oven 2 to 3 (2½ to 4) minutes or until thickened and smooth. Stir frequently.

Makes 1 cup.

Variations: Thin White Sauce: Follow recipe for Medium White Sauce reducing butter and flour to 1 tablespoon each.

Thick White Sauce: Follow recipe for Medium White Sauce increasing butter and flour to 3 to 4 tablespoons each depending upon desired thickness.

CHEESE SAUCE

1 cup Medium White Sauce (recipe page 77)
¾ cup shredded sharp Cheddar cheese
Dash cayenne pepper

1. Prepare Medium White Sauce according to recipe.
2. Add cheese and cayenne during the last 1½ (2) minutes of heating.

Makes 1½ cups sauce.

CREAMED MUSHROOM SAUCE

1 cup Medium White Sauce (recipe page 77)
1 (4-ounce) can sliced mushrooms, drained

1. Prepare Medium White Sauce according to recipe.
2. Add mushrooms during the last 1½ (2) minutes of heating.

Makes 1¼ cups.

MORNAY SAUCE

2 tablespoons butter or margarine
2 tablespoons flour
⅓ cup light cream
1 cup chicken stock or broth
¼ cup Romano cheese
¼ cup shredded Swiss cheese
2 tablespoons dried parsley flakes

1. In a 2-cup non-metallic measuring cup melt butter in Microwave Oven 30 (40) seconds.
2. Blend in flour.
3. Gradually stir in light cream and chicken stock.
4. Heat, uncovered, in Microwave Oven 2½ to 3 (3¼ to 4) minutes or until thickened and smooth. Stir frequently.
5. Add cheeses and parsley flakes and heat, uncovered, in Microwave Oven 30 (40) seconds or until cheese is melted and sauce is smooth. Allow sauce to stand until cheese has completely melted.

Makes 1½ cups.

BROWN GRAVY

2 tablespoons fat
1 cup pan drippings or beef broth
2 tablespoons flour
Salt and pepper
Brown bouquet sauce (optional)

1. After roasting meat in Microwave Oven remove meat from roasting pan and set aside. Pour pan drippings into a bowl, leaving residue in roasting pan.
2. Allow fat to rise to the top. Skim off 2 tablespoons and return to the pan. Discard any remaining fat. Reserve pan drippings and pour into a 1-cup measuring cup. Add beef broth, if necessary, to make 1 cup. Set aside.

3. Blend in flour and salt and pepper to taste; stir until smooth. Heat, uncovered, in Microwave Oven 2 to 3 (2½ to 4) minutes or until lightly browned.
4. Gradually add reserved pan drippings. Heat, uncovered, in Microwave Oven to 2 (2½) minutes or until thickened and smooth. Stir gravy every 30 (40) seconds during cooking. If desired brown bouquet sauce may be added to gravy.

Makes 1 cup.

CHICKEN GRAVY WITH MUSHROOMS

2 tablespoons chicken fat, butter or margarine
2 tablespoons flour
Salt and pepper
1 cup chicken stock or broth
1 (4-ounce) can sliced mushrooms, drained

1. Melt chicken fat or butter in a deep 1-quart non-metallic casserole in Microwave Oven 30 (40) seconds.
2. Blend in flour and salt and pepper to taste. Stir until smooth. Heat, uncovered, in Microwave Oven 1 to 2 (1¼ to 2½) minutes or until lightly browned.
3. Gradually stir in chicken stock. Add mushroom slices; stir to combine.
4. Heat, uncovered, in Microwave Oven 2 to 3 (2½ to 4) minutes or until gravy is thickened and smooth. Stir every 30 (40) seconds during cooking.

Makes 1 cup.

BARBECUE SAUCE

2 tablespoons butter or margarine
1 medium-sized onion, finely chopped
1 clove garlic, peeled and crushed
2 tablespoons finely chopped green pepper
¾ cup catsup
¼ cup water
¼ cup cider vinegar
¼ teaspoon dry mustard
¼ cup firmly packed dark brown sugar
¼ teaspoon salt
Few drops Tabasco sauce to taste

1. Place butter, onion, garlic and green pepper in a deep 1½-quart non-metallic casserole and heat in Microwave Oven 3 (4) minutes or until tender. Stir occasionally.
2. Add remaining ingredients; stir well to combine.
3. Heat, uncovered, in Microwave Oven 2 (2½) minutes or until sauce bubbles. Serve over meat or poultry.

Makes 2¼ cups.

*Parenthesis (   ) indicates 500 watt units.

MUSTARD SAUCE FOR FISH

1 tablespoon oil
1 tablespoon finely chopped shallots or onion
1 tablespoon flour
1 cup fish stock or clam juice
1 tablespoon sharp French mustard

1. In a 2-cup non-metallic measuring cup heat oil
in Microwave Oven 30 (40) seconds. Add shallots and
heat, uncovered, in Microwave Oven 1 (1¼) minute or
until shallots are tender.
2. Blend in flour; stir until smooth. Heat, uncovered,
in Microwave Oven 1 (1¼) minute or until lightly
browned.
3. Gradually stir in fish stock; stir until smooth.
4. Heat, uncovered, in Microwave Oven 2 to 3 (2½ to 4)
minutes or until thickened and smooth. Stir every
30 (40) seconds during cooking.
5. Stir in mustard.

Makes 1 cup.

Italian Tomato Sauce

APPLE JAM

1½ cups apples sliced and peeled
¾ cup sugar
1 tablespoon lemon juice
1 cup sugar

1. Pare apples; core and cut in eights.
2. In a medium size heat resistant non-metallic
bowl, combine apples, lemon juice and sugar.
Mix carefully.
3. Heat, uncovered, in Microwave Oven 10 to 12 (13
to 15½) minutes. Turn dish ½ turn after each 5 (7)
minutes.
Stir mixture occasionally.
4. Allow jam to stand 30 (40) minutes covered, at
room temperature.
5. Store in refrigerator.

Makes 1 cup.

STRAWBERRY JAM

1½ cups strawberries
1 tablespoon lemon juice
1 cup sugar

1. Wash berries—Slice in half lengthwise or quarter
large berries.
2. In a medium-size heat resistant non-metallic bowl
combine strawberries, lemon juice, and sugar. Mix
carefully.
3. Heat, uncovered, in Microwave Oven 14 to 16 (18
to 21) minutes. Turn dish ½ turn after each 5 (7)
minutes. Stir mixture occasionally. Allow jam to stand
30 (40) minutes, covered, at room temperature.
4. Store in refrigerator.

Makes 1 cup.

ITALIAN TOMATO SAUCE

2 tablespoons olive oil
1 medium-sized onion, finely chopped
1 clove garlic, peeled and crushed
1 (15-ounce) can tomato sauce
1 teaspoon sugar
½ teaspoon dried sweet basil leaves
½ teaspoon dried oregano leaves
1 teaspoon salt
¼ teaspoon pepper

1. Place olive oil, onions and garlic in a deep 1½-
quart non-metallic casserole Heat, uncovered, in
Microwave Oven 3 (4) minutes or until onion is
tender; stir occasionally.
2. Add remaining ingredients. Stir to combine.
3. Heat, covered, in Microwave Oven 5 to 7 (7 to 9)
minutes or until sauce bubbles.

Makes 2½ cups.

*Parenthesis (   ) indicates 500 watt units.

Meat, Fish and Poultry Cooking Charts/Recipes

Meat, Fish and Poultry Cooking Charts/Recipes

Cooking Times
Many factors influence the cooking times of meat, fish and poultry dishes prepared in your Microwave Oven. For instance, foods which come from the refrigerator will take longer to cook than those at room temperature. Size and shape also have an effect on cooking time. Aged or more tender meats or poultry will cook more quickly.

Roasting Meat and Poultry
Meat and poultry should be roasted in shallow non-metallic baking dishes, placed on an inverted saucer in the center of the dish to be raised above drippings. Lightly cover meat and poultry with paper towels to prevent spatter and help in basting. *Do not salt* before roasting in the Microwave Oven as salt tends to dehydrate meat and poultry and make them tough. However, pepper and other spices and herbs may be used.

Food should be turned during roasting for more even cooking. They should be turned over after half of cooking time and the baking dish should be rotated a quarter turn several times during cooking. Fats should be poured off after half the cooking time has elapsed.

At the end of the roasting time, allow meat or poultry to stand 15 to 30 minutes at room temperature. This equalizes the heat. The cooking process continues during this period and the internal temperature of the food will rise 5 to 10 degrees. The internal temperature may be checked by inserting a meat thermometer into the thickest part of the meat, away from gristle, bone or fat. The meat is done when the desired internal temperature is reached. *Never place meat or poultry in the Microwave Oven with meat thermometer inserted.*

Browning
Tough larger roasts and poultry items will brown easily in a Microwave Oven, YOU may find that smaller portions roasted in the Microwave Oven do not acquire the same degree of browning they would have if cooked by conventional means. The surface color may be enhanced by applying a 1 to 1 mixture of brown bouquet sauce and water. Meat and poultry may also be browned by searing conventionally either in a frying pan or under a broiler.

Fish
Fish should be watched very carefully during cooking in the Microwave Oven to avoid overcooking. Fish should be cooked only until it may be easily flaked with a fork.

MEAT, FISH AND POULTRY COOKING CHART

* Browning skillet may be used for these items—follow instructions provided with dish.

Meat	Time per Pound	Method	Internal Temp. After Cooking	Internal Temp. After Standing 20 to 30 Minutes
BEEF				
Rolled Roasts	rare 6 (8) min. medium 7 (9) min. well-done 8 (10) min.	Place fat-side-down in baking dish. Heat, uncovered, for ½ of cooking time. Turn roast over. Drain excess fat. Cover with paper towel or wax paper. Heat for remaining time. Let stand covered with aluminum foil.	130°F 150°F 160°F	140°F 160°F 170°F
Bone-in Roast 3 to 4 Ribs	rare 5 (6½) min. medium 6 (8) min. well-done 7 (9) min.	Cover bone ends with small pieces of foil. Place fat-side-down in baking dish. Heat, uncovered, for ½ of cooking time. Turn roast over. Drain excess fat. Cover with paper towel or wax paper. Heat for remaining time. Let stand covered with aluminum foil.	130°F 150°F 160°F	140°F 160°F 170°F
Bone-in Roast 2 Ribs	rare 5 (6½) min medium 6 (8) min. well-done 7 (9) min.	Place cut-side-down in baking dish. Heat, uncovered, for ½ of cooking time. Turn roast over and place other cut-side-down. Drain excess fat. Cover with paper towel or wax paper. Heat for remaining time. Let stand covered with aluminum foil.	130°F 150°F 160°F	140°F 160°F 170°F
Steak *	rare 3 to 4 (4 to 5) min. medium 4 (5) to 5 (6½) well-done 5 to 6 (6½ to 8) min.	Place steak in baking dish. Heat, uncovered, for ½ of cooking time. Turn steak over. Drain excess fat. Cover with paper towel. Heat for remaining time. If desired, steak may be seared conventionally. If steak is seared, reduce cooking time in Microwave Oven.	— — —	— — —
Hamburgers * and Cheeseburgers		See recipes on page 30 and 88.	—	—
LAMB				
Leg or Shoulder Roasts	well-done 10 to 12 (13 to 15½) min.	If bone is still in lamb, wrap the last 2 inches with foil. Place fat-side-down in baking dish. Heat, uncovered, for ½ of cooking time. Turn roast over. Drain excess fat. Cover with paper towel or wax paper. Heat for remaining time. Let stand covered with aluminum foil.	170°F (165°)	175°F

(Continued on next page)
*Parenthesis (   ) indicates 500 watt units.

Meat, Fish and Poultry Cooking Charts

MEAT, FISH AND POULTRY COOKING CHART—continued

* Browning skillet may be used for these items—follow instructions provided with dish.

Meat	Time per Pound	Method	Internal Temp. After Cooking	Internal Temp. After Standing 20 to 30 Minutes
Chops *	well-done 4 to 5 (5 to 6½) min.	Sear chops conventionally. Place in baking dish or on plate. Heat, uncovered, for ½ of cooking time. Turn chops over. Drain excess fat. Cover with paper towel. Heat for remaining time. Time will depend on amount of searing done before cooking in Microwave Oven.	—	—
PORK				
Fresh Loin or Fresh Shoulder	well-done 10 (13) min.	Place fat-side-down in baking dish. Heat, uncovered, for ½ of cooking time. Turn roast over. Drain excess fat. Cover with paper towel or wax paper. Let stand covered with aluminum foil.	165°F	175°F
Canned Hams	well-done 5 (6½) min.	Place fat-side-down in baking dish. Heat, uncovered, for ½ of cooking time. Turn roast over. Drain excess fat. Cover with paper towel or wax paper. Let stand covered with aluminum foil.	165°F	175°F
Chops *	well-done 5 to 6 (6 to 8) min.	Sear chops conventionally. Place in baking dish or on plate. Heat, uncovered, for ½ of cooking time. Turn chops over. Drain excess fat. Cover with paper towel. Heat for remaining time. Time will depend on amount of searing done before cooking in Microwave Oven.	—	—
VEAL				
Rolled Roast	medium 8 (10) min. well-done 9 (11½) min.	Place fat-side-down in baking dish. Place bacon, butter or margarine on top of roast. Heat, uncovered, for ½ of cooking time. Turn roast over. Place additional bacon, butter or margarine on top of roast. Heat for remaining time. Let stand covered with aluminum foil.	150°F 160°F	160°F 170°F
Chops *	well-done 5 to 6 (6 to 8) min.	Sear chops conventionally. Place in baking dish or on plate. Heat, uncovered, for ½ of cooking time. Turn chops over. Drain excess fat. Cover with paper towel. Heat for remaining time. Time will depend on amount of searing done before cooking in Microwave Oven.	— —	— —

MEAT, FISH AND POULTRY COOKING CHART—continued

* Browning skillet may be used for these items—follow instructions provided with dish.

Meat	Time per Pound	Method	Internal Temp. After Cooking	Internal Temp. After Standing 20 to 30 Minutes
FISH				
Whole Fish, Steaks and Fillets	6 (8) min.	Place in a shallow baking dish and heat, covered, for ½ of cooking time. Turn fish over. Cover and heat for remaining time or until fish flakes easily with a fork.	—	—
POULTRY				
Chicken	6 (8) min.	Place breast-side-down in a shallow baking dish and heat, uncovered, for ½ of cooking time. Turn bird over; drain excess fat. Cover with paper towel or wax paper. Heat for remaining time. Let stand covered with aluminum foil.	160°F	170°F
Turkey	*6 (8) min.	Stuff, if desired, Place breast-side-down in a shallow baking dish and heat, uncovered, for ½ of cooking time. Turn bird over. Drain excess fat. Cover with paper towel or wax paper. Heat for remaining time. Let stand covered with aluminum foil.	160°F	170°F
Duck	*6 to 7 (8 to 9) min.	Stuff, if desired. Place breast-side-down in a shallow baking dish and heat, uncovered, for ½ of cooking time. Turn bird over. Drain excess fat. Pierce skin, in many places, with the tines of a fork. Cover with paper towel or wax paper. Heat for remaining time. Let stand covered with aluminum foil.	160°F	170°F
Goose	*6 to 7 (8 to 9) min.	Stuff, if desired. Place breast-side-down in a shallow baking dish and heat, uncovered, for ½ of cooking time. Turn bird over. Drain excess fat. Pierce skin, in many places, with the tines of a fork. Cover with paper towel or wax paper. Heat for remaining time. Let stand covered with aluminum foil.	160°F	170°F

*For each pound of stuffing, add 6 min.

*Parenthesis ( ) indicates 500 watt units.

Roast Beef

ROAST BEEF

Beef roast
Garlic cloves, peeled (optional)
Pepper (optional)
Salt (optional)

1. Invert a heat-resistant non-metallic saucer or small casserole cover in the bottom of a shallow non-metallic baking dish. (The saucer keeps the meat out of the fat as it cooks.)
2. Place roast fat-side-down on the saucer.
3. Rub meat with garlic and pepper if desired.
4. Heat, uncovered, for half of the cooking time given in the chart on page 82.
5. Drain pan juices and reserve if gravy is to be made. Turn meat over, cover loosely with wax paper or paper toweling and heat for remainder of the cooking time.
6. Let roast stand covered in aluminum foil 15 to 30 minutes or until appropriate internal temperature is reached. *Do not place thermometer or aluminum foil in Microwave Oven.*
7. If necessary, return roast to Microwave Oven for a few minutes until desired internal temperature is reached.
8. Salt meat after cooking, if desired.

HOT DOGS

Frankfurters
Hot dog buns

1. Place frankfurters in buns and arrange on a paper plate or paper towel in the Microwave Oven. Heat, uncovered, according to the chart below.

Quantity	Total Cooking Time
1 frankfurter	20 (25) seconds
2 frankfurters	45 (60)seconds
3 frankfurters	1¼ (2) minutes
4 frankfurters	1½ (2) minutes

STEAKS

Steak
Pepper (optional)
Garlic salt (optional)
Salt (optional)
Brown bouquet sauce (optional)
Water (optional)

1. Place steak in a shallow non-metallic baking dish.
2. Sprinkle with pepper, garlic salt and salt, if desired.
3. For a deeper brown color, brush steak with a 1-to-1 mixture of brown bouquet sauce and water.
4. Heat, uncovered, in Microwave Oven according to the chart on page 82. Turn steak after ½ of cooking time.
5. Steak may be returned to Microwave Oven for additional cooking if necessary.

Tip: If desired, steak may be seared in a frying pan, over charcoal or under a broiler before cooking in Microwave Oven. Reduce cooking time in Step 4 if seared.
* Browning skillet may be used with these items, follow instructions provided with dish.

CHEESE DOGS

Frankfurters
Thin slices of cheese
Hot dog buns

1. Make a slit down the center of each frankfurter leaving about ¼ inch on each end uncut. Cut almost all the way through the frankfurter, making a pocket.
2. Place a thin slice of cheese (American, Swiss, Cheddar or muenster) in the pocket.
3. Place franks in buns and arrange on a paper plate or on paper toweling in Microwave Oven. Heat uncovered, according to the chart below.

Quantity	Total Cooking Time
1 frankfurter	1 (1¼) minute
2 frankfurters	1½ (2) minutes
3 frankfurters	2 (2½) minutes
4 frankfurters	2½ (3¼) minutes

MEAT LOAF

3 slices bread
Water
1 clove garlic, peeled and crushed
1 small onion, finely chopped
¼ cup finely chopped celery
½ teaspoon salt
⅛ teaspoon pepper
1 egg, slightly beaten
⅓ cup milk
1 pound lean ground beef
¼ cup catsup

1. In a small bowl soak bread in water for 5 minutes. Squeeze out extra water.
2. In a large bowl combine bread, garlic, onion, celery, salt, pepper, egg and milk. Stir until well blended. Crumble ground beef into bread mixture and stir to combine thoroughly.
3. Shape meat mixture into a loaf in a shallow non-metallic baking dish, or non-metallic loaf pan.
4. Heat, uncovered, in Microwave Oven 5 (6½) minutes turning baking dish ¼ turn every 1½ (2) minutes.
5. Spread catsup over top of meat loaf and heat, uncovered, in Microwave Oven 4 (5¼) minutes, turning baking dish occasionally.
6. Allow meat loaf to stand covered 3 to 5 minutes before cutting.

Serves 4.

Variations: Any combination of ground meats may be used in place of ground beef. If desired, you may

(Continued on next page)

*Parenthesis ( ) indicates 500 watt units.

add your own touches to meat loaf mixture; however, the addition of other ingredients may increase the cooking time. If necessary heat an additional 1 to 2 minutes after Step 5.

Tip: Meat loaf mixture may also be pressed into an 8 x 4-inch non-metallic loaf pan. Meat loaf may be prepared earlier in the day and heated at serving time.

BEEF STEW

4 tablespoons vegetable oil
2 pounds boneless lean beef chuck, cubed 1-inch
¼ cup flour
Salt and pepper
2½ cups water
2 bay leaves
2 teaspoons salt
¼ teaspoon pepper
1 clove garlic, peeled and crushed
3 medium-sized carrots, peeled and thinly sliced
6 medium-sized potatoes, peeled and cubed
2 stalks celery, cut into ½-inch slices
½ cup catsup
6 tablespoons flour
¾ cup cold water
½ to 1 teaspoon brown bouquet sauce (optional)
1 (10-ounce) package frozen peas, partially thawed (see chart page 13)

1. Heat 2 tablespoons of oil in a large skillet over moderate heat on a conventional stove.
2. Combine flour and salt and pepper in a plastic or paper bag. Shake meat cubes in seasoned flour to coat.
3. Brown beef cubes, a few at a time, on all sides in hot oil. Add the remaining 2 tablespoons of oil as needed.
4. Transfer browned beef cubes into a deep 2½ or 3-quart non-metallic casserole. Add the 2½ cups of water, bay leaves, the 2 teaspoons salt, the ¼ teaspoon pepper and garlic.
5. Heat, covered, in Microwave Oven 10 (13) minutes. Stir after 5 (6½) minutes. Skim any foam that may form.
6. Add carrots, potatoes, celery and catsup. Stir to combine.
7. Heat, covered, in Microwave Oven 25 to 30 (30 to 40) minutes or until meat and vegetables are tender.
8. While beef and vegetables are cooking, combine the 6 tablespoons flour and the ¾ cup water in a small bowl.
9. Remove bay leaves from stew.
10. Gradually stir flour mixture into stew. If desired, add brown bouquet sauce, a little at a time, until desired color is reached. Caution: color will deepen as stew cooks.
11. Add peas and heat, covered, 3 to 5 (4 to 6½) minutes or until sauce is thickened and peas are hot.

Serves 6 to 8.

Beef Stew

LAMB STEW

3½ pounds lean lamb neck meat, cut in large cubes
2 bay leaves
10 whole black peppercorns
1 teaspoon dried thyme leaves
1 tablespoon salt
1 clove garlic, peeled and crushed
3 cups water
3 medium-sized carrots, peeled and thinly sliced
3 cups potatoes cut into ½-inch cubes
6 tablespoons flour
¾ cup cold water

1. Place lamb, bay leaves, peppercorns, thyme, salt, garlic and the 3 cups of water in a 2½ or 3-quart non-metallic casserole.
2. Heat, covered, in Microwave Oven 5 (6½) minutes.
3. Skim any foam that may form.
4. Heat, covered, in Microwave Oven for an additional 25 (30) minutes or until lamb is almost tender.
5. Add carrots and potatoes and heat, covered, in Microwave Oven 20 (25) minutes or until lamb and vegetables are tender. Stir occasionally.
6. While lamb and vegetables are cooking, combine the 6 tablespoons flour and the ¾ cup water in a small bowl.
7. Remove bay leaves and peppercorns from stew.
8. Gradually stir flour mixture into stew and heat 3 to 5 (4 to 6½) minutes or until sauce is thickened and smooth.

Serves 6:

Tip: Boneless lamb may be used, however, reduce quantity of meat to 2½ pounds. Decrease cooking time in Step 4 to 20 (25) minutes.

SWEET AND SOUR LAMB CHOPS

2 tablespoons butter or margarine
4 shoulder lamb chops (about 2 pounds)
Salt and pepper
1 (8-ounce) can pineapple chunks in unsweetened
  juice, undrained
¼ cup firmly packed dark brown sugar
¼ cup white vinegar
1 tablespoon cornstarch
½ teaspoon brown bouquet sauce
2 carrots, peeled and thinly sliced
1 large green pepper, cut into 1-inch squares

1. Melt butter in a non-metallic skillet on a conventional stove. When butter is hot, sear lamb chops on both sides until lightly browned. Sprinkle with salt and pepper to taste.
2. While the chops are browning, drain pineapple juice into a small heat-resistant non-metallic bowl. Reserve pineapple chunks. Add brown sugar, vinegar, cornstarch and brown bouquet sauce to pineapple juice. Stir to combine.
3. Heat pineapple juice mixture, uncovered, in Microwave Oven 2 (2½) minutes or until thickened and clear.
4. Pour thickened sauce over browned lamb chops.
5. Add carrot slices and heat, covered, in Microwave Oven 5 (6½) minutes, turning pan ½ turn after 2½ (3¼) minutes.
6. Add pineapple chunks and heat, covered, in Microwave Oven 2½ (3¼) minutes.
7. Add green pepper squares and heat, uncovered, in Microwave Oven 2½ (3¼) minutes or until lamb and vegetables are tender.

Serves 3 to 4.

Sweet and Sour Lamb Chops

Variations: Pork chops, veal chops, boneless chicken pieces or shrimp may be substituted for the lamb chops; however, cooking times will have to be adjusted for pork, chicken and shrimp. Pork chops will require an extra 2 (2½) minutes in Step 5. Pork should always be cooked to well done. Chicken should be cooked for only 4 (5¼) minutes in Step 5. Shrimp will only require 3 (4) minutes in Step 5. Do not overcook shrimp as they will become tough.

Tip: If a non-metallic skillet is not available, any skillet may be used for browning and chops may be transferred to a 1½ or 2-quart casserole before proceeding with Step 4.

HAMBURGERS

1 pound lean ground beef
Salt (optional)
Garlic salt (optional)
Brown buquet sauce (optional)
Water (optional)

1. Shape beef into 4 patties ½-inch thick and arrange in a paper-towel-lined shallow non-metallic baking dish.
2. Sprinkle with salt and garlic salt, if desired.
3. If a deep brown color is desired, brush hamburger patties with a 1-to-1 mixture of brown bouquet sauce and water.
4. Heat, covered with paper toweling, in Microwave Oven 2 (2½) minutes.
5. Turn hamburgers and heat, covered with paper toweling, an additional 2 (2½) minutes.
6. Hamburgers may be returned to Microwave Oven for additional cooking if necessary.

Serves 4.

Quantity	Total Cooking Time
1 patty	2½ to 3 (3¼ to 4) minutes
2 patties	3½ to 4 (4½ to 5) minutes
3 patties	4 to 4½ (5 to 6) minutes
4 patties	4½ to 5 (6 to 6½) minutes
5 patties	5 to 5½ (6½ to 7) minutes
6 patties	6 to 7 (8 to 9) minutes

Variations: Cheeseburgers: Place a slice of your favorite cheese on each patty during the last 1 (1¼) minute of cooking time.

Surprise Hamburgers: Pickles, olives, relish, cheese, onion or other garnish may be sealed inside hamburger patties. Heat an additional 30 seconds to 1 minute (40 sec. to 1¼ min.) in Step 5.

The ground beef may be seasoned with Worcestershire sauce, barbecue sauce, mustard, catsup or other condiments.

If desired, hamburgers may be seared in a frying pan, over charcoal or under a broiler before cooking in Microwave Oven. Reduce cooking time in Steps 4 and 5 if seared.

*Parenthesis (   ) indicates 500 watt units.

Meat, Fish and Poultry Recipes

BACON

Bacon slices

1. Place a double layer of paper toweling in a 9-inch square non-metallic baking dish.
2. Lay bacon slices in a single layer on toweling.
3. Cover with another piece of paper toweling to prevent spattering. Heat in Microwave Oven according to the chart below.

Quantity	Total Cooking Time
1 slice	1 (1¼) minute
2 slices	1 to 1½ (1¼ to 2) minutes
4 slices	2½ to 3 (3¼ to 4) minutes
6 slices	3½ to 4 (4½ to 5) minutes

Tips: For only one or two slices, paper toweling may be placed on a paper plate.

The paper toweling is used to absorb bacon grease as it forms. If the bacon grease is desired for cooking, the layers of paper toweling underneath may be eliminated. However, bacon should still be covered lightly with a single piece of paper toweling. Drain bacon strips and blot on paper toweling before serving.

PORK CHOPS AND SAUERKRAUT

2 tablespoons vegetable oil
4 pork chops, cut 1-inch thick (about 2 pounds)
Salt and pepper
½ cup thinly sliced onion
1 (16-ounce) can sauerkraut, undrained
½ teaspoon caraway seeds
1 tart apple, peeled, cored and thinly sliced
½ cup water

1. In a non-metallic skillet, heat oil on a conventional stove until hot.
2. Sear pork chops on both sides until browned.
3. Sprinlke chops lightly with salt and pepper to taste. Drain any excess fat.
4. Arrange onions and sauerkraut over pork chops.
5. Heat, covered, in Microwave Oven 5 (6½) minutes.
6. Sprinkle caraway seeds over sauerkraut and arrange apple slices on top.
7. Add water and heat, covered, in Microwave Oven 4 (5) minutes. Turn skillet ½ turn and heat, uncovered, in Microwave Oven an additional 3 to 5 (4 to 6½) minutes or until pork chops are fork-tender.

Serves 3 to 4.

Tip: If a non-metallic skillet is not available, any skillet may be used for browning and the seared chops may be transferred to a 1½ or 2-quart non-metallic casserole after Step 3.

FRANKS AND BEANS

1 pound frankfurters
1 (32-ounce) can pork and beans
1 (8-ounce) can crushed pineapple in unsweetened juice, undrained
¼ cup chili sauce
¼ cup finely chopped onion

1. Slice frankfurters into ¼-inch rounds.
2. Place frankfurters, beans, pineapple, chili sauce and onions in a 2-quart casserole.
3. Heat, covered, in Microwave Oven 8 (10) minutes, stirring after 4 (5) minutes.
4. Allow to stand covered for 2 minutes before serving.

Serves 4 to 6.

GLAZED BAKED HAM

1 (3-pound) precooked canned ham
1 (8-ounce) can pineapple slices in unsweetened juice, undrained
½ cup firmly packed dark brown sugar
2 teaspoons dry mustard
Whole cloves

1. Remove ham from wrappings and place in a shallow non-metallic baking dish. Heat, uncovered, in Microwave Oven 10 (13) minutes.
2. Drain pineapple slices and reserve juice. In a small heat-resistant non-metallic bowl combine brown sugar, dry mustard and 3 tablespoons of the reserved pineapple juice.
3. Heat sugar mixture, uncovered, in Microwave Oven 1 (1¼) minute.
4. Score the top and sides of the ham, making diagonal cuts with a sharp knife.
5. Brush liberally with brown sugar mixture. Arrange pineapple slices on top and brush again with sugar mixture.
6. Place whole cloves in pineapple as desired.
7. Heat, uncovered, in Microwave Oven for 10 (13) minutes, brushing every 3 (4) minutes.
8. Allow to stand covered with aluminum foil 15 minutes before serving.

Serves 6 to 8.

MACARONI AND CHEESE CASSEROLE

3 tablespoons butter or margarine
3½ tablespoons flour
¾ teaspoon salt
¼ teaspoon pepper
2 teaspoons dry mustard
3 cups milk
½ pound sharp Cheddar cheese, shredded

(Continued on next page)

8 ounces elbow macaroni, cooked
1 (12-ounce) can luncheon meat, cut into ¼-inch strips
3 tablespoons melted butter or margarine
½ cup seasoned fine dry bread crumbs

1. In a deep 2½-quart non-metallic casserole melt butter in Microwave Oven 30 (40) seconds.
2. Blend in flour, salt, pepper and dry mustard, stirring until smooth.
3. Gradually stir in milk until smooth.
4. Heat, uncovered, in Microwave Oven 4 to 6 (5 to 8) minutes or until thickened and smooth. Stir frequently during last half of cooking.
5. Add shredded cheese and stir until melted.
6. Add cooked macaroni and luncheon meat. Stir until well blended.
7. In a small heat-resistant non-metallic bowl combine melted butter and bread crumbs and heat, uncovered, in Microwave Oven 3 (4) minutes or until bread crumbs are lightly browned.
8. Sprinkle bread crumb mixture over macaroni mixture.
9. Heat, uncovered, in Microwave Oven 4 to 6 (5 to 8) minutes or until heated through.

Serves 6.

Variation: 2½ cups of ham, tongue, turkey, other leftover meat or luncheon meat may be substituted for the canned luncheon meat.

SHRIMP SCAMPI

1 pound fresh jumbo shrimp
½ cup butter or margarine
2 tablespoons lemon juice
2 tablespoons dried parsley flakes
1 to 2 cloves garlic, peeled and crushed
½ teaspoon salt
Paprika (optional)

1. Under cold running water, remove the shells from the shrimp, leaving last tail section attached. Using a sharp, thin-bladed knife make a shallow cut lengthwise down the back of each shrimp and wash out the sand vein. If desired, the shrimp may be butterflied (cut lengthwise down the back of each shrimp, cutting almost completely through shrimp, removing sand vein).
2. In a shallow 2-quart non-metallic baking dish place butter, lemon juice, parsley flakes, garlic to taste and salt.
3. Heat, uncovered, in Microwave Oven 2 (2½) minutes.
4. Add shrimp and stir to coat well. If desired, sprinkle with paprika.
5. Heat, uncovered, in Microwave Oven 4 to 6 (5 to 8) minutes. Stir shrimp occasionally. Cook just until shrimp are pink and tender. Do not overcook shrimp as they well become tough.

Serves 3 to 4.

Variation: If desired, lobster, scallops, crabmeat or any combination of these may be substituted for shrimp.

Shrimp Scampi

LOBSTER NEWBURG

2 (9-ounce) lobster tails, removed from shells
Melted butter or margarine
¼ cup butter or margarine
2 tablespoons flour
½ teaspoon salt
Few grains cayenne pepper
1½ cups light cream or milk
2 egg yolks
¼ cup sherry or dry white wine
1 teaspoon lemon juice

1. Place lobster tails in a shallow non-metallic baking dish and brush liberally with melted butter.
2. Heat, covered, in Microwave Oven 6 (8) minutes or until tender. Cut lobster into bite-sized pieces. Set aside.
3. In a deep 1½-quart non-metallic casserole melt the ¼ cup butter in Microwave Oven 30 (40) seconds.
4. Blend in flour, salt and cayenne.
5. In a small bowl beat cream and egg yolks until well blended.
6. Gradually stir cream mixture into flour mixture until smooth.
7. Heat, covered, in Microwave Oven 5 to 7 (6½ to 9) minutes or until sauce thickens. Stir occasionally. Stir in lemon juice, lobster pieces and wine.
8. If necessary return to Microwave Oven 1 to 2 (1¼ to 2½) minutes or until heated through.
9. Serve over rice or toast points.
Serves 4.

Variations: If desired, shrimp, scallops, crabmeat or any combination of these may be substituted for lobster.

*Parenthesis (   ) indicates 500 watt units.

Meat, Fish and Poultry Recipes

POACHED SOLE WITH SHRIMP SAUCE

Butter or margarine
2 (12-ounce) packages frozen sole fillets
2 tablespoons finely chopped green onion or shallots
Salt and pepper
¾ cup dry white wine
4 tablespoons butter or margarine
2 tablespoons flour
1 cup light cream or milk
1 (4½-ounce) can medium-sized shrimp, rinsed
   and drained
Chopped parsley

1. Butter a shallow non-metallic baking dish lightly.
2. Place frozen fish fillets in baking dish and heat, covered, in Microwave Oven 2 (2½) minutes.
3. Separate fish fillets and arrange in baking dish. Sprinkle fish with chopped green onion, salt and pepper to taste. Pour wine over fish. Heat, covered with plastic wrap, in Microwave Oven 4 to 5 (5 to 6½) minutes or until fish flakes easily with a fork. Baste fish several times during heating.
4. Place cooked fish on a heat-resistant non-metallic serving platter, and set aside. Reserve liquid.
5. In a small heat-resistant non-metallic bowl melt the 4 tablespoons butter in Microwave Oven 30 (40) seconds.
6. Blend in flour until smooth.
7. Gradually stir in cream until smooth.
8. Return sauce to Microwave Oven and heat, uncovered, 3 to 4 (4 to 5) minutes or until thickened and smooth. Stir occasionally. Set sauce aside.
9. Return reserved fish liquid to Microwave Oven and heat, uncovered, 4 to 6 (5 to 8) minutes or until liquid has been reduced to ½ cup.
10. Stir fish liquid and shrimp into reserved sauce, until well blended.
11. Spoon shrimp sauce over fish. Heat, uncovered, in Microwave Oven 1 to 2 (1¼ to 2½) minutes or until heated through.
12. Garnish with chopped parsley.

Serves 4.

Tip: Steps 1 to 4 are basic fish poaching instructions that may be used on almost any fish. Any sauce of your choice may be used in place of shrimp sauce.

SALMON CASSEROLE

4 cups cooked noodles
1 (16-ounce) can salmon, drained and flaked
1 (4-ounce) can mushroom slices, drained
1 (10¼-ounce) can cream of celery soup
½ cup thinly sliced celery
1 (5¼-ounce) can sliced water chestnuts, drained
1 (17-ounce) can green peas, drained
1 cup coarsely broken potato chips

1. In a deep 2½-quart non-metallic casserole combine cooked noodles, salmon, mushroom slices, celery soup, celery, water chestnuts and green peas until well blended.
2. Heat, covered, in Microwave Oven 6 to 8 (8 to 10)

minutes or until heated through. Stir occasionally.
3. Just before serving sprinkle with potato chips.

Serves 6.

Variations: A number of substitutions may be made in this casserole.
1. Tuna may be substituted for salmon.
2. Cream of mushroom or cream of asparagus soup may be substituted for celery soup.
3. Green beans or corn may be used in place of peas.
4. Pimiento or green pepper may be added for color and flavor.
5. Chinese noodles, fried onion rings, broken crackers or nuts may be used in place of potato chips.

When making substitutions try to keep the volume about the same so that the cooking times will be unchanged.

POACHED FISH

Butter or margarine
2½ pounds fish fillets
Salt and pepper
¼ cup finely chopped onion
1 cup dry white wine

1. Butter a shallow non-metallic baking dish lightly.
2. Place fish fillets in baking dish.
3. Sprinkle with salt and pepper to taste. Sprinkle with onions and pour wine over fish.
4. Heat, covered tightly with clear plastic wrap, in Microwave Oven 7 to 8 (9 to 10) minutes or until fish flakes easily. Baste fish with wine and onions several times during cooking.

Serves 4 to 6.

Variation: Tomato juice, water, chicken broth or clam juice may be substituted for wine.

CHICKEN AND DUMPLINGS

1 (2 to 3-pound) broiler-fryer chicken, cut into
   serving pieces
2 cups water
6 whole black peppercorns
2 bay leaves
2 teaspoons salt
3 medium-sized carrots, peeled and thinly sliced
6 tablespoons flour
¾ cup cold water
1 teaspoon dried rubbed sage
1 cup buttermilk biscuit mix
⅓ cup milk
2 tablespoons parsley flakes
1 (4-ounce) can button mushrooms, drained
1 (10-ounce) package frozen peas, thawed
   (see chart page 13)

(Continued on next page)

1. Wash chicken and pat dry.
2. Place chicken, the 2 cups water, peppercorns, bay leaves and salt in a deep 2½ to 3-quart non-metallic casserole. Heat, covered, in Microwave Oven 10 (13) minutes. Turn casserole ½ turn and stir contents. Heat, covered, in Microwave Oven for an additional 5 (6½) minutes.
3. Add carrot slices and heat, covered, in Microwave Oven 5 (6½) minutes longer.
4. Remove chicken pieces from broth and set chicken aside until cool enough to handle. Reserve broth.
5. Remove chicken from bones and cut into bite-sized pieces.
6. Discard bones, bay leaves and peppercorns. Skim any excess fat from chicken broth.
7. Return chicken to casserole.
8. In a small bowl combine flour, the ¾ cup cold water and the sage until smooth. Gradually stir flour mixture into chicken mixture.
9. Heat, covered, in Microwave Oven 5 (6½) minutes or until gravy is thickened and smooth. Stir occasionally.
10. Prepare dumpling dough in a small bowl by combining biscuit mix, milk, and parsley flakes; stir with a fork until just blended.
11. Add mushrooms and peas to chicken and gravy mixture.
12. Drop dumpling dough by spoonfuls onto hot chicken mixture to form 6 dumplings and heat, covered, in Microwave Oven 4 (5) minutes.
13. Uncover casserole and heat an additional 2 to 4 (2½ to 5) minutes or until dumplings are no longer doughy on the underside.

Serves 4 to 6.

Chicken and Dumplings

CHICKEN CACCIATORI

1 (2½ to 3-pound) broiler-fryer chicken
1 (16-ounce) can tomato sauce
1 (6-ounce) can tomato paste
½ cup chopped onion
2 cloves garlic, peeled and crushed
1 teaspoon salt
¼ teaspoon pepper
1 teaspoon sugar
1½ teaspoons dried oregano leaves
¼ teaspoon dried thyme leaves
1½ teaspoons dried parsley flakes
1½ cups water
½ cup red wine
1 (4-ounce) can mushroom slices, drained

1. Wash chicken and pat dry. Disjoint chicken and cut into uniformly sized pieces.
2. Combine tomato sauce, tomato paste, onion, garlic, salt, pepper, sugar, oregano, thyme, parsley flakes, water and red wine in a deep 3-quart non-metallic casserole.
3. Add chicken pieces and make sure all pieces are coated.
4. Heat, covered, in Microwave Oven 10 (13) minutes. Stir.
5. Heat, covered, in Microwave Oven for an additional 10 (13) minutes. Stir occasionally.
6. Add mushroom slices and heat, uncovered, in Microwave Oven 5 to 10 (6 to 13) minutes or until chicken is tender.
7. Serve over rice or spaghetti.

Serves 4.

BARBECUED SPARERIBS

3 pounds pork or lamb spareribs, cut into serving pieces
2 cups Barbecue Sauce (see recipe page 78)
2 teaspoons chili powder
2 tablespoons lemon juice (optional)

1. Place spareribs in a large shallow non-metallic baking dish.
2. Heat, uncovered, in Microwave Oven 6 to 7 (8 to 9) minutes.
3. Drain off excess fat.
4. Turn spareribs over.
5. Combine chili powder with Barbecue Sauce.
6. Pour half of sauce over ribs.
7. Heat, uncovered, in Microwave Oven 4 (5) minutes.
8. Turn spareribs over again.
9. Sprinkle with lemon juice, if desired.
10. Pour on remaining sauce and heat, uncovered, for 6 to 8 (8 to 10) minutes or until fork-tender.
Pork should always be cooked until well done.

Serves 4 to 5.

*Parenthesis (   ) indicates 500 watt units.

BRUNSWICK STEW

1 (2-3 pound) broiler-fryer chicken, cut into serving
   pieces
2 cups water
6 whole peppercorns
2 bay leaves
2 teaspoons salt
3 ripe tomatoes, peeled and cut into 8 wedges each
1 medium-sized onion, thinly sliced
1 (10-ounce) package frozen lima beans, thawed
   (see chart page 13)
1 (10-ounce) package frozen whole kernel corn,
   thawed (see chart page 13)
1 (10-ounce) package frozen okra, thawed and sliced
   into ½-inch pieces (see chart page 13)

1. Wash chicken and pat dry.
2. Place chicken, water, peppercorns, bay leaves
and salt in a deep 2½ or 3-quart non-metallic
casserole. Stir to combine.
3. Heat, covered, in Microwave Oven 10 (13)
minutes. Turn casserole ½ turn, stir contents. Heat,
covered, in Microwave Oven an additional 5 (6½)
minutes.
4. If desired, remove chicken from bone and cut
into 1-inch pieces.
5. Discard bay leaves and peppercorns.
6. Return chicken to broth and add remaining
ingredients.
7. Heat, covered, in Microwave Oven 10 (13) minutes.
8. Uncover and heat an additional 3 to 5 (4 to 6½)
minutes or until chicken and vegetables are tender.
9. Serve in soup bowls.

Serves 4 to 6.

CHICKEN KABOBS

2 pounds boned chicken breasts
⅓ cup soy sauce
1 tablespoon sugar
1 teaspoon salt
⅛ teaspoon pepper
¼ teaspoon garlic powder
¼ teaspoon ground ginger
2 green peppers, cut into ½-inch cubes
1 (8-ounce) can mushroom caps, drained
3 tablespoons honey

1. Remove skin from chicken breasts and cut chicken
into 1-inch cubes.
2. In a large bowl combine soy sauce, sugar, salt,
pepper, garlic powder and ginger; stir to combine.
3. Add chicken pieces and toss gently to coat pieces
well.
4. Alternate chicken pieces, green peppers and
mushroom caps on wooden skewers. Reserve soy
sauce mixture.
5. Combine honey with reserved liquid.
6. Brush each kabob liberally with the mixture.
7. Place kabobs in a single layer in a shallow
non-metallic baking dish.
8. Heat, uncovered, in Microwave Oven 5 to 7 (6½ to
9) minutes, turning kabobs occasionally, until
chicken is cooked and green peppers are tender.
9. Kabobs may be served either hot or cold.

Serves 4 to 5.

*Parenthesis ( ) indicates 500 watt units.

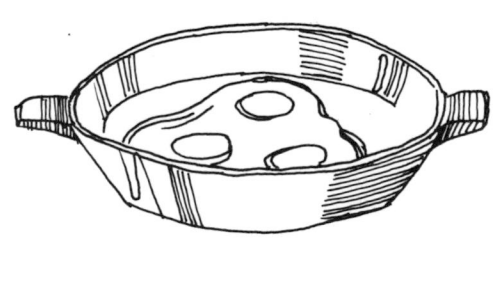

Eggs

Eggs, because of their delicate nature, require careful attention during cooking in your Microwave Oven. Here are a few hints to remember:

1. Eggs should not be boiled in the Microwave Oven because internal pressure buildup will cause them to explode.
2. Egg yolks and whites cook at different rates. For this reason the whites and yolks must be punctured with a toothpick before cooking.
3. When "frying" or scrambling eggs it helps to slow the cooking process by placing a glass of water in the Microwave Oven. Caution: the water will become hot.
4. Eggs should be slightly underdone when removed from the Microwave Oven. Allow them to stand 1 to 2 minutes before serving to allow temperatures to equalize. During this time the eggs will continue to cook.

Basic egg cooking techniques as well as recipes for more complicated dishes are included in this chapter. The times given are approximate and will vary with the kind of cookware and size and type of eggs used. Remember that eggs will always cook better if you start with them at room temperature.

SCRAMBLED EGGS

1 tablespoon butter or margarine
2 eggs
2 tablespoons light cream or milk
⅛ teaspoon salt
Few grains pepper

1. Melt butter in a non-metallic pie pan in Microwave Oven 30 (40) seconds.
2. Beat remaining ingredients until well-blended. Pour egg mixture into pie pan.
3. Heat, uncovered, in Microwave Oven 1½ (2) minutes, stirring after each 30 (40) seconds.
4. Stop cooking eggs when they are slightly softer than desired, as they will continue to cook after they are removed from the Microwave Oven. Allow to stand 1 to 2 minutes before serving.

Serves 1.

Scrambled Eggs

POACHED EGGS

2 cups water
½ teaspoon white vinegar
½ teaspoon salt
2 eggs

1. Combine water, vinegar and salt in a deep 1-quart non-metallic casserole.
2. Heat, uncovered, in Microwave Oven 1½ (2) minutes or until water mixture comes to a boil.
3. Carefully break eggs, 1 at a time, into the liquid.
4. Heat, covered with plastic wrap, in Microwave Oven 1 (1¼) minute.
5. Let stand, covered, 1 minute or until eggs reach desired degree of doneness.

Serves 1–2.

"FRIED" EGGS

Water
½ tablespoon butter or margarine
2 eggs
Salt and pepper

1. Place water in a glass and set in Microwave Oven.
2. Grease a heat-resistant non-metallic plate with the butter.
3. Carefully break eggs onto plate. Sprinkle with salt and pepper.
4. With a toothpick carefully puncture membrane around egg yolk.
5. Heat, covered with a bowl or plastic wrap, in Microwave Oven 1 to 1½ (1¼ to 2) minutes or until egg is almost cooked. Do not overcook as egg will continue cooking while standing. Let eggs stand, covered, 1 minute to finish cooking.

Serves 1–2.

OMELET

4 eggs
4 tablespoons milk or light cream
¼ teaspoon salt
Few grains pepper
1 tablespoon butter or margarine

1. In a medium-sized bowl combine eggs, milk, salt and pepper; beat until well blended.
2. Melt butter in a 10-inch non-metallic pie pan in Microwave Oven 30 (40) seconds. Rotate pan so it is completely coated with butter.
3. Pour egg mixture into pie pan and cover tightly with plastic wrap.
4. Heat in Microwave Oven 1½ (2) minutes.
5. With a rubber spatula or fork, move cooked egg toward center.
6. Heat, covered with plastic wrap, in Microwave Oven 1½ (2) minutes.
7. Let stand, covered, at least 1½ minutes.
8. Loosen egg from pie pan with a rubber spatula. Fold omelet in half and place on a heat-resistant non-metallic serving platter. If omelet is not cooked enough, return omelet to Microwave Oven for an additional 30 seconds to 1 minute (40 sec. to 1¼ min.).

Serves 2.

Variations: Cheese Omelet: Sprinkle omelet with ½ cup shredded cheese after Step 6. Cover and return to Microwave Oven for an additional 30 (40) seconds to melt cheese. Continue with Step 7.

Bacon Omelet: Cook bacon as directed on page 89 before preparing omelet. Crumble bacon into egg mixture during Step 1. If desired, some of the bacon drippings may be used in place of the butter.

(Continued on next page)

*Parenthesis ( ) indicates 500 watt units.

Western Omelet: Add ¼ cup chopped onion, ¼ cup chopped green pepper and ¼ cup diced ham to egg mixture during Step 1. Heat an additional 1 (1¼) minute during Steps 4 and 6.

Onion Omelet: Add ½ cup sauteed onions to egg mixture during Step 1.

EGGS BENEDICT

¼ cup butter or margarine
¼ cup light cream
2 egg yolks, beaten
1 tablespoon cider vinegar
¼ teaspoon salt
Few grains cayenne pepper
½ teaspoon dry mustard
1 (17-ounce) can asparagus spears, drained
4 English muffins, split and toasted conventionally
4 slices ham
4 poached eggs (see recipe page 96)

1. In a 2-cup non-metallic measuring cup melt butter in Microwave Oven 30 (40) seconds. Add light cream, egg yolks, vinegar, salt, cayenne and mustard, stir to blend thoroughly.
2. Heat, uncovered, in Microwave Oven 1 (1¼) minute or until thickened. Stir frequently. Be careful not to overcook as sauce will curdle.
3. Beat sauce until light and fluffy. Set aside.
4. Place asparagus in a shallow non-metallic baking dish and heat, uncovered, in Microwave Oven 1 to 2 (1¼ to 2½) minutes or until heated through.
5. Arrange toasted English muffin halves on a heat-resistant non-metallic serving platter. Place 1 slice of ham over 2 halves of the English muffin. Divide asparagus among the 4 muffins.
6. Heat, uncovered, in Microwave Oven 2½ to 3 (3 to 4) minutes or until muffins and ham are heated through.
7. Carefully place poached eggs on asparagus. Top with reserved sauce and heat, uncovered, in Microwave Oven 30 seconds to 1 minute (40 sec. to 1¼ min.) or until hot.

Serves 2.

EGGS RANCHEROS

2 tablespoons olive oil
1 small onion, finely chopped
1 small clove garlic, peeled and chopped
½ green pepper, finely chopped
1 cup canned tomatoes with tomato paste (see Note)
Few drops Tabasco sauce
½ teaspoon dried oregano leaves
¼ teaspoon salt
4 poached eggs (see recipe page 96)

1. In a shallow 1-quart non-metallic casserole place olive oil, onion, garlic and green pepper.
2. Heat, uncovered, in Microwave Oven 3 (4) minutes or until vegetables are tender.
3. Add canned tomatoes, Tabasco sauce, oregano and salt. Stir to combine.
4. Heat, uncovered, in Microwave Oven 3 (4) minutes or until hot.
5. Make 4 wells in tomato mixture. Carefully place one poached egg in each well.
6. Heat, uncovered, in Microwave Oven 1 to 1½ (1¼ to 2) minutes depending on desired degree of doneness. Allow to stand 2 to 3 (2½ to 4) minutes before serving. Remember eggs will continue to cook while standing at room temperature. If necessary the casserole may be returned to the Microwave Oven to cook a little longer.

Serves 2.

Note: If canned tomatoes with tomato paste are not available, 1 cup canned tomatoes plus 1 tablespoon tomato paste may be substituted.

Eggs Rancheros

POACHED EGGS AU GRATIN

2 tablespoons butter or margarine
4 poached eggs (see recipe page 96)
Grated Parmesan cheese
½ cup Medium White Sauce (see recipe page 77)

1. In a non-metallic pie pan melt butter in Microwave Oven 30 (40) seconds.
2. Carefully slide poached eggs into pie pan and sprinkle liberally with Parmesan cheese.
3. Spoon White Sauce over eggs and sprinkle again with Parmesan cheese.
4. Heat, uncovered, in Microwave Oven 1 (1¼) minute or until the sauce is hot and cheese is melted.
5. If desired, eggs may be placed under the broiler of a conventional oven for a few minutes or until browned.
Serves 2.

*Parenthesis ( ) indicates 500 watt units.

Economy Main Dishes

Economy Main Dishes

Your Microwave Oven can be a big help to your food budget. Because microwave cooking doesn't dry foods out, leftovers return to your table looking —and tasting— just as good as they did when they were first cooked. Foods are reheated so quickly that there's no problem with flavor and nutritional loss.

With a little imagination, leftovers can become something new. You can turn leftovers into exciting dishes like Chicken Divan, Ham Quiche and Shepherd's Pie.

The fast defrosting capability of your Microwave Oven enables you to defrost foods in minutes rather than hours. So you can take advantage of food sales and plan more meals around frozen foods.

Because of the rapid cooking and defrosting possible with your Microwave Oven, you can prepare two casseroles, meat loaves or other dishes in a remarkably short time: serve one now and freeze the other for quick thawing and cooking at a future date. This is not only a great budget-stretching idea but a time-saver as well.

Another good way to stretch your food dollar is through the use of "extenders" like vegetables, potatoes or pastas. Mix them with meat, and you can serve hearty stews, casseroles and other meals. Recipes elsewhere in this book include Beef, Lamb and Brunswick Stews, and Chicken and Dumplings. The Fish, Meat and Poultry Chapter suggests many nourishing casseroles.

HAM QUICHE

3 eggs
1 cup light cream
¼ teaspoon ground nutmeg
½ teaspoon salt
⅛ teaspoon pepper
Few grains cayenne pepper
½ pound cooked ham, cut into thin strips
2 cups shredded Swiss cheese
1 baked 9-inch pastry shell (in a non-metallic pie pans)

1. In a medium-sized bowl beat eggs, cream, nutmeg, salt, pepper, and cayenne pepper until well mixed.
2. Stir in ham and cheese.
3. Pour mixture into baked pastry shell.
4. Heat, uncovered, in Microwave Oven 5 (6½) minutes.
5. Move cooked edges toward center and heat an additional 5 to 7 (6½ to 9) minutes or until a knife inserted in the center comes out clean.
6. Let stand at room temperature 3 to 4 minutes to finish cooking.

Serves 6 to 8.

Ham Quiche

QUICK BEEF STEW

2 tablespoons vegetable oil
1 medium-sized onion, finely chopped
1 bay leaf
1 (8-ounce) can sliced carrots, drained
1 (16-ounce) can tiny white potatoes, drained
½ teaspoon salt
⅛ teaspoon pepper
¼ teaspoon celery salt
2 cups beef gravy (see recipe page 78)
2 to 3 cups cubed cooked beef
1 (8-ounce) can green peas, drained

1. In a deep 2-quart non-metallic casserole heat oil in Microwave Oven 2 (2½) minutes.
2. Add onion and heat, uncovered, in Microwave Oven 3 (4) minutes or until tender. Stir occasionally.
3. Add bay leaf, carrots, potatoes, salt, pepper, celery salt, beef gravy and beef; stir to combine.
4. Heat, covered, in Microwave Oven 6 to 7 (8 to 9) minutes or until almost heated. Taste and correct seasoning, if necessary, with additional salt and pepper.
5. Remove bay leaf and discard.
6. Add peas and heat, covered, in Microwave Oven 2 to 4 (2½ to 5) minutes or until heated through.

Serves 4 to 6.

CHICKEN DIVAN

2 tablespoons butter or margarine
2 tablespoons flour
2 envelopes instant chicken broth or 2 cubes chicken bouillon, crumbled
¾ cup hot water
2 tablespoons dry sherry
⅛ teaspoon ground nutmeg
¼ cup heavy cream, chilled and whipped
¼ cup grated Parmesan cheese
1 (10-ounce) package frozen broccoli, cooked (see chart page 13)
1 pound cooked chicken or turkey slices
¼ cup grated Parmesan cheese
Paprika

Chicken Divan

1. In a medium-sized heat-resistant non-metallic bowl melt butter in Microwave Oven 30 (40) seconds.
2. Blend in flour and instant chicken broth. Gradually add water, stirring until smooth.
3. Heat, uncovered, in Microwave Oven 2 (2½) minutes or until thickened and smooth.

(Continued on next page)

*Parenthesis ( ) indicates 500 watt units.

Economy Main Dishes

4. Add sherry and nutmeg.
5. Gently fold in whipped cream and the ¼ cup Parmesan cheese.
6. Line a non-metallic heat-resistant serving dish with cooked broccoli. Arrange chicken or turkey slices over broccoli.
7. Spoon sauce over chicken slices. Sprinkle with the ¼ cup of Parmesan cheese and the paprika.
8. Heat, uncovered, in Microwave Oven 4 to 5 (5 to 6½) minutes or until heated through.

Serves 3 to 4.

SHEPHERD'S PIE

2 tablespoons vegetable oil
1 medium-sized onion, thinly sliced
3 medium-sized tomatoes, peeled and thinly sliced
3 tablespoons butter or margarine
2 tablespoons flour
1½ teaspoons salt
¼ teaspoon pepper
1 cup chicken stock
1½ pounds cooked lamb, cut into 1-inch cubes
3 cups mashed potatoes, leftover, made freshly or from packaged instant potatoes

1. In a deep 2-quart non-metallic casserole place vegetable oil, onion and tomato and heat, uncovered, in Microwave Oven 4 (5¼) minutes or until tender. Set aside.
2. In a small heat-resistant non-metallic bowl melt butter in Microwave Oven 30 (40) seconds.
3. Blend in flour, salt, pepper and chicken stock.
4. Heat, uncovered, in Microwave Oven 2 (2½) minutes. or until thickened and smooth. Stir occasionally.
5. Add sauce and cooked lamb to tomato mixture. Stir to combine.
6. Heat, covered, in Microwave Oven 5 to 7 (6½ to 9) minutes or until amost heated through (time will depend on temperature of cooked lamb).
7. Top with mashed potatoes and heat, uncovered, an additional 3 to 5 (4 to 6½) minutes or until Shepherd's Pie has reached serving temperature.

Serves 4 to 6.

Variation: Cooked beef chunks, ground beef or ground lamb may be substituted for the cooked lamb.

CHICKEN FRICASSEE

2 tablespoons vegetable oil
1 medium-sized onion, thinly sliced
1 (3-pound) broiler-fryer, cut into serving pieces
1½ teaspoons salt
¼ teaspoon pepper
1 bay leaf
3 cups water
3 tablespoons butter or margarine
¼ cup flour

1 teaspoon paprika
½ cup milk
Chopped parsley

1. In a deep 3-quart non-metallic casserole heat oil in Microwave Oven 2 (2½) minutes.
2. Add onion and heat, uncovered, an additional 3 (4) minutes or until onion is tender.
3. Add chicken pieces, salt, pepper, bay leaf and water and heat, covered, in Microwave Oven 10 (13) minutes. Turn casserole ½ turn and stir contents. Continue cooking an additional 5 (6½) minutes or until chicken is tender.
4. Remove chicken pieces and set aside.
5. Strain stock and reserve 1½ cups for sauce.
6. In a medium-sized heat-resistant non-metallic bowl melt butter in Microwave Oven 30 (40) seconds.
7. Blend in flour and paprika until smooth.
8. Gradually stir in milk and reserved chicken stock.
9. Heat, uncovered, in Microwave Oven 3 (4) minutes, stirring frequently, until thickened and smooth.
10. Place reserved chicken pieces in a heat-resistant non-metallic serving dish and spoon sauce over chicken pieces.
11. Heat, uncovered, in Microwave Oven 3 (4) minutes or until heated through.
12. Sprinkle with parsley before serving.

Serves 4.

CHEESE CASSEROLE

1 (4-ounce) can green chili peppers
2 tablespoons butter or margarine
1 medium-sized onion, finely chopped
1 (8-ounce) can tomato sauce
½ teaspoon salt
2 eggs, beaten

(Continued on next page)

Cheese Casserole

1 cup half and half
1 (6-ounce) package corn chips
½ pound Cheddar cheese, shredded
1 cup commercial sour cream
½ cup shredded Cheddar cheese
3 ripe tomatoes, sliced

1. Drain chili peppers. Remove seeds and chop pepper coarsely.
2. In a medium-sized heat-resistant non-metallic bowl melt butter in Microwave Oven 30 (40) seconds.
3. Add onion and heat, uncovered, 3 (4) minutes or until tender. Add chilies, tomato sauce and salt to onion.
4. Heat, uncovered, in Microwave Oven 6 (8) minutes.
5. In a small bowl beat eggs and half and half together until well blended.
6. Gradually add egg mixture to hot sauce mixture, a very little at a time, stirring constantly.
7. Layer ½ of corn chips, ½ of tomato mixture and ½ of the ½ pound of shredded Cheddar cheese in a shallow 1½ quart non-metallic casserole.
8. Repeat with remaining corn chips, tomato mixture and the remainder of the ½ pound of cheese.
9. Carefully spread the sour cream over the top of the entire casserole.
10. Heat, uncovered, in Microwave Oven 5 (6½) minutes or until mixture begins to set.
11. Sprinkle the ½ cup of Cheddar cheese over the sour cream.
12. Arrange tomatoes in a ring around the outside edge of the casserole.
13. Heat, uncovered, in Microwave Oven 4 (5) minutes or until cheese melts and tomatoes are cooked.
Turn casserole ½ turn after 2½ (3¼) minutes.

Serves 6.

CHEESE FONDUE

1 clove garlic, peeled and cut in half
1 pound Swiss cheese, shredded
¼ cup flour
¼ teaspoon salt
Few grains pepper
¼ teaspoon nutmeg (optional)
2 cups dry white wine
2 tablespoons kirsch (optional)
French bread, cut in 1-inch cubes

1. Rub the insides and bottom of a deep 1½-quart casserole or a non-metallic fondue pot with garlic. Discard garlic.
2. Combine cheese, flour, salt, pepper and nutmeg in the prepared dish. Add wine and mix well.
3. Heat, covered, in Microwave Oven 6 (8) minutes, stirring during last half of cooking time.
4. If cheese is not completely melted, heat an additional 30 to 60 (40 to 75) seconds. If desired, stir in kirsch.

5. Spear squares of French bread with fondue forks or regular forks and dip in fondue.
6. If necessary, fondue pot may be placed on a warmer stand over low heat or returned to Microwave Oven to reheat fondue.

FISH IN WINE CASSEROLE

2 tablespoons butter or margarine
1 medium-sized onion, thinly sliced
½ cup dry white wine
2 pounds halibut fillets, cut into 2-inch pieces
Milk
3 tablespoons butter or margarine
3 tablespoons flour
1½ teaspoons salt
⅛ teaspoon pepper
1 (8½-ounce) can small peas, drained
1½ cups Chinese fired noodles

1. In a shallow 1½-quart non-metallic casserole melt the 2 tablespoons of butter in Microwave Oven 30 (40) seconds.
2. Add onion and heat, uncovered, in Microwave Oven 3 (4) minutes or until onion is tender.
3. Add wine and fish and heat, covered, in Microwave Oven 6 (8) minutes or until fish flakes easily with fork.
4. Drain juice into a measuring cup and add enough milk to pan juices to equal 2 cups. Set fish and juices aside.
5. In a small heat-resistant non-metallic bowl melt the 3 tablespoons of butter in Microwave Oven for 30 (40) seconds.
6. Stir in flour, salt and pepper. Gradually stir in reserved fish liquid mixture.
7. Heat, uncovered, in Microwave Oven 3 (4) minutes, stirring frequently until thickened and smooth.
8. Add peas to sauce.
9. Add sauce to fish in the casserole and stir gently.
10. Heat, uncovered, in Microwave Oven 2 (2½) minutes.
11. Sprinkle noodles over fish and heat, uncovered, in Microwave Oven 1 (1¼) minute.

Serves 4 to 6.

SPAGHETTI

6 cups water
1 teaspoon salt
1 tablespoon oil
1 (8-ounce) package thin spaghetti

1. Heat water, salt and oil, uncovered, in a shallow non-metallic baking dish in Microwave Oven 8 to 9 (10 to 11) minutes or until boiling.
2. Add spaghetti and heat, uncovered, in Microwave Oven 5 to 8 (6 to 10) minutes depending on desired degree of doneness. Cook until almost done.

(Continued on next page)

*Parenthesis ( ) indicates 500 watt units.

Economy Main Dishes

3. Allow to stand, covered, at room temperature in the hot water while preparing sauce (see recipes below). Spaghetti will continue to cook slightly.

Serves 4.

MEAT SAUCE

1 pound lean ground beef
1 clove garlic, peeled and crushed
½ teaspoon dried oregano leaves
½ teaspoon dried basil leaves
½ teaspoon sugar
1 teaspoon salt
¼ teaspoon pepper
1 (15-ounce) can tomato sauce

1. In a medium-sized heat-resistant non-metallic bowl crumble beef.
2. Heat, uncovered, in Microwave Oven 5 (6½) minutes, stirring frequently until meat is browned. Drain off excess fat.
3. Add remaining ingredients and stir to blend well.
4. Heat, uncovered, in Microwave Oven 5 (6½) minutes, stirring occasionally.
5. Serve over spaghetti.

Serves 4.

MEATBALLS AND TOMATO SAUCE

1 pound ground beef chuck
⅓ cup seasoned fine dry bread crumbs
½ teaspoon salt
⅛ teaspoon pepper
1 egg, slightly beaten
Italian Tomato Sauce (see recipe page 79)
Grated Parmesan cheese (optional)

1. In a medium-sized bowl combine beef, bread crumbs, salt, pepper and egg until thoroughly blended.
2. Shape meat mixture into 1-inch balls and place in a single layer in a shallow non-metallic baking dish.
3. Heat, uncovered, in Microwave Oven 5 to 6 (6½ to 8) minutes or until almost done. Drain off excess fat.
4. Prepare Italian Tomato Sauce according to directions on page 79.
5. Pour sauce over meatballs and heat, uncovered, in Microwave Oven 4 (5) minutes or until heated through.
6. Serve over spaghetti. If desired, sprinkle with Parmesan cheese.

Serves 4.

Variation: Meatballs and sauce may also be served on Italian bread.

STUFFED MEAT LOAF

1 cup fine soft bread crumbs
⅓ cup finely chopped onion
1 teaspoon salt
⅛ teaspoon pepper
¼ cup milk
1 egg, slightly beaten
½ pound ground beef chuck
½ pound lean ground pork
½ cup shredded Cheddar cheese
1 (4-ounce) can mushroom stems and pieces, drained
1½ cups seasoned mashed potatoes, leftover, made freshly or from packaged instant potatoes
Paprika (optional)

1. In a large mixing bowl combine bread crumbs, onion, salt, pepper, milk and egg; mix thoroughly using a rubber spatula.
2. Crumble the ground meats into the bread crumb mixture and gently mix until thoroughly combined.
3. In a shallow non-metallic baking dish shape about ⅓ of meat mixture into a 4 x 6-inch rectangle.
4. Sprinkle meat with ½ of shredded cheese. Arrange mushroom pieces over cheese, leaving about a ½-inch border around the edges. Sprinkle with remaining cheese.
5. Carefully shape the remaining meat over mushrooms, carefully sealing the edges.
6. Heat, uncovered, in Microwave Oven 6 (8) minutes or until almost done.
7. With a spatula frost the meat loaf with mashed potatoes, completely covering the top and sides. If desired, sprinkle with paprika.
8. Heat, uncovered, in Microwave Oven 3 (4) minutes or until potatoes are hot and meat is completely cooked.
9. Allow to stand at room temperature 4 minutes before slicing.

Serves 4.

Variations: Peas, hard-cooked eggs, artichoke hearts, olives, pimientos or many other foods may be used in place of the mushrooms.
Swiss, Muenster, Monterey Jack, Tilsit; mozzarella or any other cheese may be substituted for the Cheddar cheese.

WHITE CLAM SAUCE

½ cup olive oil
1 to 3 cloves garlic, peeled and quartered
2 (7-ounce) cans chopped clams, undrained
¼ cup chopped parsley
1 teaspoon dried oregano leaves

1. Place oil and garlic in a small heat-resistant non-metallic bowl and heat, uncovered, in Microwave Oven 3 (4) minutes.

(Continued on next page)

*Parenthesis (   ) indicates 500 watt units.

2. Remove garlic pieces.
3. Add remaining ingredients and heat, uncovered, in Microwave Oven 4 (5) minutes or until heated through. Stir occasionally.
4. Serve over spaghetti.

Serves 4.

SAUSAGE AND CABBAGE CASSEROLE

2 pounds bulk sausage
1 medium-sized onion, coarsely chopped
2 pounds cabbage, cored and cut into 1-inch pieces
1 (16-ounce) can whole peeled tomatoes, undrained
1 tablespoon sugar
½ teaspoon dried oregano leaves
1½ teaspoons salt
¼ teaspoon pepper
2 tablespoons flour
¼ cup cold water

1. Crumble sausage into a deep 2½-quart non-metallic casserole and add onion.
2. Heat, uncovered, in Microwave Oven 7 (9) minutes or until sausage is cooked and onion is tender. Stir frequently. Drain off excess fat.
3. Add cabbage, tomatoes, sugar, oregano, salt and pepper. Stir to combine.
4. Heat, covered, in Microwave Oven 8 to 10 (10 to 13) minutes or until cabbage is tender.
5. In a small cup mix flour and water until smooth.
6. Gradually stir flour mixture into sausage mixture.
7. Heat, uncovered, in Microwave Oven 3 (4) minutes, stirring frequently until thickened.

Serves 6 to 8.

LASAGNE

1 tablespoon olive oil
1½ pounds ground beef round
1 clove garlic, peeled and crushed
2 tablespoons finely chopped parsley
½ teaspoon salt
½ teaspoon dried oregano leaves
½ teaspoon dried sweet basil leaves
½ teaspoon sugar
1 (6-ounce) can tomato paste
1 (15-ounce) can tomato sauce
¼ cup water
1 (16-ounce) container cottage cheese
1 egg, slightly beaten
2 tablespoons finely chopped parsley
½ teaspoon salt
⅛ teaspoon pepper
12 to 15 cooked lasagne noodles
1 pound mozzarella cheese, thinly sliced
½ cup grated Parmesan cheese

1. In a large heat-resistant non-metallic bowl heat oil in Microwave Oven 1 (1¼) minute.

2. Add beef and heat, uncovered, in Microwave Oven, 5 (6½) minutes or until browned. Stir frequently. Drain off excess fat.
3. Stir in garlic, the 2 tablespoons parsley, the ½ teaspoon salt, oregano, basil, sugar, tomato paste, tomato sauce and water.
4. Heat, uncovered, in Microwave Oven 5 (6½) minutes.
5. In a small bowl combine cottage cheese, egg, the 2 tablespoons parsley, the ½ teaspoon salt and pepper.
6. Pour enough of the meat sauce into a shallow 2-quart non-metallic casserole to just cover the bottom.
7. Add layers of ⅓ of the noodles, ⅓ of the cottage cheese mixture, ⅓ of the mozzarella cheese slices, ⅓ of the remaining meat sauce and ⅓ of the Parmesan cheese.
8. Repeat layers twice more, ending with the Parmesan cheese.
9. Heat, uncovered, in Microwave Oven 10 (13) minutes, turning the casserole ½ turn after 5 (6½) minutes.
10. Let stand for 5 minutes before serving.

Serves 6.

CHILI PIE

1½ pounds lean ground beef chuck
1 medium-sized onion, thinly sliced
1 (12-ounce) can vacuum-pack whole kernel corn, drained
1 (16-ounce) can whole peeled tomatoes, undrained
1 (8-ounce) can tomato sauce with cheese
1 to 2 teaspoons dried chili powder
1 teaspoon salt
¼ teaspoon pepper
⅓ cup sliced stuffed olives
½ cup shredded Cheddar cheese
1½ cups coarsely crumbled tortilla chips or corn chips

1. Crumble meat into a deep 1½-quart non-metallic casserole.
2. Add onions and heat, uncovered, in Microwave Oven 7 (9) minutes or until meat is browned and onions are tender. Stir occasionally. Drain off excess fat.
3. Add corn, tomatoes, tomato sauce, chili powder to taste and salt and pepper; stir to combine.
4. Heat, uncovered, in Microwave Oven 4 (5¼) minutes, stirring occasionally.
5. Arrange olive slices on top of meat mixture and sprinkle with cheese.
6. Heat, uncovered, in Microwave Oven 2 (2½) minutes.
7. Sprinkle with tortilla chips and heat, uncovered, in Microwave Oven 1 (1¼) minute.

Serves 4 to 6.

STUFFED GREEN PEPPERS

4 medium-sized green peppers, washed
1 pound lean ground beef
½ cup quick-cooking rice, uncooked
1 teaspoon salt
¼ teaspoon pepper
½ teaspoon dried oregano leaves
⅛ teaspoon garlic powder
⅓ cup water, milk or tomato juice
1 egg, slightly beaten
1 (8-ounce) can tomato sauce with onion bits

1. Cut green peppers in half lengthwise; remove core and seeds.
2. Place peppers, hollow-side-up, in a shallow non-metallic baking dish.
3. In a medium-sized bowl crumble beef. Add rice, salt, pepper, oregano, garlic powder, water, egg and ½ cup of tomato sauce. Mix until thoroughly combined.
4. Spoon mixture into pepper halves.
5. Spoon remaining tomato sauce over peppers.
6. Heat, covered loosely with wax paper, 12 to 14 (15½ to 18) minutes in Microwave Oven or until meat is cooked and peppers are as tender as desired.
7. Turn baking dish ½ turn after 4 to 8 (5 to 10) minutes of cooking.
8. Allow to stand 4 minutes, covered, before serving.

Serves 4.

SAUCY FRANKS

1 cup chili sauce
1 cup whole-berry cranberry sauce
½ cup water
1½ pounds frankfurters, quartered
2 cups cooked rice or noodles (optional)

1. In a deep 2-quart non-metallic casserole combine chili sauce, cranberry sauce and water.
2. Heat, uncovered, in Microwave Oven 5 (6½) minutes.
3. Add frankfurters and heat, covered, in Microwave Oven 7 to 9 (9 to 11½) minutes or until frankfurters are hot and sauce is bubbly.
4. Serve over rice or noodles, if desired.

Serves 4 to 6.

Variations: For hors d'oeuvres: Cocktail franks, Vienna sausage or frankfurter slices could be used in place of quartered frankfurters.

Meatballs may also be substituted for frankfurters.

HOT DOGS IN BEER

1 (12-ounce) can of beer or ale
1 pound frankfurters
Hot dog buns, warmed
Sauerkraut, warmed

1. In a deep 1½-quart non-metallic casserole combine beer and frankfurters.
2. Heat, covered, in Microwave Oven 6 to 8 (8 to 10) minutes or until heated through.
3. Serve on hot buns with warmed sauerkraut.

Serves 4.

*Parenthesis (   ) indicates 500 watt units.

Notes

Vegetables Cooking Charts/Recipes

Vegetables Cooking Charts/Recipes

Fresh and frozen vegetables cook so quickly in the Microwave Oven that there is little loss of flavor, color or nutrients. Canned vegetables can be reheated rapidly. However, it is important to watch the vegetables carefully and check them often during cooking since the times given in these recipes are only approximate. Age, size, freshness, variety and temperature of vegetables will make a difference. Vegetables also differ from region to region. Here are a few hints to remember:

1. Vegetables may be seasoned before or after cooking. In steaming vegetables, it is better to place seasonings in the bottom of the cooking utensil.
2. Vegetables should be covered during cooking in the Microwave Oven, however, be sure to leave room so that steam can escape. Starchy vegetables tend to dehydrate more rapidly and require more water during cooking than less starchy vegetables.
3. To allow steam to escape, cooking pouches must be split or vegetables must be removed and placed in a non-metallic casserole or bowl.
4. Vegetables cooked whole in their skins, such as potatoes, must have skins punctured to prevent splitting.
5. Be careful not to overcook vegetables, as they can become tough and dehydrated. Allow all vegetables to stand, covered, for a few minutes after cooking so that temperatures may equalize.

The chart on the following pages provides cooking times and hints for fresh, frozen and canned vegetables. Recipes included range from simple vegetable preparations to more sophisticated dishes.

VEGETABLE COOKING CHART (Fresh, Frozen and Canned)

Vegetable	Amount	Time	Method
Artichokes	2 3½-inch fresh	9 (11½) minutes	Place in 1½ cups boiling water. Heat, covered. Turn ½ turn after ½ of heating time, Let stand covered 3 minutes or until bases are fork-tender.
Artichoke Hearts	10-ounce pkg. frozen 14-ounce can	5 to 6 (6½ to 8) minutes 4 (5) minutes	Add 2 tablespoons water. Heat, covered. Separate after 3 (4) minutes. Heat, covered. Stir after 2 (2½) minutes.
Asparagus	1 pound fresh 10-ounce pkg. frozen 9-ounce pouch 13-ounce can	6 (8) minutes 7 to 8 (9 to 10) minutes 5 to 6 (6½ to 8) minutes 4 (5) minutes	Add ¼ cup water. Heat, covered. Stir after 3 (4) minutes. Heat until stems are tender. Add 2 tablespoons water. Heat, covered. Separate after 4 (5) minutes. Slit pouch. Heat, uncovered. Empty pouch and separate after 3 (4) minutes. Heat, covered. Stir after 2 (2½) minutes.
Beans, Green	1 pound fresh 10-ounce pkg. frozen 10-ounce pouch 8-ounce can	10 to 12 (13 to 15½) minutes 6 to 7 (8 to 9) minutes 5 to 6 (6½ to 8) minutes 3 to 4 (4 to 5) minutes	Add ¼ cup water. Heat, covered. Stir after 4 (5) minutes and after an additional 4 (5) minutes. Heat until crisp-tender. Add 2 tablespoons water. Heat, covered. Separate after 3 (4) minutes. Slit pouch. Heat, uncovered. Empty pouch and separate after 3 (4) minutes. Heat, covered. Stir after 2 (2½) minutes.
Beans, Lima	1 pound shelled fresh 10-ounce pkg. frozen 10-ounce pouch	8 to 10 (10 to 13) minutes 9 to 10 (11½ to 13) minutes 6 to 7 (8 to 9) minutes	Add ½ cup water. Heat, covered. Stir after 4 (5) minutes. Heat until tender. Add ½ cup water. Heat, covered. Stir after 5 (6½) minutes. Slit pouch. Heat, uncovered. Empty pouch and separate after 3 (4) minutes.
Beets	1 pound fresh 14-ounce can sliced	15 to 17 (20 to 22) minutes 4 to 5 (5 to 6½) minutes	Place in water to cover. Heat, covered. Stir after 8 (10) minutes. Heat until fork-tender. Heat, covered. Stir after 2 (2½) minutes.
Broccoli	1½ pounds fresh 10-ounce pkg. frozen 10-ounce pouch	7 to 9 (9 to 11½) minutes 7 to 8 (9 to 10) minutes 6 to 7 (8 to 9) minutes	Split stems for uniform size. Add ¼ cup water. Heat, covered. Turn cooking dish ½ turn after 4 (5) minutes. Heat until stalks are fork-tender. Add 2 tablespoons water. Heat, covered. Separate after 4 (5) minutes. Slit pouch. Heat, uncovered. Empty pouch and separate after 3 (4) minutes.
Brussels Sprouts	1 pound 10-ounce pkg. frozen 10-ounce pouch	7 to 8 (9 to 10) minutes 8 to 9 (10 to 11½) minutes 5 to 6 (6 to 8) minutes	Add ¼ cup water. Heat, covered. Stir after 3 (4) minutes. Heat until tender. Add 2 tablespoons water. Heat, covered Separate after 4 (5) minutes. Slit pouch. Heat, uncovered. Empty pouch and separate after 3 (4) minutes.

*Parenthesis ( ) indicates 500 watt units.

Vegetables Cooking Charts

VEGETABLE COOKING CHART (Fresh, Frozen and Canned)—continued

Vegetable	Amount	Time	Method
Cabbage	1 medium-sized head	8 to 9 (10 to 11½) minutes	Quarter and remove stem. Add ¼ cup water. Heat, covered. Turn cooking dish ¼ turn after each 2 (2½) minutes. Heat until fork-tender.
Carrots	4 medium-sized	7 to 8 (9 to 10) minutes	Slice carrots thinly. Add ¼ cup water. Heat, covered. Stir twice during heating. Heat until fork-tender.
	10-ounce pkg. frozen	7 to 8 (9 to 10) minutes	Add 2 tablespoons water. Heat, covered. Separate after 4 (5) minutes.
	10-ounce pouch	6 to 7 (8 to 9) minutes	Slit pouch. Heat, uncovered. Empty pouch and separate after 3 (4) minutes.
Cauliflower	1 medium-sized head	7 to 8 (9 to 10) minutes	Cut into flowerets. Add 2 tablespoons water. Heat, covered. Stir after 4 (5) minutes. Heat until fork-tender.
	1 medium-sized head	8 to 9 (10 to 11½) minutes	Remove core. Place stem-end-down in non-metallic casserole. Add 2 tablespoons water. Heat, covered. Turn casserole ½ turn after 5 (6½) minutes.
	10-ounce pkg. frozen	8 to 9 (10 to 11½) minutes	Add 2 tablespoons water. Heat, covered. Separate after 4 (5) minutes.
	10-ounce pouch	6 to 7 (8 to 9) minutes	Slit pouch. Heat, uncovered. Empty pouch and separate after 4 (5) minutes.
Corn	4 ears fresh	8 to 9 (10 to 11½) minutes	Leave in husks with silk removed, wrap in wax paper, plastic wrap or place in covered casserole. Spread with butter if desired. If butter is not used, add 2 tablespoons water. Heat, covered. Turn ears after 4 (5) minutes. Heat until tender.
	4 ears frozen	12 to 14 (15½ to 18) minutes	Place in covered casserole. Add 2 tablespoons water. Turn ears after 6 (8) minutes.
	1⅓ cups kernels	5 to 6 (6½ to 8) minutes	Add 2 tablespoons water. Heat, covered. Stir after 3 (4) minutes. Heat until tender.
	10-ounce pkg. frozen	5 to 6 (6½ to 8) minutes	Add 2 tablespoons water. Heat, covered. Stir after 3 (4) minutes.
	10-ounce pouch	4 to 5 (5 to 6½) minutes	Slit pouch. Heat, uncovered. Empty pouch and stir after 3 (4) minutes.
	12-ounce can	4 (5) minutes	Heat, covered. Stir after 2 (2½) minutes.
Eggplant	1 pound	12 to 15 (15½ to 20) minutes	Cut into 1-inch cubes. Cover with water. Heat, covered. Stir after 6 (8) minutes. Until fork-tender.
Mushrooms	1 pound	6 to 7 (8 to 9) minutes	Slice. Add 4 tablespoons melted butter. Heat, covered. Stir after 3 (4) minutes.
	8-ounce can	4 (5) minutes	Heat, covered. Stir after 2 (2½) minutes.
Onions, Small White	1 pound small	6 to 7 (8 to 9) minutes	Peel. Add 1 tablespoon water. Heat, covered. Stir after 4 (5) minutes. Until fork-tender.
	10-ounce pkg. frozen	6 to 7 (8 to 9) minutes	Heat, covered. Stir after 4 (5) minutes.
	10-ounce pouch	5 to 6 (6½ to 8) minutes	Slit pouch. Heat, uncovered. Empty pouch and stir after 3 (4) minutes.
	8-ounce can	4 (5) minutes	Heat, covered. Stir after 2 (2½) minutes.

VEGETABLE COOKING CHART (Fresh, Frozen and Canned)—continued

Vegetable	Amount	Time	Method
Parsnips	4 medium	7 to 8 (9 to 10) minutes	Quarter. Add ¼ cup water. Heat, covered. Stir after 4 (5¼) minutes. Until fork-tender.
Peas	2 pounds shelled fresh	7 to 8 (9 to 10) minutes	Add 2 tablespoons water. Heat, covered. Stir after 4 (5¼) minutes.
	10-ounce pkg. frozen	5 to 6 (6½ to 8) minutes	Add 2 tablespoons water. Heat, covered. Separate after 3 (4) minutes.
	6 to 10-ounce pouch	5 to 6 (6½ to 8) minutes	Slit pouch. Heat, uncovered. Empty pouch after 3 (4) minutes and stir to separate.
	8-ounce can	3 to 4 (4 to 5) minutes	Heat, covered. Sitr after 2 (2½) minutes.
Potatoes, Baked	1 medium-sized	4 (5) minutes	Scrub potatoes and pierce skins with the tines of a fork. Leave 1 inch space between potatoes. Until tender.
	2 medium-sized	6 to 8 (8 to 10) minutes	
	3 medium-sized	8 to 10 (10 to 13) minutes	
	4 medium-sized	10 to 12 (13 to 15½) minutes	
	5 medium-sized	12 to 14 (15½ to 18) minutes	
	6 medium-sized	16 to 18 (21 to 23) minutes	
Potatoes, Boiled	4 medium-sized	15 to 18 (20 to 23) minutes	Peel and cover with water. Heat, covered. Stir occasionally. Until fork-tender.
Potatoes, Sweet	1 medium-sized	3 (4) minutes	Scrub potatoes and pierce skins with the tines of a fork. Leave 1 inch space between potatoes. Until tender.
	2 medium-sized	6 (8) minutes	
	3 medium-sized	9 (11½) minutes	
	4 medium-sized	12 (15½) minutes	
	5 medium-sized	16 (21) minutes	
	6 medium-sized	20 (25) minutes	
Spinach and Other Greens	1 pound	5 to 6 (6½ to 8) minutes	Wash and trim stems. Heat, covered, with the water that clings to the leaves. Stir after 3 (4) minutes. Until tender.
	10-ounce pkg. frozen	6 to 7 (8 to 9) minutes	Add 2 tablespoons water. Heat, covered. Separate after 3 (4) minutes.
	10-ounce pouch	6 to 7 (8 to 9) minutes	Slit pouch. Heat, uncovered. Empty pouch after 3 (4) minutes and stir to separate.
Squash, Acorn or Butternut	2 medium-sized	12 (15½) minutes plus 14 (18) minutes	Wash and cook whole for first 10 (13) minutes. Turn squash after 5 (6½) minutes. Cut in halves and remove seeds. Season and heat for additional 2 (2½) minutes or until tender.
Squash, Zucchini or Summer	2 medium	6 to 7 (8 to 9) minutes	Slice. Add ¼ cup water. Heat, covered. Stir occasionally. Until tender.
Tomatoes, Baked	2 medium	2 to 3 (2½ to 4) minutes	Cut in half crosswise. Season. Dot with butter. Heat, uncovered. Until almost tender.
Mixed Vegetables	10-ounce pkg. frozen	6 to 7 (8 to 9) minutes	Add 2 tablespoons water. Heat, covered. Separate after 3 (4) minutes.
	10-ounce pouch	6 to 7 (8 to 9) minutes	Slit pouch. Heat, uncovered. Empty pouch after 3 (4) minutes and stir to separate.
	8-ounce can	3 to 4 (4 to 5) minutes	Heat, covered. Stir after 2 (2½) minutes.

*Parenthesis (   ) indicates 500 watt units.

Vegetables Recipes

FRESH ASPARAGUS

1 pound fresh asparagus
¼ cup water

1. Place cleaned asparagus and water in a 1½-quart non-metallic casserole.
2. Heat, covered, in Microwave Oven 6 (8) minutes, stirring gently 3 times during the cooking time.
3. Drain and season to taste.

Serves 4.

Fresh Asparagus

FRESH GREEN AND WAX BEANS

1 pound fresh beans (green or wax or both)
¼ cup water

1. Wash and cut beans into 1½-inch pieces.
2. Place in a 2-quart non-metallic casserole with the water.
3. Heat, covered, in Microwave Oven 10 to 12 (13 to 15½) minutes or until tender. Stir occasionally during cooking.
4. Drain and season to taste.

Serves 4.

STEAMED CABBAGE

1 medium-sized head cabbage (about ¾ pound)
2 tablespoons water

1. Quarter cabbage.
2. Place in a 2½-quart non-metallic casserole with the water.
3. Heat, covered, in the Microwave Oven 7 to 9 (9 to 11½) minutes, stirring occasionally.
4. Drain and season to taste.
Serves 4.

FRESH CAULIFLOWER

1 medium-sized head cauliflower
2 tablespoons water

1. Wash cauliflower and separate into flowerets.
2. Place flowerets and water in a ½-quart non-metallic casserole.
3. Heat, covered, in Microwave Oven 7 to 9 (9 to 11½) minutes, turning the casserole ½ turn after 4 minutes.
4. Drain and season to taste.

Serves 4.

FRESH CORN ON THE COB

4 ears fresh corn
Butter or margarine

1. Peel back the husks and remove the silk, leaving the husks intact.
2. Brush the ears with butter. Replace the husks and fasten with string or rubber bands.
3. Place in Microwave Oven, leaving at least 1 inch between ears. Cook 4 (5) minutes.
4. Turn ears over and cook an additional 4 (5) minutes. Allow to stand 2 to 3 minutes with the husks in place.
5. Turn back the husks and use as a handle.
6. Season corn to taste.

Serves 4.

Variation: If desired, husks can be removed and corn wrapped in wax paper, plastic wrap or placed in covered casserole and cooked as in recipe above.

Fresh Corn on the Cob

FRESH SPINACH

1 pound fresh spinach

1. Wash spinach and remove any bruised leaves or thick stems. Shake excess water off leaves.
2. Place spinach in a 2-quart non-metallic casserole.
3. Heat, covered, in Microwave Oven 5 to 6 (6½ to 8) minutes. Stir after 2 minutes.
4. Drain and season to taste.

Serves 3 to 4.

BAKED TOMATOES

3 medium-sized tomatoes, washed
1 tablespoon butter or margarine
Parmesan cheese
Paprika

1. Slice tomatoes in half crosswise.
2. Place tomatoes cut-side-up on a heat-resistant non-metallic serving platter.
3. Dot each tomato half with ½ teaspoon butter and sprinkle liberally with Parmesan cheese and paprika.
4. Heat, uncovered, in Microwave Oven 3 to 5 (4 to 6½) minutes or until tomatoes are soft and cheese begins to melt. Do not overcook.

Serves 3 to 6.

ACORN SQUASH

2 (1-pound) acorn squash, washed
¼ cup hot water
4 teaspoons butter or margarine
8 teaspoons honey
¼ fresh lemon
Salt

1. Cut acorn squash in half crosswise and remove seeds with a spoon. Place squash cut-side-up in a 9-inch square non-metallic baking dish. If necessary, cut a thin slice from the bottom to prevent squash from toppling.
2. Pour hot water over the squash halves.
3. Heat, uncovered, in Microwave Oven 9 to 10 (11½ to 13) minutes. Turn dish ½ turn and heat, uncovered, in Microwave Oven 8 (10) minutes or until squash is fork tender.
4. Place 1 teaspoon butter, 2 teaspoons honey, a few drops of lemon juice and a sprinkling of salt on each half.
5. Heat, uncovered, in Microwave Oven an additional 3 (4) minutes.

Serves 2 to 4.

BAKED POTATOES

6-ounce baking potatoes

1. Select potatoes for uniform shape and size. Scrub potatoes well and pierce each potato with the tines of a fork.
2. Arrange potatoes on paper toweling leaving at least 1 inch between them.
3. Bake in Microwave Oven according to the chart below, turning potatoes after ½ of cooking time.
4. Check for doneness, as cooking times vary according to variety and shape of potatoes.

Quantity	Total Cooking Time
1 potato	4 (5) minutes
2 potatoes	6 to 8 (8 to 10) minutes
4 potatoes	10 to 12 (13 to 15½) minutes
6 potatoes	16 to 18 (21 to 23) minutes

5. Wrap potatoes in aluminum foil and allow to stand 5 minutes before serving to finish cooking.
6. If necessary, return potatoes to Microwave Oven for a few minutes. *Do not place aluminum foil in Microwave Oven.*

Tip: Potatoes can be arranged in rows or in a circle with as much space as possible between them. When placing in a circle do not place a potato in the center of the circle as it may not cook.

STUFFED BAKED POTATOES

4 (6-ounce) baked potatoes (see recipe above)
2 tablespoons butter or margarine
¾ cup milk
1 egg, slightly beaten
Salt and pepper, to taste
½ cup shredded Cheddar cheese
Paprika

(Continued on next page)

Stuffed Baked Potatoes

*Parenthesis (   ) indicates 500 watt units.

1. Allow potatoes to stand at room temperature 2 to 3 minutes after baking.
2. Cut a thin slice from the top of each potato. Caution: potatoes will be hot.
3. With a spoon, remove the potato pulp from each potato, leaving a thin shell.
4. Mash potato pulp with a fork or potato masher.
5. Add butter, milk, egg, salt, pepper and cheese. Whip potato mixture with a rotary beater or electric mixer until light and fluffy.
6. Spoon mixture into shells and sprinkle with paprika.
7. Place potatoes on a paper plate and heat, uncovered, in Microwave Oven 5 (6½) minutes.
8. If desired, after cooking in Microwave Oven, potatoes may be placed under the broiler unit of a conventional oven to brown for a few minutes. Transfer from paper plate before browning.

Serves 4.

SCALLOPED POTATOES AU GRATIN

4 medium-sized potatoes, peeled and thinly sliced
3 tablespoons flour
1 teaspoon salt
1 cup grated Cheddar cheese
1 cup milk, scalded
2 tablespoons butter or margarine
Paprika

1. Arrange ½ of the potatoes in the bottom of a shallow 1½-quart baking dish. Combine flour and salt in a small bowl and sprinkle ½ of mixture over potatoes. Sprinkle ½ of the cheese over potatoes.
2. Repeat with remaining potatoes, flour mixture, salt and cheese.
3. Pour scalded milk over last cheese layer. Dot with butter and sprinkle with paprika.
4. Heat, uncovered, in Microwave Oven 12 to 14 (15½ to 18) minutes or until potatoes are tender and cheese is melted. Turn casserole several times during cooking.

Serves 4.

Variations: If desired, fresh broccoli or cauliflower may be substituted for potatoes. The cooking time will be reduced to 8 to 10 (10 to 13) minutes in Step 4. If you prefer to use frozen broccoli or cauliflower, thaw before using according to chart on page 13. The cooking time will be reduced to 6 to 7 (8 to 9) minutes in Step 4.

GREEN BEAN CASSEROLE

2 (10-ounce) packages frozen French-style green beans
1 (10½-ounce) can cream of mushroom soup
1 (4-ounce) can mushroom slices, drained
1 (3½-ounce) can fried onion

1. Place green beans in a deep 1½-quart non-metallic casserole.
2. Heat, covered, in Microwave Oven 5 (6½) minutes.

3. Turn dish ½ turn and heat an additional 2 (2½) minutes.
4. Add cream of mushroom soup and mushrooms, stir to combine.
5. Heat, covered, in Microwave Oven 5 (6½) minutes longer or until heated through:
6. Sprinkle fried onion rings on casserole.

Serves 6.

Variations: If desired, broccoli, cauliflower, spinach or asparagus may be substituted for green beans. Cream of chicken, cream of celery or cream of asparagus soup may be used in place of mushroom soup.

RATATOUILLE

1 medium-sized eggplant, cut into ½-inch cubes (about 1½ pounds)
2 small zucchini, thinly sliced (about 1 pound)
⅓ cup olive oil
2 medium-sized onions, thinly sliced
1 clove garlic, peeled and crushed
1 large green pepper, thinly sliced
3 large ripe tomatoes, washed and cut into 8 wedges each
2 teaspoons dried basil leaves
2 teaspoons dried marjoram leaves
1 teaspoon salt
½ teaspoon pepper
1 (8-ounce) can sliced mushrooms, drained

1. In a large bowl cover eggplant and zucchini with salted water (about 1 teaspoon salt to 1 quart water). Soak for 30 (40) minutes, drain.
2. In a deep 3-quart non-metallic casserole, heat olive oil, onions and garlic, uncovered, in Microwave Oven 5 (6½) minutes or until onions and garlic are tender.

(Continued on next page)

Ratatouille

3. Add green pepper, drained eggplant and zucchini.
4. Heat, covered, in Microwave Oven 5 (6½) minutes.
5. Add remaining ingredients and stir to combine well.
6. Heat uncovered, in Microwave Oven 5 (6½) minutes longer or until vegetables are tender.
7. Ratatouille may be served either hot or cold.

Serves 6 to 8.

ORANGE GLAZED CARROTS

6 medium-sized carrots, peeled and thinly sliced
3 tablespoons firmly packed dark brown sugar
3 tablespoons butter or margarine
3 tablespoons orange juice
1 teaspoon lemon peel
¼ teaspoon salt

1. Combine all ingredients in a deep 1-quart non-metallic casserole.
2. Heat, covered, in Microwave Oven 6 to 8 (8 to 10) minutes or until carrots are tender. Stir occasionally so that carrots are well glazed.

Serves 4.

HOT POTATO SALAD

6 to 8 medium-sized potatoes, cooked and peeled (see recipe page 22)
8 slices raw bacon, cooked and crumbled (see recipe page 89)
⅓ cup olive oil or bacon fat
½ cup finely chopped onion
¼ cup wine vinegar
2 tablespoons finely chopped green onion
¼ cup chopped parsley

1. Slice potatoes into a large bowl.
2. Add crumbled bacon.
3. Place oil or bacon fat in a medium-sized heat-resistant non-metallic bowl.
4. Add the ½ cup chopped onion and heat, uncovered, in Microwave Oven 5 (6½) minutes or until lightly browned.
5. Add vineger and cook an additional 3 (4) minutes.
6. Combine all ingredients with the potatoes, toss lightly.
7. Serve hot.

Serves 6.

BAKED BEANS

½ cup chopped onion
½ cup catsup or chili sauce
1 tablespoon prepared brown mustard
¼ cup firmly packed dark brown sugar
2 (16-ounce) cans baked beans
6 slices bacon, diced and partially cooked

1. Combine onion, catsup, mustard and brown sugar in a deep 2-quart non-metallic casserole.
2. Heat, uncovered, in Microwave Oven 4 (5) minutes or until onion is tender.
3. Add beans. Stir to thoroughly combine. Top with bacon pieces.
4. Heat, covered, in Microwave Oven 12 to 15 (15½ to 20) minutes or until beans are hot and bacon has finished cooking.

Serves 4 to 6.

Notes

Dessert Cooking Chart/Recipes

Dessert Cooking Chart/Recipes

Your favorite fruit desserts are even more flavorful when prepared in the Microwave Oven. Because cooking times are greatly shortened, vitamin and nutrient losses are reduced. So fruits not only taste better, but are better for you as well.

The cooking times given are approximate since age, size, freshness, variety and temperature of the fruit will make a difference. Fruits also differ from region to region. Sugar adjustments may be necessary to suit fruit differences and personal tastes.

Because of the many new utensils which can be used in microwave cooking, desserts can be more creative than ever. Bake right in dessert dishes, even cardboard boxes. Cakes are easy to remove if you grease the utensil or carefully line it with wax paper. Do not flour.

Another advantage of microwave cooking is the fact that, unlike conventional cooking, opening the oven door does not cause cakes to fall. If cakes are not rising evenly, simply open the door and rotate baking dish as needed. Cakes baked in a Microwave Oven require more careful watching than those baked conventionally because of the rapid cooking process. But the time saved is well worth keeping a close watch. In general, once the cake has risen to full volume, cook 1 to 1½ minutes longer.

Due to the shorter cooking time, you will find that angel food cakes or other cakes leavened entirely with egg whites do not bake satisfactorily in the Microwave Oven. Also, white and yellow cakes do not brown as they would in a conventional oven. This presents no problem if cakes are to be frosted, but if browning is desired, cakes can be placed under a conventional broiler.

CAKES, COOKIES, PIES AND BREADS COOKING CHART

Item	Size/Number	Time	Method
Layer Cakes	8-inch round	6 (8) minutes	Grease pans and fill ½ full. Heat, uncovered. Turn ¼ turn every 1½ (2) minutes. Until a toothpick inserted in center comes out clean.
Layer Cakes	8-inch square	7 to 8 (9 to 10) minutes	Grease pans and fill ½ full. Heat, uncovered. Turn ¼ turn every 2 (2½) minutes. Until a toothpick inserted in center comes out clean.
Layer Cakes	12 x 7-inch	8 to 9 (10 to 11½) minutes	Grease pans and fill ½ full. Heat, uncovered. Turn ¼ turn every 2 (2½) minutes. Until a toothpick inserted in center comes out clean.
Bowl Cakes	1 large bowl	8 to 9 (10 to 11½) minutes	Prepare batter in a large heat-resistant non-metallic bowl. Press a glass, right-side-up, through batter to form tube shape. Until a toothpick inserted in center comes out clean.
Cupcakes	1 2 3 4 5 6	15 (20) seconds 30 (40) seconds 45 (60) seconds 1 (1¼) minute 1¼ (2) minutes 1½ (2) minutes	Fill paper-lined cups ½ full. Heat, uncovered. Turn ½ turn after ½ of heating time. Until a toothpick inserted in center comes out clean.
Drop Cookies	2 4 6 8 10 12	45 (60) seconds 1 (1¼) minute 1½ (2) minutes 2 (2½) minutes 2½ (3¼) minutes 3 (4) minutes	Cover a piece of cardboard with wax paper. Drop cookies by teaspoonfuls on prepared "cookie sheets". Turn "cookie sheet" after ½ of heating time.
Bar Cookies	8-inch square	7 to 8 (9 to 10) minutes	Grease pan and fill. Heat, uncovered. Turn ¼ turn every 2 (2½) minutes. Until a toothpick inserted in center comes out clean.
Bar Cookies	10 x 6-inch	5 to 6 (6½ to 8) minutes	Grease pan and fill. Heat, uncovered. Turn ¼ turn every 1½ (2) minutes. Until a toothpick inserted in center comes out clean.
Cookie Crumb Pie Crusts	9-inch	30 (40) seconds 1¾ to 2 (2¼ to 2½) minutes	Melt butter. Add 1½ to 2 cups crumbs. Press into pie pan. Heat until crisp and light brown spots appear.
Pastry Crusts	9-inch	4 (5) minutes	Roll out, flute edges and pierce sides and bottom. Heat, uncovered, until light brown spots appear.
Quick Breads	8 x 4-inch loaf	7 to 8 (9 to 10) minutes	Grease pan and fill ½ full. Heat, uncovered. Turn ¼ turn every 1½ (2) minutes. Until a toothpick inserted in center comes out clean.
Bread	8 x 4-inch loaf	5 (6½) minutes	Grease pan and add dough. Allow to raise. Heat, uncovered. Until no doughy spots remain.

*Parenthesis ( ) indicates 500 watt units.

Dessert Recipes

COFFEE CAKE

¼ cup butter or margarine
¾ cup sugar
1 egg
1½ cups sifted flour
2 teaspoons baking powder
½ teaspoon salt
½ cup milk
½ cup sugar
1½ teaspoons cinnamon

1. Grease an 8-inch square non-metallic cake pan.
2. Preheat a conventional broiler.
3. Cream butter and the ¾ cup sugar together in a large bowl until fluffy. Beat in the egg.
4. Sift the flour, baking powder and salt together.
5. Add flour mixture and milk to the sugar mixture alternately, beginning and ending with the flour.
6. Pour into the prepared cake pan. Spread evenly. Combine the ½-cup sugar and the cinnamon in a small bowl and sprinkle over the batter.
7. Heat, uncovered, in Microwave Oven 6 (8) minutes, turning the cake pan ⅓ turn after each 2 (2½) minutes.
8. Insert a wooden toothpick to test for doneness.
9. Place cake in a conventional oven 4 inches away from heating element of the broiler unit for a few minutes until topping is browned.

BREAD PUDDING

1 (3-ounce) package French vanilla pudding mix
2 cups milk
1 teaspoon cinnamon
½ cup raisins
1½ cups day-old bread cubes

1. In a deep 1-quart non-metallic casserole combine all ingredients.
2. Heat, uncovered, in Microwave Oven 6 (8) minutes or until mixture boils. Stir occasionally.
3. Serve either hot or cold.

Serves 4.

APPLE CRISP

4 cups peeled and sliced apples
2 tablespoons lemon juice
½ cup oatmeal
¼ cup flour
½ cup firmly packed dark brown sugar
½ teaspoon salt
6 tablespoons butter or margarine
1 teaspoon ground cinnamon
⅛ teaspoon ground nutmeg

1. Place apples in a 9-inch non-metallic pie pan.
2. Sprinkle with lemon juice.
3. Heat, covered, in Microwave Oven 2 (2½) minutes.
4. Combine remaining ingredients in a small heat-resistant non-metallic bowl.

5. Heat topping mixture, uncovered, in Microwave Oven 2 (2½) minutes, stirring after the first minute
6. Sprinkle topping mixture over apples.
7. Heat, uncovered, in Microwave Oven 5 (6½) minutes. Turn pie pan ½ turn and heat an additional 4 (5) minutes, or until apples are tender and topping is crisp.

Serves 4 to 6.

2-LAYER PINEAPPLE UPSIDE-DOWN CAKE

4 tablespoons butter or margarine
1 cup firmly packed dark brown sugar
2 (15¼-ounce) cans sliced pineapple, in unsweetened juice, undrained
22 maraschino cherries, drained
1 (18½-ounce) package yellow cake mix
Ingredients as called for on cake package

1. Place ½ of the butter in each of 2 8-inch round non-metallic cake pans.
2. Heat, each pan, uncovered, in Microwave Oven for 30 (40) seconds or until butter is melted.
3. Blend ½ of the brown sugar with the melted butter in each pan. Spread mixture evenly over bottom of the cake pans.
4. Drain pineapple juice into a measuring cup and reserve. Arrange pineapple slices and cherries over the brown sugar mixture in each pan.
5. Prepare cake mix according to package directions, substituting the reserved pineapple juice for the liquid called for on the package. Add water if necessary for full measure.
6. Pour ½ of batter over pineapple slices in both pans. Spread evenly.
7. Heat each layer, uncovered, in Microwave Oven for 8 (10) minutes turning pan ¼ turn after each 2 (2½) minutes.
8. Invert 1 layer onto serving plate. Invert the second layer on top of the first. Serve warm.

Serves 8.

Tip: If a browner cake is desired, after cooking in Microwave Oven, cake layers may be placed in a preheated 425° conventional oven 5 minutes or until lightly browned.

Pineapple Upside-Down Cake

FRUIT-FLAVORED GELATIN DESSERTS FROM PREPARED MIXES

1 (3½- ounce) package fruit-flavored gelatin mix
1 cup warm water
1 cup cold water

1. Empty package of gelatin mix into a deep 1-quart non-metallic casserole.
2. Gradually add warm water, stirring until thoroughly dissolved.
3. Heat, uncovered, in Microwave Oven 2 (2½) minutes or until mixture comes to a boil. Stir occasionally.
4. Stir in cold water and allow to stand at room temperature ½ hour before refrigerating.
5. Refrigerate until set.

Serves 4.

PUDDINGS FROM PREPARED MIXES

1 (3½-ounce) package pudding and pie filling mix
** (not instant)**
2 cups milk

1. Empty package of pudding mix into a deep 1-quart non-metallic casserole.
2. Gradually stir in milk until smooth.
3. Heat, uncovered, in Microwave Oven 2 (2½) minutes.
4. Stir and heat an additional 3 to 4 (4 to 5) minutes or until mixture boils. Stir occasionally.
5. Allow to cool at room temperature ½ hour before refrigerating.
Serves 4.

Fruit Flavored Gelatin from Prepared Mixes

CHOCOLATE PUDDING PIE

¼ cup butter or margarine
1½ cups chocolate cookie crumbs
3 tablespoons sugar
1 (3-ounce) package chocolate pudding and pie filling mix (not instant)
2 cups milk
1 cup miniature marshmallows

1. In a 9-inch non-metallic pie pan melt butter in Microwave Oven 30 (40) seconds.
2. Stir in cookie crumbs and sugar.
3. Press crumb mixture onto bottom and sides of pie pan.
4. Heat, uncovered, in Microwave Oven 2 (2½) minutes or until crust has crunchy texture.
5. In a deep 1-quart non-metallic casserole combine chocolate pudding mix and milk.
6. Heat, uncovered, in Microwave Oven 6 (8) minutes or until mixture boils.
7. Allow to cool for 5 minutes. Stir in marshmallows.
8. Pour chocolate mixture into pie crust.
9. Refrigerate until set.

Serves 8.

APPLESAUCE

4 cups peeled and sliced tart apples
½ cup water
¼ to ½ cup sugar
¼ to ½ teaspoon cinnamon

1. Place apples, water and sugar in a deep 1½-quart non-metallic casserole.
2. Heat, covered, in Microwave Oven 8 to 9 (10 to 11½) minutes or until apples are tender.
3. If smooth applesauce is desired, a blendor or food mill may be used. Cooked apples may also be mashed with a potato masher or fork.
4. After desired consistency is reached, add cinnamon while applesauce is still hot.

Serves 4 to 6.

BAKED APPLES

4 large baking apples
½ cup pancake syrup
2 teaspoons butter or margarine

1. Core apples and peel about 1 inch of the peel from the stem end of each apple. If necessary, cut a thin slice from the bottom of each apple so it will stand. Pierce skins in several places with the tines of a fork.
2. Arrange apples in a shallow non-metallic baking dish.
3. Pour 2 tablespoons of syrup over each apple. Put ½ teaspoon of butter into each cavity.
4. Heat, loosely covered with wax paper, in Microwave Oven 5 to 6 (6½ to 8) minutes or until apples are

(Continued on next page)
*Parenthesis ( ) indicates 500 watt units.

Dessert Recipes

tender. The time will depend on the size and kind of apples used.

Serves 4.

Variations: 4 tablespoons of sugar, fruit-flavored syrup or carbonated beverage may be substituted for the pancake syrup.

If desired, raisins or nuts may be placed in the cavities of the apples. An additional 1 to 2 (1¼ to 2½) minutes must be added to the heating time in Step 4.

STEWED APRICOTS

1 (8-ounce) package dried apricots
1 cup water
¼ cup sugar

1. Place apricots and water in a deep 1-quart non-metallic casserole.
2. Let stand at room temperature at least one hour or until apricots are softened. Stir in sugar.
3. Heat, covered, in Microwave Oven 4 (5) minutes. Stir occasionally.
4. Let stand covered until cool.

Serves 4.

Variations: Stewed Prunes: Substitute prunes for apricots and follow recipe above, omitting the sugar and increasing water to 1½ cups.

Stewed Peaches: Use recipe above substituting peaches for apricots.

BAKED GRAPEFRUIT

2 medium-sized grapefruit
4 teaspoons sugar
2 teaspoons butter or margarine
4 maraschino cherries, drained

1. Cut each grapefruit in half crosswise. Remove any pits and cut around each section with a sharp knife.
2. Sprinkle each grapefruit half with a teaspoon of sugar.
3. Dot each with a ½ teaspoon of butter. Place grapefruit halves on a paper plate.
4. Heat, uncovered, in Microwave Oven 3 to 4 (4 to 5) minutes.
5. Garnish each half with a maraschino cherry. Serve hot.

Serves 4.

FRUIT COMPOTE

2 medium-sized apples, peeled, cored and thinly sliced
3 tablespoons sugar
1 (17-ounce) can peach slices, undrained
½ cup whole-berry cranberry sauce
¼ teaspoon ground cinnamon
⅛ teaspoon ground allspice
⅛ teaspoon ground cloves
⅛ teaspoon ground nutmeg
Whipped cream

1. In a deep 1½-quart non-metallic casserole, place apples and sprinkle with sugar.
2. Heat, covered, in Microwave Oven 3 (4) minutes.
3. Add remaining ingredients; stir to combine.
4. Heat, uncovered, 4 (5) minutes or until apples are tender.
5. Serve with dollops of whipped cream.

Serves 4.

Variations: Pineapple, apricots, pears or plums may be substituted for apples or peach slices.

If desired, ½ cup walnut or pecan pieces may be added to compote in Step 3.

CHERRY PIE

Ingredients for 9-inch, 2-crust pie, from package pie crust mix of favorite recipe
2 (16-ounce) cans water-packed, pitted, tart red cherries
1 cup sugar
⅓ cup flour
⅛ teaspoon salt
½ teaspoon lemon extract
Few drops red food coloring (optional)
2 tablespoons butter or margarine
Water
Sugar

1. Prepare pie crust pastry according to package directions or favorite recipe.
2. Roll out ½ of the pastry and line a 9-inch non-metallic pie pan.
3. Roll out remaining dough and cut into 10 strips ½-inch wide and set aside, covered with a clean cloth towel.
4. Drain cherries and set aside. Reserve ½ cup of the liquid.
5. Mix together the 1 cup of sugar, the ⅓ cup flour and the salt in a medium-sized heat-resistant non-metallic bowl.
6. Gradually add the cherry liquid; mix until smooth.
7. Heat, uncovered, in Microwave Oven 2 (2½) minutes or until thickened and smooth; stir frequently.
8. Stir in lemon extract and red food coloring, if desired.
9. Add cherries to sauce and mix gently.
10. Pour cherries into lined pie pan.

(Continued on next page)

11. Dot with butter.
12. To make a lattice top, place 5 strips of pastry at equal intervals across the top of cherries, using one of the longest strips for the center and the shorter ones for the sides. The ends should extend over the edges of the lower crust.
13. Lay remaining five strips crosswise to form lattice, weaving if desired.
14. Trim strips to fit the edge of the lower crust.
15. Turn the pastry edge from the lower crust over the ends of the strips. Pinch or flute, as desired, to seal the edge.
16. Brush strips with water and sprinkle with granulated sugar.
17. Preheat a conventional oven to 450°F.
18. Heat pie, uncovered, in Microwave Oven 7 to 8 (9 to 10) minutes or until juice starts bubbling and fruit is just about tender.
19. Cook in the preheated conventional oven 10 to 15 (13 to 20) minutes or until the top crust is golden brown.

Serves 8.

IRISH SODA BREAD

4 cups unsifted flour
¼ cup sugar
3 teaspoons baking powder
1 teaspoon salt
¼ cup butter or margarine
2 cups dark raisins
1⅓ cups buttermilk
1 egg
1 teaspoon baking soda
1 egg yolk
1 tablespoon water

1. Grease a deep 2½-quart non-metallic casserole and set aside.
2. Sift flour, sugar, baking powder and salt together into a large bowl.
3. With a pastry blender or two knives, cut in butter until mixture resembles corn meal.
4. Stir in raisins.
5. Combine buttermilk, egg and baking soda in a small bowl until thoroughly blended.
6. Stir buttermilk mixture into dry ingredients, stirring until well blended.
7. Turn out into a lightly floured board and knead lightly about 3 minutes or until dough is smooth.
8. Shape dough into a ball and place in prepared casserole.
9. With a sharp knife cut an X about ½-inch deep into the top of the dough.
10. Beat egg yolk and water together.
11. Brush mixture over top of dough.
12. Heat, uncovered, in Microwave Oven 10 (13) minutes or until a cake tester inserted in the center comes out clean. Turn casserole ¼ turn after each 2 (3) minutes of cooking time. Cool 10 minutes in casserole; turn out of pan and allow to cool completely.

Tip: If desired, bread may be placed in a very hot conventional oven (475°F) for few minutes to brown.

LOG CABIN CAKE

1 (18½-ounce) package devil's food cake mix
Ingredients as called for on cake package
3 egg whites, at room temperature
¼ teaspoon salt
6 tablespoons sugar
1 cup plus 2 tablespoons light corn syrup
3 tablespoons sweetened cocoa
2 teaspoons vanilla extract
Black licorice strings

1. Grease two 8-inch square non-metallic cake pans and set aside.
2. Prepare cake mix according to package directions.
3. Pour ½ of batter into each prepared pan.
4. Heat each layer, uncovered, in Microwave Oven 7 (9) minutes, turning ¼ turn each 2 (2½) minutes.
5. Allow cake to cool 10 minutes before removing from pan.
6. While cakes are cooling prepare frosting.
7. In a small mixer bowl beat egg whites with salt until foamy. Add sugar 1 tablespoon at a time, beating until stiff peaks form.
8. In a 2-cup heat-resistant non-metallic measuring cup combine corn syrup and cocoa.
9. Heat, uncovered, in Microwave Oven 3 to 4 (4 to 5¼) minutes or until mixture comes to a boil.
10. Gradually pour boiling mixture over egg whites, beating constantly until frosting is cool and very stiff. Beat in vanilla.
11. Cut one of the cake layers in half diagonally.
12. Spread some of the frosting on one of the triangular layers. Place the other half-layer on top to form a 2-layer triangle.
13. Cut the other layer in half crosswise to form two 8 x 4-inch rectangles.
14. Spread some of the frosting on the top one of the rectangles. Set the other half on top to form a 2-layer rectangle, place on a serving tray.
15. Spread some of the frosting on the top of the rectangle.
16. Place the triangle, long-side down, on top of the rectangle to form the "roof" of the log cabin.
17. Spread the entire cake with frosting.
18. With a thin-bladed spatula, make ridges horizontally in the frosting to resemble logs.
19. With licorice strings, form windows and doors.

Tips: Frosting will be neater if you place strips of wax paper under the bottom edges of the cake before frosting the sides. Remember to gently remove wax paper before serving cake.
Any leftover frosting can be used on cupcakes or stored in the refrigerator for later use.

*Parenthesis (   ) indicates 500 watt units.

Dessert Recipes

STRAWBERRY SOUFFLÉ CHILLED

2 pints fresh strawberries, washed and hulled
2 envelopes unflavored gelatine (2 tablespoons)
¼ cup water
⅔ cup sugar
4 egg yolks, well beaten
⅛ teaspoon salt
1 tablespoon lemon juice
4 egg whites, at room temperature
½ cup sugar
1 cup heavy cream, chilled and whipped
Whipped cream (optional)

1. Puree strawberries in an electric blender or press through a sieve or food mill.
2. In a 1-quart heat-resistant non-metallic measuring cup combine 1 cup of strawberries, gelatine, water, the ⅔ cup sugar, egg yolks and salt. Stir to combine.
3. Heat, uncovered, in Microwave Oven 4 (5) minutes or until mixture just begins to boil. Stir frequently.
4. Cool mixture slightly.
5. Add remaining strawberries and lemon juice.
6. Chill mixture until it is the consistency of unbeaten egg whites.
7. While mixture is chilling, beat egg whites in a large bowl until stiff peaks form. Add the ½ cup sugar one tablespoon at a time, beating constantly, until egg whites are stiff and glossy.
8. Fold whipped cream and chilled berry mixture into egg whites.
9. Pour mixture into a 2-quart heat-shaped mold.
10. Chill at least 3 to 4 hours.
11. Unmold, if desired. Garnish with whipped cream, if desired.

*Parenthesis (   ) indicates 500 watt units.

Super Snacks

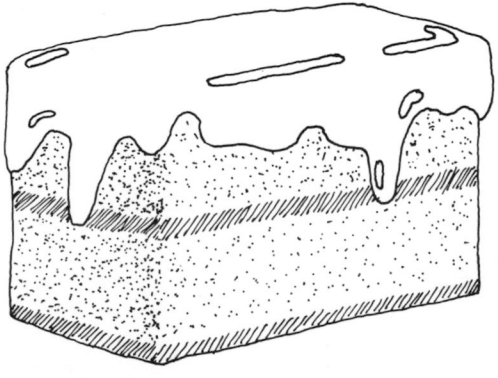

Super Snacks

What to feed a hungry group of snackers. It's no longer a problem with your Microwave Oven. Snacks can be made quickly and often with very little fuss or cleaning up afterwards since they can be cooked and served in the same container. Here are some ideas on how to handle "I'm hungry, what's to eat?"

Cakes, cookies and pies can be reheated in the Microwave Oven to recapture their just-baked flavor. Place the cake slice, cookies or pie wedge on a paper or cloth-lined plate. Heat, uncovered, in Microwave Oven 30 to 60 (40 to 75) seconds or until warmed. *Do not overcook*. It is better to underheat and reheat than to overcook.

Soggy potato chips, pretzels and nuts taste fresh again after heating in the Microwave Oven for 15 to 30 (20 to 40) seconds.

CINNAMON CANDY APPLES

1 (5-ounce) candy apple kit
2 cups sugar
1 cup water
½ cup cinnamon candies
8 to 10 medium-sized apples, washed, dried and
 stems removed

1. Place contents of candy apple kit, sugar, water and cinnamon candies in a deep 1-quart non-metallic casserole; stir to combine.
2. Heat, uncovered in Microwave Oven 20 (25) minutes or until a candy thermometer registers 295°F. (If a candy thermometer is not available, drop a small amount of mixture into very cold water. The mixture should separate into threads which are hard and brittle.) *Do not place thermometer in Microwave Oven.*
3. While candy mixture is cooking, insert wooden sticks into stem end of clean dry apples.
4. Dip each apple into candy mixture until well coated. Place dipped apples on greased wax paper.
5. If mixture becomes too stiff, return it to Microwave Oven for 30 (40) seconds.
6. Refrigerate apples until candy coating is set.

Makes 8 to 10.

CARAMEL APPLES

1 (14-ounce) package caramel candies
1 tablespoon hot water
5 to 6 medium-sized apples, washed, dried and
 stems removed

1. Unwrap caramels and place in a deep 1½-quart. non-metallic casserole.
2. Add hot water and heat, uncovered, in Microwave Oven 1½ (2) minutes or until melted; stir occasionally.
3. While candy mixture is cooking, insert wooden sticks into stem end of clean, dry apples.
4. Dip each apple into caramel mixture until well coated, turning and tipping casserole to coat apples. Place dipped apples on greased wax paper.
5. If mixture becomes too stiff, return to Microwave Oven for 30 (40) seconds.
6. Refrigerate apples until caramel coating is set.

Makes 5 to 6.

ROCKY ROAD CANDY

1 (6-ounce) package semisweet chocolate pieces
1 tablespoon butter or margarine
2 eggs, beaten until foamy
1¼ cups confectioners' sugar
½ teaspoon salt
1½ cups unsalted shelled peanuts
2 cups miniature marshmallows
1 cup shredded coconut
1½ teaspoon vanilla extract

1. In a large heat-resistant non-metallic bowl melt chocolate and butter in Microwave Oven 3 (4) minutes.
2. While chocolate and butter are melting, in a small bowl combine eggs, confectioners' sugar, salt, and vanilla until well blended.
3. Stir peanuts, marshmallows, and coconut into chocolate mixture.
4. Add egg mixture; stir until well blended.
5. Drop by teaspoonfuls onto greased wax paper.
6. If mixture becomes too stiff, return to Microwave Over for 30 (40) seconds.
7. Chill candies to set.

Makes 2 to 3 dozen.

POPCORN

½ cup unpopped popcorn, chilled
Melted butter and salt, to taste

1. Line a deep 3-quart non-metallic casserole with a paper towel. Do not use glass casserole.
2. Spread popcorn evenly in casserole bottom.
3. Heat, covered tightly, 6 (8) minutes or until most kernels are popped. Shake casserole occasionally.
4. Remove paper towel. Pour butter and sprinkle salt over popped corn.

Tip: If all the popcorn hasn't popped at the end of the cooking time, remove the popped popcorn and heat remaining corn an additional 2 to 4 (2½ to 5) minutes. If it still hasn't popped discard. Do not continue to re-heat the popcorn and do not put butter or oil on popcorn before popping.
Caution: Do not cook popcorn any other way as it may harm oven or utensils.

Candy Apples Page 127

*Parenthesis ( ) indicates 500 watt units.

POPCORN BALLS

¾ cup granulated sugar
¾ cup dark brown sugar, firmly packed
½ cup light corn syrup
½ cup water
¼ teaspoon salt
1 teaspoon white vinegar
¾ cup butter or margarine
2 quarts unbuttered popped popcorn (recipe on page 128)

1. Place sugar, brown sugar, corn syrup, water, salt and vinegar in a deep 3-quart non-metallic casserole.
2. Heat, uncovered, stirring occasionally, in Microwave Oven 15 (20) minutes or until a candy thermometer registers 260°F. (If a candy thermometer is not available, drop a small amount of mixture into very cold water. The mixture should form a hard ball which holds its shape but is pliable.) *Do not place thermometer in Microwave Oven.*
3. Stir in butter until melted.
4. Add popcorn and stir until well mixed. Mixture will be sticky.
5. With well-buttered hands, shape into 3-inch balls. Place shaped popcorn balls on greased wax paper.

Makes 10 to 14.

PANAJACKS

Butter or margarine
Ingredients for Popcorn Balls (see recipe at above)
1 cup salted peanuts

1. Butter a jelly-roll sheet and set aside.
2. Prepare Popcorn Balls up to Step 4. Add peanuts with popcorn.
3. Stir until well coated.
4. Spread mixture on prepared jelly-roll sheet.
5. Cool and break into bite-sized pieces.

TEN-MINUTE CHOCOLATE MINT FUDGE

3 cups sugar
¾ cup butter or margarine
1 (5-ounce) can evaporated milk
2 (6-ounce) packages chocolate mint pieces
1 (7-ounce) jar marshmallow cream
1 cup coarsely chopped walnuts
1 teaspoon vanilla extract

1. Grease a shallow 1½-quart baking dish and set aside.
2. Place sugar, butter, and evaporated milk in a deep 2½-quart non-metallic casserole and heat, uncovered, in Microwave Oven 8 (10) minutes.
3. Stir occasionally.
4. Stir in remaining ingredients until chocolate melts.
5. Pour mixture into prepared baking dish.
6. Cool and cut into squares.

PEANUT BRITTLE

1½ teaspoons baking soda
1 teaspoon water
1 teaspoon vanilla extract
1½ cups sugar
1 cup water
1 cup light corn syrup
3 tablespoons butter or margarine
1 pound shelled raw peanuts

1. Combine baking soda, water and vanilla in a small dish and set aside.
2. Place sugar, water, and corn syrup in a deep 3-quart non-metallic casserole; stir to blend.
3. Heat, uncovered in Microwave Oven 12 (15½) minutes or until a candy thermometer registers 240°F. (If a candy thermometer is not available, drop a small amount of the mixture into very cold water. The mixture should form a soft ball which flattens when removed from the water.) *Do not place thermometer in Microwave Oven.*
4. Stir in butter until melted.
5. Add peanuts and return to Microwave Oven and heat, uncovered, 20 (25) minutes or until a candy thermometer registers 300°F. (If a candy thermometer isn't available, drops small amount of mixture into very cold water. The mixture should separate into threads which are hard and brittle.) Stir occasionally with a wooden spoon.
6. Grease 2 cookie sheets and warm them in a conventional oven set at 250°F while peanut mixture is heating.
7. Stir the reserved baking soda mixture into hot candy mixture. Pour hot peanut brittle onto prepared cookie sheets and spread evenly to ¼ inch.
8. When peanut brittle has cooled, break into bite-sized pieces.

PARTY MIX

½ cup butter or margarine
2 tablespoons Worcestershire sauce
Few drops Tabasco sauce, to taste
½ teaspoon salt
2 cups bite-sized shredded corn biscuits
2 cups bite-sized shredded wheat biscuits
2 cups bite-sized shredded rice biscuits
1 cup salted peanuts
1 cup thin pretzel sticks

1. In a deep 3-quart non-metallic casserole, melt butter in Microwave Oven 45 (60) seconds.
2. Add Worcestershire sauce, Tabasco sauce and salt. Stir to combine thoroughly.
3. Mix remaining ingredients together and stir into butter mixture.
4. Heat, uncovered, stirring frequently, in Microwave Oven 4 (5) minutes or until cereal mixture is well coated and crisp.
5. Turn mixture onto a paper-towel-lined tray and spread evenly.
6. Allow to cool.

SPICED NUTS

½ cup firmly packed dark brown sugar
½ teaspoon salt
½ teaspoon ground cinnamon
¼ teaspoon ground allspice
⅛ teaspoon ground nutmeg
⅛ teaspoon ground cloves
1½ tablespoons water
1½ cups walnut halves, pecan halves or cashews
  or a combination of these

1. In a deep 2-quart non-metallic casserole, combine first 7 ingredients.
2. Heat, uncovered, in Microwave Oven 1½ (2) minutes; stir occasionally.
3. Add ½ cup nuts at a time to syrup mixture. Stir until well coated. With a slotted spoon lift out nuts; drain extra syrup. Place nuts in a shallow 1½-quart non-metallic baking dish. Repeat with remaining nuts.
4. Heat coated nuts, uncovered, in Microwave Oven for 5 (6½) minutes or until syrup begins to harden slightly.
5. Transfer nuts to greased wax paper and allow to cool and harden.

DOUBLE BUTTERSCOTCH BROWNIES

¼ cup butter or margarine
1 cup firmly packed dark brown sugar
1 egg, slightly beaten
¼ teaspoon salt
¾ cup unsifted flour
1 teaspoon baking powder
1 teaspoon vanilla extract
¾ cup coarsely broken pecans or walnuts
1 (6-ounce) package butterscotch pieces

1. Generously grease an 8-inch square non-metallic baking dish.
2. Place butter in a medium sized heat-resistant non-metallic bowl and heat in Microwave Oven 30 (40) seconds or until melted.
3. Mix in brown sugar, egg, salt, flour, baking powder and vanilla until smooth.
4. Stir in pecans.
5. Pour batter into prepared baking dish.
6. Heat, uncovered, in Microwave Oven 8 (10) minutes, turning baking dish ¼ turn after each 2 (2½) minutes cooking time.
7. Place butterscotch pieces in a small heat-resistant non-metallic bowl and heat in Microwave Oven 2 (2½) minutes.
8. Spread melted butterscotch pieces over brownies. When cool, cut into bars.

Makes 32 small bars.

PEANUT BUTTER COOKIES

¼ cup softened butter or margarine
¾ cup peanut butter
½ cup sugar
½ cup firmly packed dark brown sugar
2 eggs

3 cups unsifted flour
¾ teaspoon baking soda
½ teaspoon salt

1. Cover 29x12 inch pieces of cardboard with wax paper to use as cookie sheets.
2. In a large mixing bowl cream butter and peanut butter together until smooth. Add sugar and beat until fluffy.
3. Add eggs, 1 at a time, beating well after each addition.
4. Add remaining ingredients and beat until well combined.
5. Chill dough 1 hour.
6. Roll dough into 1-inch balls and place on cookie sheets. Place 9 dough balls on each sheet.
7. Press each dough ball with a 4-tined fork in two directions to flatten.
8. Bake in Microwave Oven 2 to 2½ (2½ to 3¼) minutes or until no longer doughy.

Makes 4 dozen.

Cookies Page 130 and 131

JAM CRUMBLE BARS

¾ cup butter or margarine
1 cup firmly packed dark brown sugar
1¾ cups unsifted flour
1 teaspoon salt
½ teaspoon baking soda
1½ cups quick cooking oats
¾ cup raspberry jam

1. Generously grease an 8-inch square non-metallic baking dish.
2. In a medium-sized bowl, cream butter and sugar together until fluffy. Stir in flour, salt, baking soda and oats; combine until well blended.
3. Press ½ of mixture into bottom of prepared baking dish.

(Continued on next page)
*Parenthesis (   ) indicates 500 watt units.

4. Heat, uncovered, in Microwave Oven 4 (5) minutes, turning dish ½ turn after 2 (2½) minutes.
5. Spread jam evenly over baked oat mixture.
6. Crumble remaining oat mixture over jam and press lightly.
7. Heat, uncovered, in Microwave Oven an additional 4 (5) minutes, turning dish after 2 (2½) minutes. Test for doneness with a toothpick.
8. Allow to cool and cut into bars.

Makes 32 small bars.

GINGERBREAD KIDS

5 cups unsifted flour
1½ teaspoons salt
2 teaspoons ground ginger
1 teaspoon baking soda
½ teaspoon ground nutmeg
½ teaspoon ground allspice
½ teaspoon ground cinnamon
1 cup soft shortening
1 cup sugar
1 cup dark molasses
½ cup water
Decorator's Icing (see recipe at below)

1. Cover 29x12 inch pieces of cardboard with wax paper to use as cookie sheets.
2. Sift flour, salt, baking soda, ginger, nutmeg, allspice and cinnamon together onto a piece of wax paper.
3. In the large bowl of an electric mixer, cream shortening and sugar together until light and fluffy. Blend in molasses and water.
4. Add sifted dry ingredients, blending until smooth.
5. Chill dough 2 to 3 hours or until firm.
6. Roll dough out on a well-floured board until ⅛-inch thick.
7. Cut with gingerbread girl or boy cookie cutters. Carefully place on prepared cookie sheets.
8. Bake according to chart below.
9. Allow to cool. Decorate as desired with icing.

Quantity	Total Cooking Time
3 3'' cookies	1¼ (2) minutes
1 8'' cookie	1 (1¼) minutes
15 1½'' cookies	2½ (3¼) minutes

DECORATOR'S ICING

4 cups sifted confectioner's sugar
2 tablespoons cold water
Water
Food coloring

1. Mix sifted confectioners' sugar with the 2 tablespoons cold water. Add additional water by ½ teaspoonfuls until desired consistency is reached.
2. Divide and color as desired with food coloring.

CHOCOLATE CANDY CHIP COOKIES

1 (23-ounce) package double fudge brownie mix (with chocolate flavor packet)
¾ cup unsifted flour
6 tablespoons vegetable oil
2 eggs
2 tablespoons water
¾ cup coarsely chopped nuts
1 (6-ounce) package candy-coated chocolate bits

1. Cover 29x12 inch pieces of cardboard with wax paper to use as cookie sheets.
2. In a medium-sized bowl, combine brownie mix, chocolate flavor packet, flour, oil, eggs and water. Stir until well mixed.
3. Fold in chopped nuts and candy-coated chocolate bits.
4. Drop by teaspoonfuls onto prepared cookie sheets.
5. Bake 12 at a time in Microwave Oven for 2 to 2½ (2½ to 3¼) minutes.

Makes 5 to 6 dozen.

SAMORES

8 graham cracker squares
8 squares of milk chocolate candy bar, cut to fit graham cracker squares
4 large marshmallows

1. Place 4 paper napkins on table.
2. Arrange 1 graham cracker square in the center of each napkin. Top each graham cracker with 1 square of milk chocolate. Top chocolate with a marshmallow, another chocolate square and the other graham cracker square.
3. Wrap each samore in its paper napkin as tightly as possible. (This helps hold the cookies together as marshmallow melts.)
4. Place in Microwave Oven, seam side down, and heat 1 (1¼) minute or until marshmallow melts.
5. Let stand 1 minute to melt chocolate.

Serves 4.

PETIT FOURS

1 (18½-ounce) package golden cake mix
Ingredients as called for on cake package
9 cups sifted confectioners' sugar (about 2 pounds)
½ cup water
½ cup light corn syrup
1 teaspoon vanilla extract
Food coloring (optional)

1. Lightly grease 2 8-inch square non-metallic baking dishes and set aside.
2. Prepare golden cake mix according to package directions.
3. Pour ⅓ of the prepared batter into the baking dish and smooth with a spatula.
4. Heat, uncovered, in Microwave Oven 6 (8) minutes or until cake tests done with a toothpick. Turn pan ¼ turn after each 1½ (2) minutes.

(Continued on next page)

5. Allow cake to cool 10 minutes. Remove cake from baking dish.

6. Repeat process twice using ½ of remaining batter each time.

7. When cake layers have cooled, cut into desired shapes with a knife or cookie cutters.

8. In a large heat-resistant non-metallic bowl combine confectioners' sugar, water, corn syrup and vanilla.

9. Heat, uncovered, in Microwave Oven 2 (2½) minutes or until warm.

10. If desired, divide icing into separate bowls and tint with food coloring to delicate pastel colors.

11. Glaze cake pieces a few at a time by placing on a wire rack over wax paper. Spoon icing over top so entire cake piece is covered at one time. (Glaze that drips off cake may be reused. If glaze becomes too stiff return to Microwave Oven for 30 (40) seconds.)

12. Decorate as desired.

Apple Brown Betty

Petit Fours and Cupcakes

APPLE BROWN BETTY

½ **cup sugar**
1 **teaspoon ground cinnamon**
¼ **cup raisins**
¼ **cup coarsely broken nuts**
4 **medium-sized apples, peeled and thinly sliced**
1 **tablespoon lemon juice**
⅓ **cup corn flakes**

1. In a small bowl, combine sugar, cinnamon, raisins and broken nuts.

2. Layer apples slices, lemon juice and sugar mixture in a deep 1-quart non-metallic casserole. Reserve ¼ of sugar mixture for the topping.

3. Heat, covered, in Microwave Oven 4 (5) minutes or until apples are almost tender.

4. While the casserole is heating, combine remaining sugar mixture with corn flakes.

5. Sprinkle topping mixture over cooked apples and heat, uncovered, 1 to 2 (1¼ to 2½) minutes or until topping is crisp.

Serves 4.

CUPCAKES

1. Prepare cake batter as directed in recipe above.

2. Place paper muffin liners in small custard or coffee cups and fill half full with batter. Bake in Microwave Oven according to chart below. Turn ½ turn after half of baking time.

Quantity	Total Cooking Time
6 cupcakes	3 (4) minutes
4 cupcakes	2 (2½) minutes
2 cupcakes	1 (1¼) minutes

3. Test for doneness with a toothpick.

4. Ice and decorate as desired.

Tip: When baking 3 or more cupcakes, place in a circle. Never place a cupcake in the center of the circle as it will not bake properly.

CRAZY CAKE

1 **package fruit-flavored gelatin (4-serving size)**
¾ **cup boiling water**
½ **cup cold water**
1 **(18-ounce) package golden cake mix**
Ingredients as called for on cake package
Whipped cream (optional)

1. Lightly grease a shallow 1½-quart non-metallic baking dish and set aside.

2. In a small bowl, dissolve gelatin in the ¾ cup boiling water. Stir in the ½ cup cold water. Set gelatin mixture aside.

3. Prepare golden cake mix according to package directions. Pour ⅔ of batter into prepared baking dish and smooth with a spatula. (Remaining batter may be used to make cupcakes. See recipe above).

4. Heat, uncovered, in Microwave Oven for 6 (8) minutes or until cake tests done with a toothpick. Turn pan ¼ turn after 1½ (2) minutes.

(Continued on next page)
*Parenthesis ( ) indicates 500 watt units.

5. With a meat fork or a toothpick poke holes in cake 1 inch apart. (Cake should still be in pan.)
6. Carefully pour gelatin into holes. Refrigerate until gelatin is set.
7. Cut into squares and serve topped with whipped cream, if desired.

Variation: Cold fruit juice or fruit-flavored carbonated beverage may be subsituted for cold water.

ANN'S DUTCH CARROT BREAD

2 cups unsifted flour
2 teaspoons baking soda
1 teaspoon ground cinnamon
1½ cups sugar
3 eggs
1½ cups vegetable oil
2 teaspoons vanilla extract
2 cups finely grated carrots

1. Lightly grease 2 8½x4½x2½ inch non-metallic loaf pans and set aside.
2. Sift flour, baking soda, cinnamon and sugar together into a large bowl.
3. Stir with a spoon. Make a well in center with the back of the spoon.
4. Place eggs in well and beat just the eggs with a rotary beater or hand electric mixer until thoroughly blended. Try to keep dry ingredients on the sides of the bowl.
5. Add vegetable oil and beat thoroughly with eggs, again trying to keep dry ingredients on the sides of the bowl.
6. Add vanilla to egg-oil mixture.
7. Beat in flour mixture until all ingredients are combined and smooth.
8. Fold carrots into mixture.
9. Pour mixture into prepared loaf pans.
10. Bake each loaf, uncovered, in Microwave Oven 7 (9) minutes, turning pan ¼ turn after each 2 minutes of cooking time. Bread is done when a toothpick inserted in the bread comes out clean.
11. Allow bread to cool 10 minutes before removing from loaf pans.

STICKY BUNS

1 (14-ounce) package hot roll mix
Ingredients as called for on package
Melted butter or margarine
½ cup sugar
½ teaspoon ground cinnamon
¼ cup butter or margarine
½ cup firmly packed dark brown sugar
½ cup walnut pieces

1. Prepare hot roll mix according to package directions.
2. Allow to raise as package directs.
3. Divide dough into 2 equal parts. Roll each part on a liberally floured board until it forms an 8x16-inch rectangle.

4. Brush each rectangle liberally with melted butter.
5. In a small bowl combine granulated sugar and cinnamon.
6. Sprinkle ½ of sugar mixture over each rectangle.
7. Roll dough up in jellyroll fashion from the long side. Cut into 8 slices and set aside.
8. Repeat procedure with remaining dough, melted butter and sugar mixture.
9. Melt ½ of the ¼ cup butter in each of 2 9-inch non-metallic pie pans in Microwave Oven 30 (40) seconds each. Pans will have to be placed in the oven one at a time.
10. Sprinkle ½ of brown sugar and ½ of the walnuts in each pan.
11. Arrange 8 dough slices in each pan and allow to raise, covered with a clean towel, until double in size.
12. Heat each pan, uncovered, in Microwave Oven 6 (8) minutes, turning ⅓ turn after each 2 minutes. Dough will not brown during cooking. Test for doneness with a toothpick.
13. Allow to cool 5 minutes before inverting onto a serving plate. Allow topping to drip over buns.

Makes 16 buns.

Tip: Buns may be browned for a few minutes under the broiler of a conventional oven.

BANANA BREAD

3½ cups unsifted flour
3 teaspoons baking powder
1 teaspoon baking soda
1 teaspoon salt
2 cups mashed ripe bananas
2 tablespoons lemon juice
¾ cup softened butter or margarine
1½ cups sugar
3 eggs
¾ cup milk
1 cup coarsely broken walnuts

1. Lightly grease 2 8½x4½x2½ inch non-metallic loaf pans and set aside.
2. Sift together flour, baking powder, baking soda and salt; set aside. In a small bowl, combine mashed bananas and lemon juice and set aside.
3. In the large bowl of an electric mixer, cream butter and sugar until light and fluffy. Add eggs, 1 at a time, beating well after each addition.
4. Add milk and dry ingredients alternately, beginning and ending with dry ingredients.
5. Fold in walnuts and banana mixture.
6. Pour batter into prepared loaf pans and bake each loaf, uncovered, in Microwave Oven 7 (9) minutes, turning pan ½ turn after each 2 (2½) minutes of cooking time.
7. Bread is done when a toothpick inserted in the bread comes out clean.
8. Allow bread to cool 10 minutes before removing from loaf pans.

*Parenthesis ( ) indicates 500 watt units.

Breads and Sticky Buns Page 133

BLUEBERRY BETTY

1 quart fresh blueberries, washed and drained
1 tablespoon lemon juice
2 to 4 tablespoons granulated sugar
1 tablespoon cornstarch
1 cup unsifted flour
Few grains salt
¼ teaspoon ground cinnamon
1 cup firmly packed dark brown sugar
½ cup butter or margarine

1. Place berries in a deep 1½-quart non-metallic casserole.
2. Sprinkle with lemon juice and granulated sugar to taste.
3. Heat, covered, in Microwave Oven 3 (4) minutes.
4. Stir in cornstarch until smooth.
5. Sift flour, salt, cinnamon and brown sugar together into a small bowl. With a pastry blender or 2 knives cut in butter until mixture is crumbly.
6. Sprinkle mixture over berries.
7. Heat, uncovered, in Microwave Oven 5 to 6 (6½ to 8) minutes or until topping is no longer doughy.

Serves 4 to 6.

Tip: If a browner topping is desired, Blueberry Betty may be placed under the broiler of a conventional oven for several minutes.

BRANDIED PEACHES

1 (29-ounce) can peach halves, undrained
⅔ cup pineapple preserves
⅓ cup brandy
1 teaspoon lemon juice
¼ cup toasted coconut

1. Drain peach halves and reserve ½ cup syrup.
2. In a small bowl combine reserved syrup, pineapple preserves, brandy and lemon juice.
3. Arrange peaches in a shallow non-metallic baking dish.
4. Pour sauce over peaches. Sprinkle with coconut.
5. Heat, uncovered, in Microwave Oven 4 to 5 (5 to 6½) minutes.
6. Serve either warm or chilled.

Serves 4.

GREMLIN GOODIES

¼ cup butter or margarine
1 (10-ounce) package large marshmallows
5 cups crispy rice cereal
Butter or margarine
Red and yellow food coloring
Candy corn
Large black and orange gumdrops
Sugar
Light corn syrup.

1. In a large heat-resistant non-metallic bowl melt butter in Microwave Oven 30 (40) seconds.
2. Stir marshmallows into melted butter until well coated.
3. Heat, uncovered, in Microwave Oven 30 (40) seconds or until melted. Stir until smooth.
4. Add cereal and stir until well combined. Mixture will be sticky.
5. Add red and yellow food coloring until desired shade of orange is reached. If desired, a portion of the mixture can be colored differently or remain uncolored. (This can be done by dividing the mixture into separate bowls.)
6. Butter an 8-inch square pan and press ½ of the mixture into the pan with well-buttered hands.
7. Cool and cut into serving-sized squares.
8. Shape remaining marshmallow mixture into 2-inch balls.
9. Press a candy corn kernel into the center of each ball for a nose and cut black gumdrops for eyes.
10. To decorate squares, cut patterns for a cat, pumpkin or other seasonal designs out of thin cardboard. Roll out gumdrops on a well-sugared board to $\frac{1}{16}$-inch thick. Sprinkle sugar over rolled gumdrops as they are rolled out. With a sharp knife cut out designs. With light corn syrup attach gumdrop cutouts to squares.
11. Refrigerate goodies to set decorations.

Makes 12 squares and 10 gremlin goodies.

*Parenthesis (   ) indicates 500 watt units.

Convenience Food Chart

Item	Size	Method	Time	Comments
Appetizers				
Frozen Crab Puffs	7 oz.	Remove from package and arrange in a circle on a paper plate.	1—2 (1¼—2½) min.	Will not have a crisp crust.
Frozen Pizza Rolls	6 oz.	Remove from package and arrange in a circle on a paper plate.	2 (2½) min.	Will not have a crisp crust.
Frozen Pizza Rounds	17 oz.	Remove from package and arrange in a circle on a paper towel-lined paper plate.	2—3 (2½—4) min.	Will not have a crisp crust.
Main Courses				
Frozen Entrees (meat and potato)	9—10 oz.	Remove foil cover. Place foil tray with food in it back in original box or cover with wax paper.	6—7 (8—9) min.	Foods will heat faster if removed from foil tray.
2 Course Dinners	15—16 oz.	Remove foil cover. Place foil tray with food in it back in original box or cover with wax paper.	7—8 (9—10) min.	Foods will heat faster if removed from foil tray.
3 or 4 Course Dinners (without soup)	15—16 oz.	Remove foil cover. Place foil tray with food in it back in original box or cover with wax paper.	7—8 (9—10) min.	Foods will heat faster if removed from foil tray.
3 or 4 Course Dinners (with soup)	16 oz.	Heat soup first in separate bowl. Remove foil cover. Place foil tray with food in it back in original box or cover with wax paper.	2 (2½) min. + 7 (9) min.	Foods will heat faster if removed from foil tray. Place soup in a separate bowl.
Low Calorie Dinners	16 oz.	Remove foil cover. Place foil tray with food in it back in original box or cover with wax paper.	8 (10) min.	Foods will heat faster if removed from foil tray.
Pot Pies	8 oz.	Remove from carton. Place pie, in its containers, on a non-metallic plate. If a crisp crust is desired heat in a conventional oven at 425°F 15 minutes after heating in Microwave Oven.	7—9 (9—11½) min.	Do not use a paper plate.
Main Dishes				
Frozen in Cooking Pouches	6—8 oz.	Place pouch in a non-metallic casserole for first half of heating. Pierce pouch in several places. Empty pouch into casserole for last half of heating.	5—7 (6½—9) min.	Stir occasionally during last half of heating.
Frozen Casseroles	6—10 oz.	Remove from metal dish and place on a non-metallic plate.	7—12 (9—15½) min.	Press bottom of metal dish to pop food out. Stir if needed.
Frozen Breakfast				
French Toast	4—5 oz.	Remove from tray and place on paper towel-lined non-metallic plate. Cover with wax paper.	2 (2½) min.	Press bottom of tray to pop food out.
Eggs and Potatoes	4—5 oz.	Remove foil cover. Place foil tray with food in it back in original box or cover with wax paper.	3 (4) min.	Foods will heat faster if removed from foil tray.
Desserts				
Frozen Cake	11 oz.	Place on paper towel-lined plate.	45 (60) sec. + (Rest 1 min.) +Heat an additional min.	Cake will be warm. Do not overheat.

*Parenthesis ( ) indicates 500 watt units.

Conventional Recipe Conversion

Cooking in the Microwave Oven is different from conventional cooking. In this section we have defined some basic cooking terms and methods for use in the Microwave Oven.

You will find that in most cases the cooking methods are quite similar.

Wherever possible we have referred you to cooking charts in the earlier chapters of this book.

You will find that with a little planning almost any conventional recipe can be easily adapted for Microwave Oven use. The cooking times, of course, will be shortened.

Bake, Cakes

To cook by dry heat. Pour batter into cake pan and fill ½ full. Heat according to cooking chart.

Bake, Meats

To cook by dry heat. Also called roasting. Place meat in Microwave Oven. Cover loosely with paper toweling or wax paper. Heat according to cooking charts.

Bake, Vegetables

To cook without moisture. Place vegetables in utensil or at least 1 inch apart on oven shelf. Heat according to cooking chart.

Barbecue

To roast on a rack or revolving spit in a highly seasoned sauce. Spoon sauce over meat and heat, uncovered, in Microwave Oven. Use cooking times in Meat, Fish and Poultry cooking chart as a guide.

Blanch

To pour boiling water over food or to place food in water, bring to a boil and then drain. It is sometimes advisable to pour cold water over food to stop the cooking. Heat water in Microwave Oven according to the chart in Beverage Chapter. When bringing water to boil with food in it add an additional 2 to 5 (2½ to 6½) minutes to time needed to boil just the water. The time depends on the amount of food added to the water.

Boil

To cook in liquid at boiling temperature. Boiling is reached when bubbles rise continuously and break at the surface. For a guide to time needed to boil water in Microwave Oven see chart in Beverage Chapter.

Braise

To brown meat and vegetables in hot fat (can be done conventionally) and then cover and cook with a small amount of liquid until tender. Heat, covered, in Microwave Oven using cooking times in Meat, Fish and Poultry cooking chart as a guide.
Microwave Browning Dish may be used to braise foods.

Broil

To cook under direct heat or over hot coals. This step should be done conventionally to obtain the crisp texture associated with grilled foods. The cooking time can be reduced greatly by simply searing meats conventionally under the broiler unit of a stove and then finishing cooking in Microwave Oven. *Microwave Browning Dish may be used to obtain a crisp texture.*

To Candy (Fruit and Fruitpeels)

To cook in a heavy sugar syrup until transparent, then drain and allow to dry. Sugar syrups can be made easily in Microwave Oven by simply boiling sugar and water together until desired temperature is reached.

To Candy (Vegetables)

To cook vegetables in a sugar or honey syrup to give a coating or glaze. See recipe for Glaze Carrots as a guide.

Caramelizing

To heat sugar slowly until it melts and turns a golden brown. See recipe for Caramel Custard as a guide. Remember to stir frequently to keep sugar from burning.

Deep-Fat Fry

To cook in a deep container in enough fat to cover food. Do not attempt to deep fat fry in a Microwave Oven as the temperature of oil will not stay constant enough to produce an even browning.

Flambé

To cover or combine food with warmed alcoholic spirits such as brandy or cognac and ignite before serving. The alcohol can be warmed easily in Microwave Oven. See recipe for Cherry Sauce Variation as a guide.

Fricassée

To cook meat or fowl cut into serving pieces in liquid then thicken the liquid. See recipe for Chicken Fricassee as a guide.

Fry

To cook in hot fat. (See Sauté, Pan-Fry and Deep-Fat Fry.)
Microwave Browning Dish may be used to obtain a fried product in the Microwave Oven.

Grill

See Broil.

Melt

To reduce solids to liquids. To melt butter or margarine, heat 1 to 8 tablespoons uncovered, in Microwave Oven 30 to 90 seconds (40 sec. to 2 min.) depending on amount of butter used.

Pan-Broil

To cook uncovered in a hot skillet pouring off fat as it accumulates. This should be done conventionally to obtain the proper grilled texture associated with pan-broiled foods. The conventional time can be reduced greatly by simply searing meats in the hot skillet and then transfering them to Microwave Oven to finish cooking.
Microwave Browning Dish may be used to obtain a broiled appearance.

Pan-Fry

To cook in a skillet with a small amount of fat.
This should be done conventionally for best results. However, the conventional time can be reduced greatly by simply searing food on both sides and then transfering to Microwave Oven to finish cooking.

Parboil

To boil in liquid until partially cooked. Heat liquid according to the chart in Beverage Chapter. Then add food and continue to cook a few additional minutes until desired degree of doneness is reached.

Poach

To cook in simmering liquid. See recipes for Poached Fish and Poached Eggs.

Roast

See Bake, Meat.

Sauté

To cook in a small amount of hot fat in a skillet.
Melt fat in Microwave Oven and add ingredients to be sautéed. Heat, uncovered 3 to 10 (4 to 13) minutes depending on amount of food added and desired degree of doneness.
Sautéing can also be done is the Browning Dish.

Sear

To brown the surface of meat quickly by intense heat.
(See Broil, Pan-Fry and Pan-Broil.)
Searing can be obtained in the Browning Dish.

Simmer

To cook in liquid just below boiling point. Heat food and liquid in Microwave Oven, covered, until desired degree of doneness is reached. It may be necessary to stop the cooking occasionally to keep liquid from boiling.

Steam

To cook with only enough water to generate steam.
Heat food, tightly covered, in Microwave Oven with just a little water in the bottom of the pan.

Steep

To cover with boiling water and let stand without additional heating or stirring. For a guide to time needed to boil water see chart in Beverage Chapter.

Stew

To cook foods in simmering liquid. Heat, covered, in Microwave Oven using cooking times in Meat, Fish and Poultry Chart as a guide.

Toast

To brown by direct heat in toaster or conventional oven. Bread will not toast in a Microwave Oven but may be reheated. (See recipe for reheating toast.) Following is a glossary of additional cooking terms used in both conventional and Microwave Oven recipes:

Baste

To moisten foods while they are cooking. Spoon butter or margarine, pan drippings or sauce over meats as they cook. Basting addc flavor and prevents drying out.

Chill

To allow to become thoroughly cold, usually in the refrigerator.

Chop

To cut into small pieces, usually about a ¼ to ½ inch.

Cool

To let stand at room temperature until no longer warm to the touch.

Cube

To cut into small evenly sized cubes.

Dice

To cut into ¼-inch cubes.

Dollop

A heaping spoonful of garnish used as a topping, such as sour cream or whipped cream.

Flake

To break into small pieces. Usually done with a fork. A good test to see if fish is cooked.

Fold

To combine a delicate ingredient such as a meringue with a solid mixture such as a batter using a gentle under-and-over motion with a rubber spatula.

Garnish

To decorate, usually with an edible accompaniment.

Glaze

To coat with sugar syrup, honey syrup or melted jelly, either during or after cooking.

Grease

To coat the inside of a cooking utensil with a fat such as butter, margarine or shortening before filling it with food.

Hull

To remove strip of outer covering or stems of certain fruits and vegetables. As to remove the stem end of a strawberry.

Mince

To cut or chop into very fine pieces.

Pare

To cut away outside surfaces of fruits and vegetables with a knife or other utensil.

Peel

To strip off the outer covering of certain fruits and vegetables.

Purée

To press food through a sieve or food mill until smooth.

Shred

To cut into long narrow pieces or grate coarsely.

Index

Index

Index

Index

Our sincere thanks to
Gordon E. Smith for photographs
Royal Copenhagen for china and
silver

Printed in Japan